MAIN
KANSAS CITY KANSAS
PUBLIC LIBRARY

DATE:

DOVER·THRIFT EDITIONS

Essays on Teaching

EDITED BY
BOB BLAISDELL

DOVER PUBLICATIONS, INC.
Mineola, New York

DOVER THRIFT EDITIONS

GENERAL EDITOR: MARY CAROLYN WALDREP
EDITOR OF THIS VOLUME: JANET BAINE KOPITO

ACKNOWLEDGMENTS: SEE PAGES VI–VIII

Copyright

Copyright © 2013 by Dover Publications, Inc.
All rights reserved.

Bibliographical Note

Essays on Teaching is a new compilation, first published by Dover Publications, Inc., in 2013. Bob Blaisdell has selected and arranged the essays and provided all of the introductory material. For the sake of authenticity, inconsistencies in spelling, capitalization, and punctuation have been retained in the texts.

Library of Congress Cataloging-in-Publication Data

Essays on teaching / edited by Bob Blaisdell.
      p. cm. — (Dover thrift editions)
   Summary: "These reflections on the teaching experience include selections from letters, diaries, and memoirs in addition to essays and poems. A wide range of authors and educators includes Plato, Erasmus, Rousseau, Tolstoy, and Emerson as well as Dewey, Montessori, Bertrand Russell, A. S. Neill, and several contemporary American writers"—Provided by publisher.
   ISBN-13 978-0-486-48901-8 (pbk.)
   ISBN-10 0-486-48901-9
   1. Education. 2. Education in literature. I. Blaisdell, Robert.
   LB41.E7495 2013
   371.102—dc23

2012030163

Manufactured in the United States by Courier Corporation
48901901   2013
www.doverpublications.com

Note

IF THERE IS one thing that effective teachers have in common, it seems to be—based on the accounts and reflections recorded and described in this anthology—imagination. What does she, my student, already understand, and what can she already do? That's the question that teachers are constantly responding to, gauging, wondering about. Teaching may become routine, but because it is a continuously evolving relationship between a teacher and his or her students, it is neither mechanical nor formulaic; it does not allow complacency any more than parenting does. Even for the best teachers, it's hit and miss, a mixture of good days and worse, with constant adjustments and continual ingrained mistakes. I, for example, have been teaching for more than thirty years, and it has always been interesting but never, except on the best days, easy. D. H. Lawrence describes, in "Best of School" (in his "Schoolmaster" sequence), one of those rare, glorious afternoons:

> Oh, sweet it is
> To feel the lads' looks light on me.
> Then back in a swift, bright flutter to work,
> As birds who are stealing turn and flee.

"Sweet it is," but we teachers don't expect such moments; rather, we get used to failing: we don't like it, but we get used to it, and we keep trying to figure out how not to fail quite so much, with not quite so many students. At our worst, our imaginations draw a blank; we see students as our adversaries or as empty receptacles rather than as our sources of interest, information, and inspiration. Our students really do change, and we teachers really do get older. Rash and idealistic when young, we become more practical; we, perhaps, make fewer gaffes, though obviously (time is cruel) we lose some zip, too. The political science professor Stephen Leacock reminds us, based

on his experience as a rookie teacher in late nineteenth-century On-
tario, that things haven't changed much: ". . . the whole profession
is chaotic. It is made up of young men and old men, good men and
bad men, enthusiasts and time workers, martyrs and drones. They
are in it, men of all types and ages. Here is a young man fresh out of
college with clothes made by a city tailor and with hope still written upon his face; and beside him in the next class room is a poor
ancient thing in a linen duster fumbling a piece of chalk in his hand,
with the resigned pathos of intellectual failure stamped all over him."

It's true, as Ralph Waldo Emerson says, that "a treatise on education, a convention for education, a lecture, a system, affects us
with slight paralysis and a certain yawning of the jaws," so these
are not—except here and there, when a teacher is clever enough
to put one over on us—treatises but essays, attempts at explaining and describing moments of uncertainty, moments of mystery,
moments of *teaching*, based on very particular events or upon years
and years of experience. "The imagination must be addressed,"
Emerson reminds us. The accounts given here of imaginatively
addressed teaching experiences range from those by the most renowned of the Western world's educators, Pestalozzi and Froebel
and Montessori and Neill, to the great philosophers, Plato and
Rousseau and Dewey and Russell, to famous authors, Tolstoy and
Emerson and D. H. Lawrence, to the most extraordinary everyday teachers, from Helen Keller's Anne Sullivan to the slam-poet
teacher-advocate Taylor Mali, who have written amusingly, honestly,
and amazedly about that personally revealing experience of teaching. It's a demanding job. We learn from what doesn't work, and
sometimes we see that those frustrating days make good stories. This
book is full of good stories.

I present these selections chronologically based on the date of
publication. Among the "essays" are an interview, a series of letters,
a transcript of a class, diaries, a compilation of commencement addresses, sections of memoirs, and a handful of poems—all of which
seek the heart of the dynamics of teaching. Some of the pieces are indeed theoretical, but when they are, they, for the most part, *dramatize*
that theory. The opening of Plato's *Protagoras*, for example, dramatizes
how Socrates accompanies an admiring pupil on his initial interview
with a flashy teacher. (We teachers are often skeptical of our students'
new favorites.) Personal essays on teaching allow for the revelation
of every kind of experience, from overwhelming and confusing (see,

for example, Elizabeth Gold's "Every Child Has a Voice" or Gerry Albarelli's "Questions") to shocking (Mark Salzman's "Somebody") to a consciousness of those pedagogical habits that begin to define us as human beings (e.g., John Ridland's "Grading").

The essay that convinced me as a graduate student that teaching, so exciting, so unpredictable, so elusive in its achievements, was actually an art and thereby impossible but worthwhile to continually attempt to master, was Lev Tolstoy's "Who Is to Teach Whom to Write, We the Peasant-Children or the Peasant-Children Us?" He describes, for instance, how those children composed a beautiful and moving story before his eyes: "It seemed to me so strange that a half-educated peasant-boy suddenly revealed such a conscious artistic power that, in all his immeasurable development, Goethe could not achieve. It seemed to me so strange and insulting that I, the author of *Childhood*, who have achieved some success and been recognized for my artistic talent by the cultivated Russian public, that I, in the matter of art, not only could not direct or help eleven-year-old Semka and Fedka, but could only just barely in a happy moment of excitement follow along and understand them."

I warmly thank the generous writers and rights-holders who have granted us permission to include their work. I recommend the books and periodicals where these essays first appeared, as well as one of the best collections on teaching, Claude M. Fuess and Emory S. Basford's *Unseen Harvests: A Treasury of Teaching* (New York: 1947). There also have been a number of excellent anthologies published by Teachers & Writers Collaborative, among them *Educating the Imagination*, Volumes 1 and 2, edited by Christopher Edgar and Ron Padgett (New York, 1994).

—Bob Blaisdell
Kingsborough Community College
City University of New York

Acknowledgments

D. H. Lawrence: "A Lesson on a Tortoise," from PHOENIX II: UN-COLLECTED PAPERS OF D. H. LAWRENCE by D. H. Lawrence, edited by Warren Roberts and Harry T. Moore, copyright © 1959, 1963, 1968 by the Estate of Frieda Lawrence.

Bernard Darwin: "The Schoolmaster's Profession through a Layman's Eyes," from *The English Public School*. London: Longman, Green and Co., 1929. [This excerpt appeared in *Unseen Harvests: A Treasury of Teaching,* edited by Claude M. Fuess and Emory S. Basford. New York: Macmillan. 1947.]

Bertrand Russell: "Education and Discipline," by Bertrand Russell, from *In Praise of Idleness and Other Essays.* New York: Simon and Schuster. 1935. Reproduced by permission of The Bertrand Russell Peace Foundation, Ltd. 1996 and Taylor & Francis Books UK.

Irwin Edman: "Former Students," from *Philosopher's Holiday.* New York: Viking Press. 1938.

Mary Ellen Chase: "The Teaching of English," from *A Goodly Fellowship.* New York: Macmillan. 1939. [An excerpt appeared as "The Teaching of English" in *Unseen Harvests: A Treasury of Teaching.* Edited by Claude M. Fuess and Emory S. Basford. New York: Macmillan. 1947.]

L. S. Simckes: "Want to See My Bottom?," by L. S. Simckes, from *Writers as Teachers: Teachers as Writers.* Edited by Jonathan Baumbach. New York: Holt, Rinehart and Winston. 1970. Used here by the kind permission of Dr. Simckes.

Ron Padgett: "The Care and Feeding of a Child's Imagination," reprinted from *The Straight Line: Essays on Poetry and Poets* (University of Michigan Press, 2000), copyright © by Ron Padgett. Used by permission of the author.

John Ridland:"Grading," from *Writing Poems*. 2nd edition. Edited by Robert Wallace. Glenview, Illinois: Scott, Foresman and Co., 1987. Copyright © 1984 by John Ridland. Reprinted with the permission of the author.

Marvin Mudrick: "'Week One': A Class in Eighteenth-Century English Prose," from *Mudrick Transcribed: Classes and Talks by Marvin Mudrick*. Edited by Lance Kaplan. Santa Barbara. 1989. Reprinted by the kind permission of the Mudrick family and Lance Kaplan.

Stephen Vincent:"In Class," from *Educating the Imagination: Essays and Ideas for Teachers and Writers. Vol. 2*. Edited by Christopher Edgar and Ron Padgett. New York: Teachers and Writers Collaborative. 1994. Reprinted by permission of Stephen Vincent.

Kenneth Koch/Judy Kravis: "The Butterfly and the Rhinoceros," from *Teaching Literature: Writers and Teachers Talking*. Cork, Ireland: Cork University Press. 1995. Reprinted by permission of Judy Kravis.

Billy Collins: "Introduction to Poetry," from *The Apple That Astonished Paris*. Copyright © 1988, 1996 by Billy Collins. Reprinted with the permission of The Permissions Company, Inc., on behalf of the University of Arkansas Press, www.uapress.com

Gerry Albarelli:"Questions," from *Teacha! Stories from a Yeshiva*. Thetford, Vermont: Glad Day Books. 2000. Reprinted with the permission of the author.

Jervey Tervalon: "A Novel Education," from the *Los Angeles Times*. January 23, 2000. Copyright © by Jervey Tervalon. Used by permission of the author.

Jean Trounstine:"Rose," from *Shakespeare Behind Bars: One Teacher's Story of the Power of Drama in a Women's Prison,* by Jean Trounstine. Reprinted by permission of The University of Michigan Press: Ann Arbor, 2004. Copyright © 2004 by The University of Michigan Press.

Taylor Mali:"What Learning Leaves: Four Poems." Copyright © by Taylor Mali. Reprinted from *What Learning Leaves,* Newtown, CT: Hanover Press, Ltd. 2002. Reprinted by permission of the author.

Elizabeth Gold: "Every Child Has a Voice": *Brief Intervals of Horrible Sanity*. Copyright © by Elizabeth Gold. Reprinted from *Brief Intervals of Horrible Sanity: One Season in a Progressive School*. New York: Jeremy P. Tarcher / Penguin. 2003. Reprinted by permission of the author.

Jennifer Nauss: "The Long Answer," from *Bearing Witness: Poetry by Teachers about Teaching*. Edited by Margaret Hatcher. Tucson: Zephyr Press. 2002. Reprinted by permission of the author.

Mark Salzman: "Somebody," from *True Notebooks: A Writer's Year at Juvenile Hall*. New York: Vintage. 2003. Excerpt, Chapter 1, reprinted with the permission of the author.

Elizabeth Stone: "Acts of Revelation," from *The Chronicle of Higher Education*. October 24, 2003. Reprinted with the permission of the author.

Dan Brown: "September: The Disharmony," from *The Great Expectations School: A Rookie Year in the New Blackboard Jungle,* by Dan Brown. Copyright © by Dan Brown. Reprinted by permission of the author and by arrangement with Skyhorse Publishing.

Philip Schultz: From *My Dyslexia,* by Philip Schultz. Copyright © 2011 by Philip Schultz. Used by permission of W. W. Norton and Company: New York. 2011. Reprinted by permission of W. W. Norton and Company, Inc.

Contents

Note iii

Acknowledgments vi

Plato
from *Protagoras* (c. 380 B.C.) 1

Desiderius Erasmus
from *The Argument That Children Should Straightway
from Their Earliest Years Be Trained in Virtue and Sound
Learning* (1529) 13

Michel de Montaigne
from "Of the Education of Children" (1575) 17

Thomas Fuller
"The Good Schoolmaster" (1642) 24

Jean-Jacques Rousseau
from *Emile, or On Education*, "Children Require the Naked
Truth" (1762) 28

Johann Heinrich Pestalozzi
"A Letter on Early Education" (1819) 39

Catharine E. Beecher
from *Suggestions Respecting Improvements in Education* (1829) ... 42

Friedrich Froebel
"Account of the German Kindergarten" (1843) 49

Lev Tolstoy
"Who Is to Teach Whom to Write, We the Peasant-Children
or the Peasant-Children Us?" (1862) 52

Matthew Arnold
from "General Report for the Year 1880" (1880)   76

Ralph Waldo Emerson
"Education" (1883)   79

John Dewey
"My Pedagogic Creed" (1897)   95

Arthur Christopher Benson
"Training of Teachers" (1902)   106

Anne Mansfield Sullivan
"The Education of Helen Keller" (1903)   110

George Herbert Palmer
from *The Ideal Teacher* (1908)   124

D. H. Lawrence
"A Lesson on a Tortoise" (1909)   128

Maria Montessori
"History of Methods" (1912)   134

William Lyon Phelps
"Imagination in Teaching" (1912)   141

D. H. Lawrence
"The Schoolmaster": Three Poems (1913)   148

A. S. Neill
from *A Dominie's Log* (1915)   152

Stephen Leacock
"The Lot of the Schoolmaster" (1916)   159

Bernard Darwin
"The Schoolmaster's Profession through a Layman's
Eyes" (1929)   171

Bertrand Russell
"Education and Discipline" (1935)   174

Irwin Edman
"Former Students" (1938)   179

Mary Ellen Chase
"The Teaching of English" (1939)   187

L. S. Simckes
"Want to See My Bottom?" (1970)   192

Ron Padgett
"The Care and Feeding of a Child's Imagination" (1976)   201

John Ridland
"Grading" (1984)   212

Marvin Mudrick
"'Week One': A Class in Eighteenth-Century English
Prose" (1989)   214

Bob Blaisdell
"It's Greek to Me" (1994)   226

Stephen Vincent
"In Class" (1994)   232

Kenneth Koch
"The Butterfly and the Rhinoceros" (1995)   234

Billy Collins
"Introduction to Poetry" (1996)   242

Gerry Albarelli
"Questions" (2000)   243

Jervey Tervalon
"A Novel Education" (2000)   250

Jean Trounstine
from *Shakespeare behind Bars*: "Rose" (2001)   253

Taylor Mali
from *What Learning Leaves*: Four Poems (2002)   259

Elizabeth Gold
from *Brief Intervals of Horrible Sanity*: "Every Child Has a
Voice" (2003)   265

Jennifer Nauss
The Long Answer (2003)   272

Mark Salzman
from *True Notebooks*: "Somebody" (2003)   274

Elizabeth Stone
"Acts of Revelation" (2003)   279

Dan Brown
from *The Great Expectations School*: "September:
The Disharmony" (2007)   284

Philip Schultz
from *My Dyslexia* (2011)   301

Essays on Teaching

PLATO

from *Protagoras*
(c. 380 B.C.)

The philosopher Plato (c. 427–347 B.C.) dramatizes the great teacher Socrates (469–399 B.C.) relating to his young, eager, naïve companion how he (Socrates) scrutinized the pedagogical claims of Protagoras for another young, eager Athenian, Hippocrates: "You are going to commit your soul to the care of a man whom you call a Sophist. And yet I hardly think that you know what a Sophist is; and if not, then you do not even know to whom you are committing your soul and whether the thing to which you commit yourself be good or evil." One of the pleasures of this Socratic dialogue is the humor and the dramatic tension Plato builds, as well as his representation of the character of Socrates, whose delight in argument and wisdom and his love of youth's earnestness allow him to captivate his listeners.

COMPANION: Where do you come from, Socrates? And yet I need hardly ask the question, for I know that you have been in chase of the fair Alcibiades. I saw the day before yesterday; and he had got a beard like a man—and he is a man, as I may tell you in your ear. But I thought that he was still very charming.

SOCRATES: What of his beard? Are you not of Homer's opinion, who says "Youth is most charming when the beard first appears"? And that is now the charm of Alcibiades.

COMPANION: Well, and how do matters proceed? Have you been visiting him, and was he gracious to you?

SOCRATES: Yes, I thought that he was very gracious; and especially today, for I have just come from him, and he has been helping me in an argument. But shall I tell you a strange thing? I paid no attention to him, and several times I quite forgot that he was present.

COMPANION: What is the meaning of this? Has anything happened between you and him? For surely you cannot have discovered a fairer love than he is; certainly not in this city of Athens.

SOCRATES: Yes, much fairer.

1

COMPANION: What do you mean—a citizen or a foreigner?

SOCRATES: A foreigner.

COMPANION: Of what country?

SOCRATES: Of Abdera.

COMPANION: And is this stranger really in your opinion a fairer love than the son of Cleinias?

SOCRATES: And is not the wiser always the fairer, sweet friend?

COMPANION: But have you really met, Socrates, with some wise one?

SOCRATES: Say rather, with the wisest of all living men, if you are willing to accord that title to Protagoras.

COMPANION: What! Is Protagoras in Athens?

SOCRATES: Yes; he has been here two days.

COMPANION: And do you just come from an interview with him?

SOCRATES: Yes; and I have heard and said many things.

COMPANION: Then, if you have no engagement, suppose that you sit down tell me what passed, and my attendant here shall give up his place to you.

SOCRATES: To be sure; and I shall be grateful to you for listening.

COMPANION: Thank you, too, for telling us.

SOCRATES: That is thank you twice over. Listen then.

Last night, or rather very early this morning, Hippocrates, the son of Apollodorus and the brother of Phason, gave a tremendous thump with his staff at my door; someone opened to him, and he came rushing in and bawled out: "Socrates, are you awake or asleep?"

I knew his voice, and said: "Hippocrates, is that you? And do you bring any news?"

"Good news," he said; "nothing but good."

"Delightful," I said; "but what is the news? And why have you come hither at this unearthly hour?"

He drew nearer to me and said: "Protagoras is come."

"Yes," I replied; "he came two days ago: have you only just heard of his arrival?"

"Yes, by the gods," he said; "but not until yesterday evening."

At the same time he felt for the truckle-bed, and sat down at my feet, and then he said: "Yesterday quite late in the evening, on my return from Oenoe whither I had gone in pursuit of my runaway slave Satyrus, as I meant to have told you, if some other matter had not come in the way; on my return, when we had done supper and were about to retire to rest, my brother said to me: 'Protagoras is come.' I was going to you at once, and then I thought that the night was far spent. But the moment sleep left me after my fatigue, I got up and came hither direct."

I, who knew the very courageous madness of the man, said: "What is the matter? Has Protagoras robbed you of anything?"

He replied, laughing: "Yes, indeed he has, Socrates, of the wisdom which he keeps from me."

"But, surely," I said, "if you give him money, and make friends with him, he will make you as wise as he is himself."

"Would to heaven," he replied, "that this were the case! He might take all that I have, and all that my friends have, if he pleased. But that is why I have come to you now, in order that you may speak to him on my behalf; for I am young, and also I have never seen nor heard him; (when he visited Athens before I was but a child) and all men praise him, Socrates; he is reputed to be the most accomplished of speakers. There is no reason why we should not go to him at once, and then we shall find him at home. He lodges, as I hear, with Callias the son of Hipponicus: let us start."

I replied: "Not yet, my good friend; the hour is too early. But let us rise and take a turn in the court and wait about there until daybreak; when the day breaks, then we will go. For Protagoras is generally at home, and we shall be sure to find him; never fear."

Upon this we got up and walked about in the court, and I thought that I would make trial of the strength of his resolution. So I examined him and put questions to him. "Tell me, Hippocrates," I said, "as you are going to Protagoras, and will be paying your money to him, what is he to whom you are going? And what will he make of you? If, for example, you had thought of going to Hippocrates of Cos, the Asclepiad, and were about to give him your money, and someone had said to you: 'You are paying money to your namesake Hippocrates, O Hippocrates; tell me, what is he that you give him money?' how would you have answered?"

"I should say," he replied, "that I gave money to him as a physician."

"And what will he make of you?"

"A physician," he said.

"And if you were resolved to go to Polycleitus the Argive, or Pheidias the Athenian, and were intending to give them money, and someone had asked you: 'What are Polycleitus and Pheidias? And why do you give them this money?' How would you have answered?"

"I should have answered that they were sculptors."

"And what will they make of you?"

"A sculptor, of course."

"Well now," I said, "you and I are going to Protagoras, and we are ready to pay him money on your behalf. If our own means are sufficient, and we can gain him with these, we shall be only too glad; but if not, then we are to spend the money of your friends as well. Now suppose, that while we are thus enthusiastically pursuing our object someone were to say to us: 'Tell me, Socrates, and you Hippocrates, what is Protagoras, and why are you going to pay him money?' How should we answer? I know that Pheidias is a sculptor, and that Homer is a poet; but what appellation is given to Protagoras? How is he designated?"

"They call him a Sophist, Socrates," he replied.

"Then we are going to pay our money to him in the character of a Sophist?"

"Certainly."

"But suppose a person were to ask this further question: 'And how about yourself? What will Protagoras make of you, if you go to see him?'"

He answered, with a blush upon his face (for the day was just beginning to dawn, so that I could see him): "Unless this differs in some way from the former instances, I suppose that he will make a Sophist of me."

"By the gods," I said, "and are you not ashamed at having to appear before the Greeks in the character of a Sophist?"

"Indeed, Socrates, to confess the truth, I am."

"But you should not assume, Hippocrates, that the instruction of Protagoras is of this nature: may you not learn of him in the same way that you learned the arts of the grammarian, musician, or trainer, not with the view of making any of them a profession, but only as a part of education, and because a private gentleman and freeman ought to know them?"

"Just so," he said; "and that, in my opinion, is a far truer account of the teaching of Protagoras."

I said: "I wonder whether you know what you are doing?"

"And what am I doing?"

"You are going to commit your soul to the care of a man whom you call a Sophist. And yet I hardly think that you know what a Sophist is; and if not, then you do not even know to whom you are committing your soul and whether the thing to which you commit yourself be good or evil."

"I certainly think that I do know," he replied.

"Then tell me, what do you imagine that he is?"

"I take him to be one who knows wise things," he replied, "as his name implies."

"And might you not," I said, "affirm this of the painter and of the carpenter also: Do not they, too, know wise things? But suppose a person were to ask us: 'In what are the painters wise?' We should answer: 'In what relates to the making of likenesses, and similarly of other things.' And if he were further to ask: 'What is the wisdom of the Sophist, and what is the manufacture over which he presides?' How should we answer him?"

"How should we answer him, Socrates? What other answer could there be but that he presides over the art which makes men eloquent?"

"Yes," I replied, "that is very likely true, but not enough; for in the answer a further question is involved: Of what does the Sophist make a man talk eloquently? The player on the lyre may be supposed to make a man talk eloquently about that which he makes him understand, that is about playing the lyre. Is not that true?"

"Yes."

"Then about what does the Sophist make him eloquent? Must not he make him eloquent in that which he understands?"

"Yes, that may be assumed."

"And what is that which the Sophist knows and makes his disciple know?"

"Indeed," he said, "I cannot tell."

Then I proceeded to say: "Well, but are you aware of the danger which you are incurring? If you were going to commit your body to someone who might do good or harm to it, would you not carefully consider and ask the opinion of your friends and kindred, and deliberate many days as to whether you should give him the care of your body? But when the soul is in question, which you hold to be of far more value than the body, and upon the good or evil of which depends the well-being of your all, about this never consulted either with your father or with your brother or with anyone of us who are your companions. But no sooner does this foreigner appear, than you instantly commit your soul to his keeping. In the evening, as you say, you hear of him, and in the morning you go to him, never deliberating or taking the opinion of anyone as to whether you ought to entrust yourself to him or not. You have quite made up your mind that you will at all hazards be a pupil of Protagoras, and are prepared to expend all the property of yourself and of your friends in carrying out at any price this determination, although, as you admit, you do not know him, and have never spoken with him: and you call him a Sophist, but are manifestly ignorant of what a Sophist is; and yet you are going to commit yourself to his keeping."

When he heard me say this, he replied: "No other inference, Socrates, can be drawn from your words."

I proceeded: "Is not a Sophist, Hippocrates, one who deals wholesale or retail in the food of the soul? To me that appears to be his nature."

"And what, Socrates, is the food of the soul?"

"Surely," I said, "knowledge is the food of the soul; and we must take care, my friend, that the Sophist does not deceive us when he praises what he sells, like the dealers wholesale or retail who sell the food of the body; for they praise indiscriminately all their goods, without knowing what are really beneficial or hurtful: neither do their customers know, with the exception of any trainer or physician who may happen to buy of them. In like manner those who carry about the wares of knowledge, and make the round of the cities, and sell or retail them to any customer who is in want of them, praise them all alike; though I should not wonder, O my friend, if many of them were really ignorant of their effect upon the soul; and their customers equally ignorant, unless he who buys of them happens to be a physician of the soul. If, therefore, you have understanding of what is good and evil, you may safely buy knowledge of Protagoras or of anyone; but if not, then, O my friend, pause, and do not hazard your dearest interests at a game of chance. For there is far greater peril in buying knowledge than in buying meat and drink: the one you purchase of the wholesale or retail dealer, and carry them away in other vessels, and before you receive them into the body as food, you may deposit them at home and call in any experienced friend who knows what is good to be eaten or drunken, and what not, and how much, and when; and then the danger of purchasing them is not so great. But you cannot buy the wares of knowledge and carry them away in another vessel; when you have paid for them you must receive them into the soul and go your way, either greatly harmed or greatly benefited; and therefore we should deliberate and take counsel with our elders; for we are still young—too young to determine such a matter. And now let us go, as we were intending, and hear Protagoras; and when we have heard what he has to say, we may take counsel of others; for not only is Protagoras at the house of Callias, but there is Hippias of Elis, and, if I am not mistaken, Prodicus of Ceos, and several other wise men."

To this we agreed, and proceeded on our way until we reached the vestibule of the house; and there we stopped in order to conclude a discussion which had arisen between us as we were going along; and we stood talking in the vestibule until we had finished and come to an understanding. And I think that the doorkeeper, who was a eunuch, and who was probably annoyed at the great inroad of the Sophists, must have heard us talking. At any rate, when we knocked at the door, and he opened and saw us, he grumbled: "They are Sophists—he is not at home," and instantly gave the door a hearty bang with both his hands. Again we knocked, and he answered without opening: "Did you not hear me say that he is not at home, fellows?" "But, my friend," I said, "you need not be alarmed; for we are not Sophists, and we are not come to see Callias, but we want to see Protagoras; and I must request you to announce us." At last, after a good deal of difficulty, the man was persuaded to open the door.

When we entered, we found Protagoras taking a walk in the cloister; and next to him, on one side, were walking Callias, the son of Hipponicus, and Paralus, the son of Pericles, who, by the mother's side, is his half-brother, and Charmides, the son of Glaucon. On the other side of him were Xanthippus, the other son of Pericles, Philippides, the son of Philomelus; also Antimoerus of Mende, who of all the disciples of Protagoras is the most famous, and intends to make sophistry his profession. A train of listeners followed him; the greater part of them appeared to be foreigners, whom Protagoras had brought with him out of the various cities visited by him in his journeys, he, like Orpheus, attracting them by his voice, and they following. I should mention also that there were some Athenians in the company. Nothing delighted me more than the precision of their movements: they never got into his way at all; but when he and those who were with him turned back, then the band of listeners parted regularly on either side; he was always in front, and they wheeled round and took their places behind him in perfect order.

After him, as Homer says, "I lifted up my eyes and saw" Hippias the Elean sitting in the opposite cloister on a chair of state, and around him were seated on benches Eryximachus, the son of Acumenus, and Phaedrus the Myrrhinusian, and Andron the son of Androtion, and there were strangers whom he had brought with him from his native city of Elis, and some others: they were putting to Hippias certain physical and astronomical questions, and he, upon his "throne," was determining their several questions to them, and discoursing of them.

Also, "my eyes beheld Tantalus"; for Prodicus the Cean was at Athens: he had been lodged in a room which, in the days of Hipponicus, was a storehouse; but, as the house was full, Callias had cleared this out and made the room into a guest-chamber. Now Prodicus was still in bed, wrapped up in sheepskins and bed-clothes, of which there seemed to be a great heap; and there was sitting by him, on the couches near, Pausanias of Cerameis, and with Pausanias was a youth quite young, who is certainly remarkable for his good looks, and, if I am not mistaken, is also of a fair and gentle nature. I thought that I heard him called Agathon, and my suspicion is that he is the beloved of Pausanias. There was this youth, and also there were the two Adeimantuses, one the son of Cepis, and the other of Leucolophides, and some others. I was very anxious to hear what Prodicus was saying, for he seems to me to be an all-wise and inspired man; but I was not able to get into the inner circle, and his fine deep voice made an echo in the room which rendered his words inaudible.

No sooner had we entered than there followed us Alcibiades the beautiful, as you say, and I believe you; and also Critias the son of Callaeschrus.

On entering we stopped a little, in order to look about us, and then walked up to Protagoras, and I said: "Protagoras, my friend Hippocrates and I have come to see you."

"Do you wish," he said, "to speak with me alone, or in the presence of the company?"

"Whichever you please," I said; "you shall determine when you have heard the purpose of our visit."

"And what is your purpose?" he said.

"I must explain," I said, "that my friend Hippocrates is a native Athenian; he is the son of Apollodorus, and of a great and prosperous house, and he is himself in natural ability quite a match for anybody of his own age. I believe that he aspires to political eminence; and this he thinks that conversation with you is most likely to procure for him. And now you can determine whether you would wish to speak to him of your teaching alone or in the presence of the company."

"Thank you, Socrates, for your consideration of me. For certainly a stranger finding his way into great cities, and persuading the flower of the youth in them to leave company of their kinsmen or any other acquaintances, old or young, and live with him, under the idea that they will be improved by his conversation, ought to be very cautious; great jealousies are aroused by his proceedings, and he is the subject of many enmities and conspiracies. Now the art of the Sophist is, as I believe, of great antiquity; but in ancient times those who practiced it, fearing this odium, veiled and disguised themselves under various names, some under that of poets, as Homer, Hesiod, and Simonides, some, of hierophants and prophets, as Orpheus and Musaeus, and some, as I observe, even under the name of gymnastic-masters, like Iccus of Tarentum, or the more recently celebrated Herodicus, now of Selymbria and formerly of Megara, who is a first-rate Sophist. Your own Agathocles pretended to be a musician, but was really an eminent Sophist; also Pythocleides the Cean; and there were many others; and all of them, as I was saying, adopted these arts as veils or disguises because they were afraid of the odium which they would incur. But that is not my way, for I do not believe that they effected their purpose, which was to deceive the government, who were not blinded by them; and as to the people, they have no understanding, and only repeat what their rulers are pleased to tell them. Now to run away, and to be caught in running away, is the very height of folly, and also greatly increases the exasperation of mankind; for they regard him who runs away as a rogue, in addition to any other objections which they have to him; and therefore I take an entirely opposite course, and acknowledge myself to be a Sophist and instructor of mankind; such an open acknowledgment appears to me to be a better sort of caution than concealment. Nor do I neglect other precautions, and therefore I hope, as I may say, by the favour of heaven that no harm will come of the acknowledgment that I am a Sophist. And I have been now many years in the profession—for all my years when added up are many: there is no one here present of whom I might not be the father. Wherefore I should much prefer conversing with you, if you want to speak with me, in the presence of the company."

As I suspected that he would like to have a little display and glorification in the presence of Prodicus and Hippias, and would gladly show us to them in the light of his admirers, I said: "But why should we not summon Prodicus and Hippias and their friends to hear us?"

"Very good," he said.

"Suppose," said Callias, "that we hold a council in which you may sit and discuss?" This was agreed upon, and great delight was felt at the prospect of hearing wise men talk; we ourselves took the chairs and benches, and arranged them by Hippias, where the other benches had been already placed. Meanwhile Callias and Alcibiades got Prodicus out of bed and brought in him and his companions.

When we were all seated, Protagoras said: "Now that the company are assembled, Socrates, tell me about the young man of whom you were just now speaking."

I replied: "I will begin again at the same point, Protagoras, and tell you once more the purport of my visit: this is my friend Hippocrates, who is desirous of making your acquaintance; he would like to know what will happen to him if he associates with you. I have no more to say."

Protagoras answered: "Young man, if you associate with me, on the very first day you will return home a better man than you came, and better on the second day than on the first, and better every day than you were on the day before."

When I heard this, I said: "Protagoras, I do not at all wonder at hearing you say this; even at your age, and with all your wisdom, if anyone were to teach you what you did not know before, you would become better no doubt: but please do answer in a different way. I will explain how by an example. Let me suppose that Hippocrates, instead of desiring your acquaintance, wished to become acquainted with the young man Zeuxippus of Heraclea, who has lately been in Athens, and he had come to him as he has come to you, and had heard him say, as he has heard you say, that every day he would grow and become better if he associated with him: and then suppose that he were to ask him, 'In what shall I become better, and in what shall I grow?' Zeuxippus would answer, 'In painting.' And suppose that he went to Orthagoras the Theban, and heard him say the same thing, and asked him, 'In what shall I become better day by day?' he would reply, 'In flute-playing.' Now I want you to make the same sort of answer to this young man and to me, who am asking questions on his account. When you say that on the first day on which he associates with you he will return home a better man, and on every day will grow in like manner, in what, Protagoras, will he be better? And about what?"

When Protagoras heard me say this, he replied: "You ask questions fairly, and I like to answer a question which is fairly put. If Hippocrates comes to me he will not experience the sort of drudgery with which other Sophists are in the habit of insulting their pupils; who, when they have just escaped from the arts, are taken and driven back into them by these teachers, and made to learn calculation, and astronomy, and geometry, and music (he gave a look at Hippias as he said this); but if he comes to me, he will learn that which he comes to learn. And this is prudence in affairs private as well as public; he will learn to order his own house in the best manner, and he will be able to speak and act for the best in the affairs of the state."

"Do I understand you," I said; "and is your meaning that you teach the art of politics, and that you promise to make men good citizens?"

"That, Socrates, is exactly the profession which I make."

"Then," I said, "you do indeed possess a noble art, if there is no mistake about this; for I will freely confess to you, Protagoras, that I have a doubt whether this art is capable of being taught, and yet I know not how to disbelieve your assertion. And I ought to tell you why I am of opinion that this art cannot be taught or communicated by man to man. I say that the Athenians are an understanding people, and indeed they are esteemed to be such by the other Hellenes. Now I observe that when we are met together in the assembly, and the matter in hand relates to building, the builders are summoned as advisers; when the question is one of shipbuilding, then the shipwrights; and the like of other arts which they think capable of being taught and learned. And if some person offers to give them advice who is not supposed by them to have any skill in the art, even though he be good-looking, and rich, and noble, they will not listen to him, but laugh and hoot at him, until either he is clamored down and retires of himself; or if he persist, he is dragged away or put out by the constables at the command of the executive officers. This is their way of behaving about professors of the arts. But when the question is an affair of state, then everybody is free to have a say: carpenter, tinker, cobbler, sailor, passenger; rich and poor, high and low—anyone who likes gets up, and no one reproaches him, as in the former case, with not having learned, and having no teacher, and yet giving advice; evidently because they are under the impression that this sort of knowledge cannot be taught. And not only is this true of the state, but of individuals; the best and wisest of our citizens are unable to impart their political wisdom to others: as for example, Pericles, the father of these young men, who gave them excellent instruction in all that could be learned from masters, in his own department of politics neither taught them, nor gave them teachers; but they were allowed to wander at their own free will in a sort of hope that they would light upon virtue of their own accord. Or take another example: there was Cleinias the younger brother of our friend Alcibiades, of whom this very same Pericles was the guardian; and he being in fact under the apprehension that Cleinias would be corrupted by Alcibiades, took him away, and placed him in the house of Ariphron to be educated; but before six months had elapsed, Ariphron sent him back, not knowing what to do with him. And I could mention numberless other instances of persons who were good themselves, and never yet made anyone else good, whether friend or stranger. Now I, Protagoras, having these examples before me, am inclined to think that virtue cannot be taught. But then again, when I listen to your words, I waver; and am disposed to think that there must be something in what you say, because I know that you have great experience, and learning, and invention. And I wish that you would, if possible, show me a little more clearly that virtue can be taught. Will you be so good?"

"That I will, Socrates, and gladly. But what would you like? Shall I, as an elder, speak to you as younger men in an apologue or myth, or shall I argue out the question?"

To this several of the company answered that he should choose for himself.

"Well, then," he said, "I think that the myth will be more interesting. . . ."

—Translated from the Greek by Benjamin Jowett

SOURCE: *The Dialogues of Plato*. New York: The Colonial Press. 1899.

DESIDERIUS ERASMUS

from *The Argument That Children Should Straightway from Their Earliest Years Be Trained in Virtue and Sound Learning*
(1529)

Desiderius Erasmus (1466–1536) of Rotterdam was a Greek and Latin scholar of the Renaissance who became a professor at Cambridge University. His treatise on education, "De Pueris Statim ac Liberaliter Instituendis," written in Latin, was addressed to William, Duke of Cleves.

I desire to urge upon you, Illustrious Duke, to take into your early and serious consideration the future nurture and training of the son lately born to you. For, with Chrysippus, I contend that the young child must be led to sound learning whilst his wit is yet unwarped, his age tender, his mind flexible and tenacious. In manhood we remember nothing so well as the truths which we imbibed in our youth. Wherefore I beg you to put aside all idle chatter which would persuade you that this early childhood is unmeet for the discipline and the effort of studies.

The arguments which I shall enlarge upon are the following:

First, the beginnings of learning are the work of memory, which in young children is most tenacious. Next, as nature has implanted in us the instinct to seek for knowledge, can we be too early in obeying her behest? Thirdly, there are not a few things which it imports greatly that we should know well, and which we can learn far more readily in our tender years. I speak of the elements of Letters, Grammar, and the fables and stories found in the ancient Poets. Fourthly, since children, as all agree, are fit to acquire manners, why may they not acquire the rudiments of learning? And seeing that they must needs be busy about something, what else can be better approved? For how much wiser to amuse their hours with Letters, than to see them frittered away in aimless trifling!

It is, however, objected, first, that such knowledge as can be thus early got is of slight value. But even so, why despise it, if so be it serve as the foundation for much greater things? For if in early childhood

13

a boy acquire such useful elements he will be free to apply his youth to higher knowledge, to the saving of his time. Moreover, whilst he is thus occupied in sound learning he will perforce be kept from some of the temptations which befall youth, seeing that nothing engages the whole mind more than studies. And this I count a high gain in such times as ours.

Next, it is urged that by such application health may be somewhat endangered. Supposing this to be true, still the compensation is great, for by discipline the mind gains far more in alertness and in vigor than the body is ever likely to lose. Watchfulness, however, will prevent any such risk as is imagined. Also, for this tender age you will employ a teacher who will win and not drive, just as you will choose such subjects as are pleasant and attractive, in which the young mind will find recreation rather than toil.

Furthermore, I bid you remember that a man ignorant of Letters is no man at all, that human life is a fleeting thing, that youth is easily enticed into sin, that early manhood is absorbed by clashing interests, that old age is unproductive, and that few reach it. How then can you allow your child, in whom you yourself live again, to lose even one of those precious years in which he may begin to acquire those means whereby he may elevate his whole life and keep at arm's length temptation and evil?

The First Law: Education Must Begin from the Very Earliest Years. I rejoice at your determination that your son shall be early initiated into the arts of true learning and the wisdom of sound philosophy. Herein consists the full duty of fatherhood, the care and guidance of the spirit of him for whose creation you are responsible. And now for my first precept. Do not follow the fashion, which is too common amongst us, of allowing the early years of childhood to pass without fruit of instruction, and of deferring its first steps until the allurements of indulgence have made application more difficult.

I urge you, therefore, to look even now for a scholar of high character and attainment to whom you may commit the charge of your boy's mind and disposition, leaving to wisely chosen nurses the care of his bodily welfare. By thus dividing control the child will be saved from the mischievous kindnesses and indulgence of foolish serving-women, and of weak relatives, who decry learning as so much poison, and babble about the unfitness of the growing boy for Letters. To such chatter you will turn a deaf ear. For, remembering that the welfare of your son demands not less circumspection from you than a man will gladly bestow upon his horse, his castle, his estate, you will take heed only to the wisest counsel which you can secure, and ponder that with yourself. Consider, in this regard, the care which a boy's mother will lavish upon his bodily frame, how she will take thought should she but faintly suspect in him a tendency to become wry-necked, cross-eyed, crookbacked or splay-footed, or by any mischance prove ill-formed in proportions of his figure. Think, too, how she is apt to busy herself about his milk, his meat, his bath, his exercise, following herein the wise foresight of Galen; will she defer this carefulness until the seventh year? No, from the very day of his birth charge is taken lest mischief hap, and wisely, knowing that a weakly manhood may be thus avoided. Nay, even before the child be born, how diligent is the wise mother to see that no harm come to herself for her child's sake, provides for a son who is worthily educated, provides means to virtue: but whoso saves for a child endowed with rude temper and uncultivated wit is but ministering to opportunities of indulgence and mischief. It is the height of folly that one should train the body to be comely, and wholly neglect that excellence of mind which alone can guide it aright. For I hesitate not to affirm that those things which men covet for their sons—health, riches, and repute—are more surely secured by virtue and learning—the gifts of education—than by any other means. True, the highest gifts of all no man can give to another, even to his child; but we can store his mind with that sound wisdom and learning whereby he may attain to the best.

No one blames this as undue or untimely care for the young life. Why then do men neglect that part of our nature, the nobler part, whereby we are rightly called men; we bestow, justly, our effort upon the mortal body; yet have we but slight regard for the immortal spirit.

Are other instances needed? Then think of the training of a colt, how early it is begun; or of the work of the husbandman who fashions and trains the sapling to suit his taste or to further the fruitfulness of the tree. This is a task of human skill and purpose; and the sooner these are applied the more sure the result.

To dumb creatures Mother Nature has given an innate power or instinct, whereby they may in great part attain to their right capacities. But Providence in granting to man alone the privilege of reason has thrown the burden of development of the human being upon training. Well, therefore, has it been said that the first means, the second, and the third means to happiness is right training or education. Sound education is the condition of real wisdom. And if an education which is soundly planned and carefully carried out is the very fount of all human excellence, so, on the other hand, careless and unworthy training is the true source of folly and vice. This capacity for training is, indeed, the chief aptitude which has been bestowed upon humanity. Unto the animals nature has given swiftness of foot or of wing, keenness of sight, strength or size of frame, and various weapons of defense. To Man, instead of physical powers, is given a mind apt for training; in this single gift all others are comprised, for him, at least, who turns it to due profit. We see that where native instinct is strong—as in squirrels or bees—capacity for being taught is wanting. Man, lacking instinct, can do little or nothing of innate power; scarce can he eat, or walk, or speak, unless he be guided thereto. How then can we expect that he should become competent to the duties of life unless straightway and with much diligence he be brought under the discipline of a worthy education? Let me enforce this by the well-known story of Lycurgus, who, to convince the Spartans, brought out two hounds, one of good mettle, but untrained and therefore useless in the field, and the other poorly bred and well-drilled at his work; "Nature," he said, "may be strong, yet Education is more powerful still."

—Translated from the Latin by William Harrison Woodward

SOURCE: William Harrison Woodward. *Desiderius Erasmus: Concerning the Aim and Method of Education*. Liverpool: University Press. 1904.

MICHEL DE MONTAIGNE

from "Of the Education of Children"
(1575)

*Montaigne (1533–1592) was the great French essayist and philosopher of
the Renaissance. In this essay, he typically modestly confesses his ignorance:
"How inconsiderable soever these essays of mine may be, I will say I never
intended to conceal them, no more than my old bald grizzled pate before
them, where the painter has presented you not with a perfect face, but with
mine. For these are my own particular opinions and fancies, and I deliver
them as only what I myself believe, and not for what is to be believed by
others. I have no other end in this writing, but only to discover myself, who,
also, shall, peradventure, be another thing tomorrow, if I chance to meet any
new instruction to change me. I have no authority to be believed, neither do
I desire it, being too conscious of my own inerudition to be able to instruct
others." Despite his lack of "authority," he addresses his very compelling,
wandering and erudite instructions in this essay to Madame Diane de Foix,
Comtesse de Gurson, on the education of her as-yet unborn son.*

I see better than any other, that all I write here are but the idle
reveries of a man that has only nibbled upon the outward crust of
sciences in his nonage, and only retained a general and formless image of them; who has got a little snatch of everything, and nothing
of the whole, a la Francoise. For I know, in general, that there is
such a thing as physic, as jurisprudence; four parts in mathematics,
and, roughly, what all these aim and point at; and peradventure, I yet
know farther, what sciences in general pretend unto, in order to the
service of our life: but to dive farther than that, and to have cudgeled
my brains in the study of Aristotle, the monarch of all modern learning, or particularly addicted myself to any one science, I have never
done it; neither is there any one art of which I am able to draw the
first lineaments and dead color; insomuch that there is not a boy of
the lowest form in a school, that may not pretend to be wiser than I,

who am not able to examine him in his first lesson, which, if I am at any time forced upon, I am necessitated, in my own defense, to ask him, unaptly enough, some universal questions, such as may serve to try his natural understanding; a lesson as strange and unknown to him, as his is to me.

I never seriously settled myself to the reading any book of solid learning but Plutarch and Seneca; and there, like the Danaides, I eternally fill, and it as constantly runs out; something of which drops upon this paper, but little or nothing stays with me. History is my particular game as to matter of reading, or else poetry, for which I have particular kindness and esteem: for, as Cleanthes said, as the voice, forced through the narrow passage of a trumpet, comes out more forcible and shrill; so, methinks, a sentence pressed within the harmony of verse, darts out more briskly upon the understanding, and strikes my ear and apprehension with a smarter and more pleasing effect. As to the natural parts I have, of which this is the essay, I find them to bow under the burden; my fancy and judgment do but grope in the dark, tripping and stumbling in the way, and when I have gone as far as I can, I am in no degree satisfied; I discover still a new and greater extent of land before me, with a troubled and imperfect sight and wrapped up in clouds, that I am not able to penetrate. And taking upon me to write indifferently of whatever comes into my head, and therein making use of nothing but my own proper and natural means, if it befall me, as oft-times it does, accidentally to meet in any good author, the same heads and commonplaces upon which I have attempted to write . . . to see myself so weak and so forlorn, so heavy and so flat, in comparison of those better writers, I at once pity or despise myself. Yet do I please myself with this, that my opinions have often the honor and good fortune to jump with theirs, and that I go in the same path, though at a very great distance, and can say, "Ah, that is so." I am farther satisfied to find, that I have a quality, which everyone is not blessed withal, which is, to discern the vast difference between them and me; and notwithstanding all that, suffer my own inventions, low and feeble as they are, to run on in their career, without mending or plastering up the defects that this comparison has laid open to my own view. . . .

[. . .]

But, be it how it will, and how inconsiderable soever these essays of mine may be, I will say I never intended to conceal them, no more than my old bald grizzled pate before them, where the painter has presented you not with a perfect face, but with mine. For these are my own particular opinions and fancies, and I deliver them as only what I myself believe, and not for what is to be believed by others. I have no other end in this writing, but only to discover myself, who, also, shall, peradventure, be another thing tomorrow, if I chance to meet any new instruction to change me. I have no authority to be believed, neither do I desire it, being too conscious of my own inerudition to be able to instruct others.

A friend of mine, then, having read the preceding chapter, the other day told me, that I should a little farther have extended my discourse on the education of children. Now, madame, if I had any sufficiency in this subject, I could not possibly better employ it, than to present my best instructions to the little gentleman that threatens you shortly with a happy birth (for you are too generous to begin otherwise than with a male); for having had so great a hand in the treaty of your marriage, I have a certain particular right and interest in the greatness and prosperity of the issue that shall spring from it; besides that, your having had the best of my services so long in possession, sufficiently obliges me to desire the honor and advantage of all wherein you shall be concerned. But, in truth, all I understand as to that particular is only this, that the greatest and most important difficulty of human science is the education of children. For as in agriculture, the husbandry that is to precede planting, as also planting itself, is certain, plain, and well known; but after that which is planted comes to life, there is a great deal more to be done, more art to be used, more care to be taken, and much more difficulty to cultivate and bring it to perfection; so it is with men; it is no hard matter to get children; but after they are born, then begins the trouble, solicitude, and care rightly to train, principle, and bring them up. The symptoms of their inclinations in that tender age are so obscure, and the promises so uncertain and fallacious, that it is very hard to establish any solid judgment or conjecture upon them. . . .

[. . .]

For a boy of quality then, who pretends to letters not upon the account of profit (for so mean an object as that is unworthy of the grace and favor of the Muses, and moreover, in it a man directs his service to and depends upon others), nor so much for outward ornament, as for his own proper and peculiar use, and to furnish and enrich himself within, having rather a desire to come out an accomplished cavalier than a mere scholar or learned man; for such a one, I say, I would, also, have his friends solicitous to find him out a tutor, who has rather a well-made than a well-filled head; seeking, indeed, both the one and the other, but rather of the two to prefer manners and judgment to mere learning, and that this man should exercise his charge after a new method.

'Tis the custom of pedagogues to be eternally thundering in their pupil's ears, as they were pouring into a funnel, while the business of the pupil is only to repeat what the others have said: now I would have a tutor to correct this error, and, that at the very first, he should, according to the capacity he has to deal with, put it to the test, permitting his pupil himself to taste things, and of himself to discern and choose them, sometimes opening the way to him, and sometimes leaving him to open it for himself; that is, I would not have him alone to invent and speak, but that he should also hear his pupil speak in turn. Socrates, and since him Arcesilaus, made first their scholars speak, and then they spoke to them. *"Obest plerumque iis, qui discere volunt, auctoritas eorum, qui docent."*[1] It is good to make him, like a young horse, trot before him that he may judge of his going and how much he is to abate of his own speed, to accommodate himself to the vigor and capacity of the other. For want of which due proportion we spoil all; which also to know how to adjust, and to keep within an exact and due measure, is one of the hardest things I know, and 'tis the effect of a high and well-tempered soul to know how to condescend to such puerile motions and to govern and direct them. I walk firmer and more secure up hill than down.

Such as, according to our common way of teaching, undertake, with one and the same lesson, and the same measure of direction, to instruct several boys of differing and unequal capacities, are infinitely mistaken; and 'tis no wonder, if in a whole multitude of scholars, there are not found above two or three who bring away any good account of their time and discipline. Let the master not only examine him about the grammatical construction of the bare words of his lesson, but about the sense and substance of them, and let him judge of the profit he has made, not by the testimony of his memory, but by that of his life. Let him make him put what he has learned into a hundred several forms, and accommodate it to so many several subjects, to see if he yet rightly comprehends it, and has made it his

---

1. Montaigne quotes from Cicero's *On the Nature of the Gods*: "The authority of those who teach often hinders those who wish to learn."

own, taking instruction of his progress by the pedagogic institutions of Plato. 'Tis a sign of crudity and indigestion to disgorge what we eat in the same condition it was swallowed; the stomach has not performed its office unless it have altered the form and condition of what was committed to it to concoct. Our minds work only upon trust, when bound and compelled to follow the appetite of another's fancy, enslaved and captivated under the authority of another's instruction; we have been so subjected to the trammel, that we have no free, nor natural pace of our own; our own vigor and liberty are extinct and gone: *"Nunquam tutelae suae fiunt."*[2] . . .

Let him make him examine and thoroughly sift everything he reads, and lodge nothing in his fancy upon simple authority and upon trust. Aristotle's principles will then be no more principles to him, than those of Epicurus and the Stoics: let this diversity of opinions be propounded to, and laid before him; he will himself choose, if he be able; if not, he will remain in doubt. *"Che, non men che saper, dubbiar m' aggrata,"*[3] for, if he embrace the opinions of Xenophon and Plato, by his own reason, they will no more be theirs, but become his own. Who follows another, follows nothing, finds nothing, nay, is inquisitive after nothing.

"Non sumus sub rege; sibi quisque se vindicet."[4] Let him at least, know that he knows. It will be necessary that he imbibe their knowledge, not that he be corrupted with their precepts; and no matter if he forgot where he had his learning, provided he know how to apply it to his own use. Truth and reason are common to everyone, and are no more his who spake them first, than his who speaks them after: 'tis no more according to Plato, than according to me, since both he and I equally see and understand them. Bees cull their several sweets from this flower and that blossom, here and there where they find them, but themselves afterward make the honey, which is all and purely their own, and no more thyme and marjoram: so the several fragments he borrows from others, he will transform and shuffle together to compile a work that shall be absolutely his own; that is to say, his judgment: his instruction, labor and study, tend to nothing else but to form that. He is not obliged to discover whence he got the materials that have assisted him, but only to produce what he

2. Montaigne quotes from Seneca's *Letters*: "They never learn to learn on their own."
3. Montaigne quotes from Dante's *Inferno*. That is, "No less it pleases me to doubt than wise to be."
4. Montaigne quotes from Seneca's *Letters*. That is, "We are not under a king's command. Everyone may challenge himself; for let him at least know that he knows."

has himself done with them. . . . To know by rote, is no knowledge, and signifies no more but only to retain what one has intrusted to our memory. That which a man rightly knows and understands, he is the free disposer of at his own full liberty, without any regard to the author from whence he had it or fumbling over the leaves of his book. A mere bookish learning is a poor, paltry learning; it may serve for ornament, but there is yet no foundation for any superstructure to be built upon it, according to the opinion of Plato, who says that constancy, faith, and sincerity, are the true philosophy, and the other sciences, that are directed to other ends, mere adulterate paint. . .

[. . .]

. . . this method of education ought to be carried on with a severe sweetness, quite contrary to the practice of our pedants, who, instead of tempting and alluring children to letters by apt and gentle ways, do in truth present nothing before them but rods and ferules, horror and cruelty. Away with this violence! away with this compulsion! than which, I certainly believe nothing more dulls and degenerates a well-descended nature. If you would have him apprehend shame and chastisement, do not harden him to them: inure him to heat and cold, to wind and sun, and to dangers that he ought to despise; wean him from all effeminacy and delicacy in clothes and lodging, eating and drinking; accustom him to everything, that he may not be a Sir Paris, a carpet-knight, but a sinewy, hardy, and vigorous young man. I have ever from a child to the age wherein I now am, been of this opinion, and am still constant to it. But among other things, the strict government of most of our colleges has evermore displeased me; peradventure, they might have erred less perniciously on the indulgent side. 'Tis a real house of correction of imprisoned youth. They are made debauched, by being punished before they are so. Do but come in when they are about their lesson, and you shall hear nothing but the outcries of boys under execution, with the thundering noise of their pedagogues drunk with fury. A very pretty way this, to tempt these tender and timorous souls to love their book, with a furious countenance, and a rod in hand! A cursed and pernicious way of proceeding! Besides what Quintilian has very well observed, that this imperious authority is often attended by very dangerous consequences, and particularly our way of chastising. How much more decent would it be to see their classes strewed with green leaves and fine flowers, than with the bloody stumps of birch and willows? Were it left to my ordering, I should paint the school with the pictures of joy and gladness; Flora and the Graces, as the philosopher Speusippus did his. Where their profit is, let them there have their pleasure too. Such viands as are proper and wholesome for children, should be sweetened with sugar, and such as are dangerous to them, embittered with gall. 'Tis marvelous to see how solicitous Plato is in his Laws concerning the gayety and diversion of the youth of his city, and how much and often he enlarges upon their races, sports, songs, leaps, and dances: of which, he says, that antiquity has given the ordering and patronage particularly to the gods themselves, to Apollo, Minerva, and the Muses. . . .

—*Translated from the French by Charles Cotton*

SOURCE: *The Essays of Montaigne.* Translated by Charles Cotton. Edited by William Carew Hazlitt. London: Reeves and Turner. 1877.

THOMAS FULLER

"The Good Schoolmaster"
(1642)

The English historian and essayist was born in 1608. Fuller attended Queen's College, Cambridge. He died in 1661. This essay first appeared as a passage in The Holy State and the Prophane State.

There is scarce any profession in the commonwealth more necessary, which is so slightly performed. The reasons whereof I conceive to be these: First, young scholars make this calling their refuge; yea, perchance, before they have taken any degree in the university, commence schoolmasters in the country, as if nothing else were required to set up this profession but only a rod and a ferula. Secondly, others who are able, use it only as a passage to better preferment, to patch the rents in their present fortune, till they can provide a new one, and betake themselves to some more gainful calling. Thirdly, they are disheartened from doing their best with the miserable reward which in some places they receive, being masters to their children and slaves to their parents. Fourthly, being grown rich, they grow negligent, and scorn to touch the school but by the proxy of the usher. But see how well our schoolmaster behaves himself.

His genius inclines him with delight to his profession. Some men had as well be schoolboys as schoolmasters, to be tied to the school, as Cooper's *Dictionary* and Scapula's *Lexicon* are chained to the desk therein; and though great scholars, and skilful in other arts, are bunglers in this. But God, of His goodness, hath fitted several men for several callings, that the necessity of Church and State, in all conditions, may be provided for. So that he who beholds the fabric thereof, may say, God hewed out the stone, and appointed it to lie in this very place, for it would fit none other so well, and here it doth most excellent. And thus God mouldeth some for a schoolmaster's life, undertaking it with desire and delight, and discharging it with dexterity and happy success.

He studieth his scholars' natures as carefully as they their books; and ranks their dispositions into several forms. And though it may seem difficult for him in a great school to descend to all particulars, yet experienced schoolmasters may quickly make a grammar of boys' natures, and reduce them all—saving some few exceptions—to these general rules:

Those that are ingenious and industrious. The conjunction of two such planets in a youth presage much good unto him. To such a lad a frown may be a whipping, and a whipping a death; yea, where their master whips them once, shame whips them all the week after. Such natures he useth with all gentleness.

Those that are ingenious and idle. These think with the hare in the fable, that running with snails so they count the rest of their schoolfellows they shall come soon enough to the post, though sleeping a good while before their starting. Oh, a good rod would finely take them napping.

Those that are dull and diligent. Wines, the stronger they be, the more lees they have when they are new. Many boys are muddy-headed till they be clarified with age, and such afterwards prove the best. Bristol diamonds are both bright, and squared, and pointed by nature, and yet are soft and worthless; whereas orient ones in India are rough and rugged naturally. Hard, rugged, and dull natures of youth, acquit themselves afterwards the jewels of the country, and therefore their dullness at first is to be borne with, if they be diligent. That schoolmaster deserves to be beaten himself who beats nature in a boy for a fault. And I question whether all the whipping in the world can make their parts which are naturally sluggish rise one minute before the hour nature hath appointed.

Those that are invincibly dull, and negligent also. Correction may reform the latter, not amend the former. All the whetting in the world can never set a razor's edge on that which hath no steel in it. Such boys he consigneth over to other professions. Shipwrights and boat-makers will choose those crooked pieces of timber which other carpenters refuse. Those may make excellent merchants and mechanics which will not serve for scholars.

He is able, diligent, and methodical in his teaching; not leading them rather in a circle than forwards. He minces his precepts for children to swallow, hanging clogs on the nimbleness of his own soul, that his scholars may go along with him.

He is and will be known to be an absolute monarch in his school. If cockering mothers proffer him money to purchase their sons' exemption from his rod (to live, as it were, in a peculiar, out of their master's jurisdiction), with disdain he refuseth it, and scorns the late custom in some places of commuting whipping into money, and ransoming boys from the rod at a set price. If he hath a stubborn youth, correction-proof, he debaseth not his authority by contesting with him, but fairly, if he can, puts him away before his obstinacy hath infected others.

He is moderate in inflicting deserved correction. Many a schoolmaster better answereth the name *paidotribes* than *paidagogos*[5], rather tearing his scholars' flesh with whipping than giving them good education. No wonder if his scholars hate the muses, being presented unto them in the shape of fiends and furies. Junius complains "of the executioner of the insolent," of the schoolmaster by whom "he is torn by whips seven or eight times a day." Yea, hear the lamentable verses of poor Tusser in his own life:

> From Paul's I went, to Eton sent.
> To learn straightways the Latin phrase
> Where fifty-three stripes given to me
> At once I had.
>
> For fault but small, or none at all,
> It came to pass thus beat I was;
> See Udall, see the mercy of thee
> To me, poor lad.

Such an Orbilius mars more scholars than he makes. Their tyranny hath caused many tongues to stammer which spake plain by nature, and whose stuttering at first was nothing else but fears quavering on their speech at their master's presence; and whose mauling them about their heads hath dulled those who in quickness exceeded their master.

He makes his school free to him who sues to him *in forma pauperis*[6]. And surely learning is the greatest alms that can be given. But he is a beast who, because the poor scholar cannot pay him his wages, pays the scholar in his whipping; rather are diligent lads to be encouraged with all excitements to learning. This minds me of what

5. *Paidotribes* and *paidagogos*: Greek for "physical-educator" and "educator."
6. *In forma pauperis*: Latin for "as a poor person."

I have heard concerning Mr. Bust, that worthy late schoolmaster of Eton, who would never suffer any wandering begging scholar such as justly the statute hath ranked in the fore-front of rogues to come into his school, but would thrust him out with earnestness however privately charitable unto him lest his schoolboys should be disheartened from their books, by seeing some scholars after their studying in the university preferred to beggary.

He spoils not a good school to make thereof a bad college, therein to teach his scholars logic. For, besides that logic may have an action, of trespass against grammar for encroaching on her liberties, syllogisms are solecisms taught in the school, and oftentimes they are forced afterwards in the university to unlearn the fumbling skill they had before.

Out of his school he is no way pedantical in carriage or discourse; contenting himself to be rich in Latin, though he doth not jingle with it in every company wherein he comes.

To conclude, let this, amongst other motives, make schoolmasters careful in their place—that the eminences of their scholars have commended the memories of their schoolmasters to posterity, who, otherwise in obscurity, had altogether been forgotten.

SOURCE: *A Book of English Literature*. Edited by Franklyn Bliss Snyder and Robert Grant Martin. New York: Macmillan. 1916.

JEAN-JACQUES ROUSSEAU

from *Emile, or On Education*
"Children Require the Naked Truth"
(1762)

The most famous philosopher of the Enlightenment was the Swiss-born Rousseau (1712–1778). He was a man of feeling and trusted those feelings to lead his thoughts through discourses on politics, music, literature and education. He was not a successful teacher but was able to conjure up what kind of teacher he would have had to be to follow through on the education of an imaginary boy like Emile. He writes in Book 1 of Emile: *"I have had enough experience of the task to convince myself of my own unfitness, and my circumstances would make it impossible, even if my talents were such as to fit me for it. . . . If I am unable to undertake the more useful task, I will at least venture to attempt the easier one; I will follow the example of my predecessors and take up, not the task, but my pen; and instead of doing the right thing I will try to say it. . . . I have therefore decided to take an imaginary pupil, to assume on my own part the age, health, knowledge, and talents required for the work of his education, to guide him from birth to manhood, when he needs no guide but himself." The excerpt below, wherein Rousseau picks apart a fable of La Fontaine's, is from Book 2.*

Remember, reader, that he who speaks to you is neither a scholar nor a philosopher, but a plain man and a lover of truth; a man who is pledged to no one party or system, a hermit, who mixes little with other men, and has less opportunity of imbibing their prejudices, and more time to reflect on the things that strike him in his intercourse with them. My arguments are based less on theories than on facts, and I think I can find no better way to bring the facts home to you than by quoting continually some example from the observations which suggested my arguments.

I had gone to spend a few days in the country with a worthy mother of a family who took great pains with her children and their education. One morning I was present while the eldest boy had his lessons. His tutor, who had taken great pains to teach him ancient history, began upon the story of Alexander and lighted on the well-known anecdote of Philip the Doctor. There is a picture of it, and the story is well worth study. The tutor, worthy man, made several reflections which I did not like with regard to Alexander's courage, but I did not argue with him lest I should lower him in the eyes of his pupil. At dinner they did not fail to get the little fellow talking, French fashion. The eager spirit of a child of his age, and the confident expectation of applause, made him say a number of silly things, and among them from time to time there were things to the point, and these made people forget the rest. At last came the story of Philip the Doctor. He told it very distinctly and prettily. After the usual meed of praise, demanded by his mother and expected by the child himself, they discussed what he had said. Most of them blamed Alexander's rashness, some of them, following the tutor's example, praised his resolution, which showed me that none of those present really saw the beauty of the story. "For my own part," I said, "if there was any courage or any steadfastness at all in Alexander's conduct I think it was only a piece of bravado." Then every one agreed that it was a piece of bravado. I was getting angry, and would have replied, when a lady sitting beside me, who had not hitherto spoken, bent towards me and whispered in my ear. "Jean Jacques," said she, "say no more, they will never understand you." I looked at her, I recognized the wisdom of her advice, and I held my tongue.

Several things made me suspect that our young professor had not in the least understood the story he told so prettily. After dinner I took his hand in mine and we went for a walk in the park. When I had questioned him quietly, I discovered that he admired the vaunted courage of Alexander more than anyone. But in what do you suppose he thought this courage consisted? Merely in swallowing a disagreeable drink at a single draught without hesitation and without any signs of dislike. Not a fortnight before the poor child had been made to take some medicine which he could hardly swallow, and the taste of it was still in his mouth. Death, and death by poisoning, were for him only disagreeable sensations, and senna was his only idea of poison. I must admit, however, that Alexander's resolution had made a great impression on his young mind, and he was determined that next time he had to take medicine he would be an Alexander. Without entering upon explanations which were clearly beyond his grasp, I confirmed him in his praiseworthy intention, and returned home smiling to myself over the great wisdom of parents and teachers who expect to teach history to children.

Such words as king, emperor, war, conquest, law, and revolution are easily put into their mouths; but when it is a question of attaching clear ideas to these words the explanations are very different from our talk with Robert the gardener.

I feel sure some readers dissatisfied with that "Say no more, Jean Jacques," will ask what I really saw to admire in the conduct of Alexander. Poor things! if you need telling, how can you comprehend it? Alexander believed in virtue, he staked his head, he staked his own life on that faith, his great soul was fitted to hold such a faith. To swallow that draught was to make a noble profession of the faith that was in him. Never did mortal man recite a finer creed. If there is an Alexander in our own days, show me such deeds.

If children have no knowledge of words, there is no study that is suitable for them. If they have no real ideas they have no real memory, for I do not call that a memory which only recalls sensations. What is the use of inscribing on their brains a list of symbols which mean nothing to them? They will learn the symbols when they learn the things signified; why give them the useless trouble of learning them twice over? And yet what dangerous prejudices are you implanting when you teach them to accept as knowledge words which have no meaning for them. The first meaningless phrase, the first thing taken for granted on the word of another person without seeing its use for himself, this is the beginning of the ruin of the child's judgment. He may dazzle the eyes of fools long enough before he recovers from such a loss.[7]

No, if nature has given the child this plasticity of brain which fits him to receive every kind of impression, it was not that you should imprint on it the names and dates of kings, the jargon of heraldry,

---

7. The learning of most philosophers is like the learning of children. Vast erudition results less in the multitude of ideas than in a multitude of images. Dates, names, places, all objects isolated or unconnected with ideas are merely retained in the memory for symbols, and we rarely recall any of these without seeing the right or left page of the book in which we read it, or the form in which we first saw it. Most science was of this kind till recently. The science of our times is another matter; study and observation are things of the past; we dream and the dreams of a bad night are given to us as philosophy. You will say I too am a dreamer; I admit it, but I do what the others fail to do, I give my dreams as dreams, and leave the reader to discover whether there is anything in them which may prove useful to those who are awake. [Rousseau's footnote.]

the globe and geography, all those words without present meaning or future use for the child, which flood of words overwhelms his sad and barren childhood. But by means of this plasticity all the ideas he can understand and use, all that concern his happiness and will some day throw light upon his duties, should be traced at an early age in indelible characters upon his brain, to guide him to live in such a way as befits his nature and his powers.

Without the study of books, such a memory as the child may possess is not left idle; everything he sees and hears makes an impression on him, he keeps a record of men's sayings and doings, and his whole environment is the book from which he unconsciously enriches his memory, till his judgment is able to profit by it.

To select these objects, to take care to present him constantly with those he may know, to conceal from him those he ought not to know, this is the real way of training his early memory; and in this way you must try to provide him with a storehouse of knowledge which will serve for his education in youth and his conduct throughout life. True, this method does not produce infant prodigies, nor will it reflect glory upon their tutors and governesses, but it produces men, strong, right-thinking men, vigorous both in mind and body, men who do not win admiration as children, but honor as men.

Emile will not learn anything by heart, not even fables, not even the fables of La Fontaine, simple and delightful as they are, for the words are no more the fable than the words of history are history. How can people be so blind as to call fables the child's system of morals, without considering that the child is not only amused by the apologue but misled by it? He is attracted by what is false and he misses the truth, and the means adopted to make the teaching pleasant prevent him profiting by it. Men may be taught by fables; children require the naked truth.

All children learn La Fontaine's fables, but not one of them understands them. It is just as well that they do not understand, for the morality of the fables is so mixed and so unsuitable for their age that it would be more likely to incline them to vice than to virtue. "More paradoxes!" you exclaim. Paradoxes they may be; but let us see if there is not some truth in them.

I maintain that the child does not understand the fables he is taught, for however you try to explain them, the teaching you wish to extract from them demands ideas which he cannot grasp, while the poetical form which makes it easier to remember makes it harder to understand, so that clearness is sacrificed to facility. Without quoting the host of wholly unintelligible and useless fables which are taught to children because they happen to be in the same book as the others, let us keep to those which the author seems to have written specially for children.

In the whole of La Fontaine's works I only know five or six fables conspicuous for child-like simplicity; I will take the first of these as an example, for it is one whose moral is most suitable for all ages, one which children get hold of with the least difficulty, which they have most pleasure in learning, one which for this very reason the author has placed at the beginning of his book. If his object were really to delight and instruct children, this fable is his masterpiece. Let us go through it and examine it briefly.

THE FOX AND THE CROW: A FABLE

"Maitre corbeau, sur un arbre perche" (Mr. Crow perched on a tree).

"Mr.!" what does that word really mean? What does it mean before a proper noun? What is its meaning here? What is a crow? What is "un arbre perche"? We do not say "on a tree perched," but perched on a tree. So we must speak of poetical inversions, we must distinguish between prose and verse.

"Tenait dans son bec un fromage" (Held a cheese in his beak)

What sort of a cheese? Swiss, Brie, or Dutch? If the child has never seen crows, what is the good of talking about them? If he has seen crows will he believe that they can hold a cheese in their beak? Your illustrations should always be taken from nature.

"Maitre renard, par l'odeur alleche" (Mr. Fox, attracted by the smell).

Another Master! But the title suits the fox—who is master of all the tricks of his trade. You must explain what a fox is, and distinguish between the real fox and the conventional fox of the fables.

"Alleche." The word is obsolete; you will have to explain it. You will say it is only used in verse. Perhaps the child will ask why people talk differently in verse. How will you answer that question?

"Alleche, par l'odeur d'un fromage." The cheese was held in his beak by a crow perched on a tree; it must indeed have smelt strong if the fox, in his thicket or his earth, could smell it. This is the way you train your pupil in that spirit of right judgment, which rejects all but reasonable arguments, and is able to distinguish between truth and falsehood in other tales.

"Lui tient a peu pres ce langage" (Spoke to him after this fashion).

"Ce langage." So foxes talk, do they! They talk like crows! Mind what you are about, oh, wise tutor; weigh your answer before you give it, it is more important than you suspect.

"*Eh! Bonjour, Monsieur le Corbeau!*" ("*Good-day, Mr. Crow!*")

Mr.! The child sees this title laughed to scorn before he knows it is a title of honor. Those who say "Monsieur du Corbeau" will find their work cut out for them to explain that "du."

"*Que vous etes joli! Que vous me semblez beau!*" ("*How handsome you are, how beautiful in my eyes!*")

Mere padding. The child, finding the same thing repeated twice over in different words, is learning to speak carelessly. If you say this redundance is a device of the author, a part of the fox's scheme to make his praise seem all the greater by his flow of words, that is a valid excuse for me, but not for my pupil.

"*Sans mentir, si votre ramage*" ("*Without lying, if your song*").

"Without lying." So people do tell lies sometimes. What will the child think of you if you tell him the fox only says "Sans mentir" because he is lying?

"*Se rapporte a votre plumage*" ("*Answered to your fine feathers*").

"Answered!" What does that mean? Try to make the child compare qualities so different as those of song and plumage; you will see how much he understands.

"*Vous seriez le phenix des hotes de ces bois!*" ("*You would be the phoenix of all the inhabitants of this wood!*")

The phoenix! What is a phoenix? All of a sudden we are floundering in the lies of antiquity—we are on the edge of mythology.

"The inhabitants of this wood." What figurative language! The flatterer adopts the grand style to add dignity to his speech, to make it more attractive. Will the child understand this cunning? Does he know, how could he possibly know, what is meant by grand style and simple style?

"*A ces mots le corbeau ne se sent pas de joie*" (At these words, the crow is beside himself with delight).

To realise the full force of this proverbial expression we must have experienced very strong feeling.

"*Et, pour montrer sa belle voix*" (And, to show his fine voice).

Remember that the child, to understand this line and the whole fable, must know what is meant by the crow's fine voice.

"*Il ouvre un large bec, laisse tomber sa proie*" (He opens his wide beak and drops his prey).

This is a splendid line; its very sound suggests a picture. I see the great big ugly gaping beak, I hear the cheese crashing through the branches; but this kind of beauty is thrown away upon children.

"*Le renard s'en saisit, et dit, 'Mon bon monsieur'*" (*The fox catches it, and says, "My dear sir"*).

So kindness is already folly. You certainly waste no time in teaching your children.

"*Apprenez que tout flatteur*" ("*You must learn that every flatterer*").

A general maxim. The child can make neither head nor tail of it.

"*Vit au depens de celui qui l'ecoute*" ("*Lives at the expense of the person who listens to his flattery*").

No child of ten ever understood that.

"*Ce lecon vaut bien un fromage, sans doute*" ("*No doubt this lesson is well worth a cheese*").

This is intelligible and its meaning is very good. Yet there are few children who could compare a cheese and a lesson, few who would not prefer the cheese. You will therefore have to make them understand that this is said in mockery. What subtlety for a child!

"*Le corbeau, honteux et confus*" (*The crow, ashamed and confused*).

A nothing pleonasm, and there is no excuse for it this time.

"*Jura, mais un peu tard, qu'on ne l'y prendrait plus*" (*Swore, but rather too late, that he would not be caught in that way again*).

"Swore." What master will be such a fool as to try to explain to a child the meaning of an oath?

What a host of details! but much more would be needed for the analysis of all the ideas in this fable and their reduction to the simple and elementary ideas of which each is composed. But who thinks this analysis necessary to make himself intelligible to children? Who of us is philosopher enough to be able to put himself in the child's place? Let us now proceed to the moral.

Should we teach a six-year-old child that there are people who flatter and lie for the sake of gain? One might perhaps teach them that there are people who make fools of little boys and laugh at their foolish vanity behind their backs. But the whole thing is spoilt by the cheese. You are teaching them how to make another drop his cheese rather than how to keep their own. This is my second paradox, and it is not less weighty than the former one.

Watch children learning their fables and you will see that when they have a chance of applying them they almost always use them exactly contrary to the author's meaning; instead of being on their guard against the fault which you would prevent or cure, they are disposed to like the vice by which one takes advantage of another's defects. In the above fable children laugh at the crow, but they all love the fox. In the next fable you expect them to follow the example of the grasshopper. Not so, they will choose the ant. They do not care to abase themselves, they will always choose the principal part—this is the choice of self-love, a very natural choice. But what a dreadful lesson for children! There could be no monster more detestable than a harsh and avaricious child, who realized what he was asked to give and what he refused. The ant does more; she teaches him not merely to refuse but to revile.

In all the fables where the lion plays a part, usually the chief part, the child pretends to be the lion, and when he has to preside over some distribution of good things, he takes care to keep everything for himself; but when the lion is overthrown by the gnat, the child is the gnat. He learns how to sting to death those whom he dare not attack openly.

From the fable of the sleek dog and the starving wolf he learns a lesson of licence rather than the lesson of moderation which you profess to teach him. I shall never forget seeing a little girl weeping bitterly over this tale, which had been told her as a lesson in obedience. The poor child hated to be chained up; she felt the chain chafing her neck; she was crying because she was not a wolf.

So from the first of these fables the child learns the basest flattery; from the second, cruelty; from the third, injustice; from the fourth, satire; from the fifth, insubordination. The last of these lessons is no more suitable for your pupils than for mine, though he has no use for it. What results do you expect to get from your teaching when it contradicts itself! But perhaps the same system of morals which furnishes me with objections against the fables supplies you with as many reasons for keeping to them. Society requires a rule of morality in our words; it also requires a rule of morality in our deeds; and these two rules are quite different. The former is contained in the Catechism and it is left there; the other is contained in La Fontaine's fables for children and his tales for mothers. The same author does for both.

Let us make a bargain, M. de la Fontaine. For my own part, I undertake to make your books my favorite study; I undertake to love you, and to learn from your fables, for I hope I shall not mistake their meaning. As to my pupil, permit me to prevent him studying any one of them till you have convinced me that it is good for him to learn things three-fourths of which are unintelligible to him, and until you can convince me that in those fables he can understand he will never reverse the order and imitate the villain instead of taking warning from his dupe.

When I thus get rid of children's lessons, I get rid of the chief cause of their sorrows, namely their books. Reading is the curse of childhood, yet it is almost the only occupation you can find for children. Emile, at twelve years old, will hardly know what a book is. "But," you say, "he must, at least, know how to read."

When reading is of use to him, I admit he must learn to read, but till then he will only find it a nuisance.

If children are not to be required to do anything as a matter of obedience, it follows that they will only learn what they perceive to be of real and present value, either for use or enjoyment; what other motive could they have for learning? The art of speaking to our absent friends, of hearing their words; the art of letting them know at first hand our feelings, our desires, and our longings, is an art whose usefulness can be made plain at any age. How is it that this art, so useful and pleasant in itself, has become a terror to children? Because the child is compelled to acquire it against his will, and to use it for purposes beyond his comprehension. A child has no great wish to perfect himself in the use of an instrument of torture, but make it a means to his pleasure, and soon you will not be able to keep him from it.

People make a great fuss about discovering the best way to teach children to read. They invent "bureaux"[8] and cards, they turn the nursery into a printer's shop. Locke would have them taught to read by means of dice. What a fine idea! And the pity of it! There is a better way than any of those, and one which is generally overlooked—it consists in the desire to learn. Arouse this desire in your scholar and have done with your "bureaux" and your dice—any method will serve.

Present interest, that is the motive power, the only motive power that takes us far and safely. Sometimes Emile receives notes of invitation from his father or mother, his relations or friends; he is invited to a dinner, a walk, a boating expedition, to see some public entertain-

8. The "bureau" was a sort of case containing letters to be put together to form words. It was a favorite device for the teaching of reading and gave its name to a special method, called the bureau-method, of learning to read. [Translator's footnote.]

ment. These notes are short, clear, plain, and well written. Someone must read them to him, and he cannot always find anybody when wanted; no more consideration is shown to him than he himself showed to you yesterday. Time passes, the chance is lost. The note is read to him at last, but it is too late. Oh! if only he had known how to read! He receives other notes, so short, so interesting, he would like to try to read them. Sometimes he gets help, sometimes none. He does his best, and at last he makes out half the note; it is something about going tomorrow to drink cream—Where? With whom? He cannot tell—how hard he tries to make out the rest! I do not think Emile will need a "bureau." Shall I proceed to the teaching of writing? No, I am ashamed to toy with these trifles in a treatise on education.

I will just add a few words which contain a principle of great importance. It is this—What we are in no hurry to get is usually obtained with speed and certainty. I am pretty sure Emile will learn to read and write before he is ten, just because I care very little whether he can do so before he is fifteen; but I would rather he never learnt to read at all, than that this art should be acquired at the price of all that makes reading useful. What is the use of reading to him if he always hates it? . .

The more I urge my method of letting well alone, the more objections I perceive against it. If your pupil learns nothing from you, he will learn from others. If you do not instil truth he will learn falsehoods; the prejudices you fear to teach him he will acquire from those about him, they will find their way through every one of his senses; they will either corrupt his reason before it is fully developed or his mind will become torpid through inaction, and will become engrossed in material things. If we do not form the habit of thinking as children, we shall lose the power of thinking for the rest of our life.

I fancy I could easily answer that objection, but why should I answer every objection? If my method itself answers your objections, it is good; if not, it is good for nothing. I continue my explanation.

If, in accordance with the plan I have sketched, you follow rules which are just the opposite of the established practice, if instead of taking your scholar far afield, instead of wandering with him in distant places, in far-off lands, in remote centuries, in the ends of the earth, and in the very heavens themselves, you try to keep him to himself, to his own concerns, you will then find him able to perceive, to remember, and even to reason; this is nature's order. As the sentient being becomes active his discernment develops along

with his strength. Not till his strength is in excess of what is needed
for self-preservation is the speculative faculty developed, the faculty
adapted for using this superfluous strength for other purposes. Would
you cultivate your pupil's intelligence, cultivate the strength it is
meant to control. Give his body constant exercise, make it strong
and healthy, in order to make him good and wise; let him work, let
him do things, let him run and shout, let him be always on the go;
make a man of him in strength, and he will soon be a man in reason.

Of course by this method you will make him stupid if you are
always giving him directions, always saying come here, go there,
stop, do this, don't do that. If your head always guides his hands, his
own mind will become useless. But remember the conditions we
laid down; if you are a mere pedant it is not worth your while to
read my book.

—*Translated from the French by Barbara Foxley*

SOURCE: Jean-Jacques Rousseau. *Emile, or On Education*. New York:
J. M. Dent and Sons. 1921.

JOHANN HEINRICH PESTALOZZI

"A Letter on Early Education"
(1819)

The "Father of Modern Education" was a Swiss from Zurich, born in 1746. He ran an orphanage before creating the school in Yverdon, Switzerland, that he made famous. He believed in universal education for the poor, for both boys and girls. His educational influence on Lev Tolstoy's pedagogical ideas is apparent (see Tolstoy's essay below); his influence continues today. "The only influence to which the heart is accessible for a long time before the mind can appreciate it," he writes elsewhere, "is that of affection." Pestalozzi died in 1827.

February 4, 1819

My Dear Greaves—

If education is understood to be the work, not of a certain course of exercises resumed at stated times, but of a continual and benevolent superintendence; if the importance of development is acknowledged not only in favor of the memory, and the intellect, and a few abilities which lead to indispensable attainments, but in favor of all the faculties, whatever may be their names, or nature, or energy, which Providence has implanted; its province, thus enlarged, will yet be with less difficulty surveyed from one point of view, and will have more of a systematic and truly philosophical character, than an incoherent mass of exercises, arranged without unity of principle, and gone through without interest, which frequently, not very appropriately, receives the name of education.

We must bear in mind, that the ultimate end of education is not a perfection in the accomplishments of the school, but fitness for life; not the acquirement of habits of blind obedience, and of prescribed diligence, but a preparation for independent action. We must bear in mind, that whatever class of society a pupil may belong to, whatever calling he may be intended for, there are certain faculties in human nature common to all, which constitute the stock of the fundamen-

39

tal energies of man. We have no right to withhold from anyone the opportunities of developing all their faculties. It may be judicious to treat some of them with marked attention, and to give up the idea of bringing others to high perfection. The diversity of talent and inclination, of plans and pursuits, is a sufficient proof for the necessity of such a distinction. But I repeat, that we have no right to shut out the child from the development of those faculties also, which we may not for the present conceive to be very essential for his future calling or station in life.

Who is not acquainted with the vicissitudes of human fortune, which have frequently rendered an attainment valuable, that was little esteemed before, or led to regret the want of application to an exercise that had been treated with contempt? Who has not at some time or other experienced the delight of being able to benefit others by his advice or assistance, under circumstances when, but for his interference, they must have been deprived of that benefit? And who, even if in practice he is a stranger to it, would not at least in theory acknowledge, that the greatest satisfaction that man can obtain, is a consciousness that he is preeminently qualified to render himself useful?

But even if all this were not deserving of attention; if the sufficiency of ordinary acquirements for the great majority were vindicated on grounds, perhaps, of partial experience, and of inference from well-known facts; I would still maintain, that our systems of education have for the most part been laboring under this inconvenience, that they did not assign the due proportion to the different exercises proposed by them.

The only correct idea of this subject is to be derived from the examination of human nature with *all its faculties.* We do not find, in the vegetable or the animal kingdom, any species of objects gifted with certain qualities which are not, in some stage of its existence, called into play, and contribute to the full development of the character of the species in the individual. Even in the mineral kingdom, the wonders of Providence are incessantly manifested in the numberless combinations of crystallization; and thus even in the lowest department of created things, as far as we are acquainted with them, a constant law, the means employed by Supreme Intelligence, decides upon the formation, the shape, and the individual character of a mineral, according to its inherent properties. Although the circumstances under which a mineral may have been formed, or a plant may have grown, or an animal brought up, may influence and modify, yet they can never destroy that result, which the combined agency of its natural energies or qualities will produce.

Thus education, instead of merely considering what is to be imparted to children, ought to consider first what they may be said already to possess, if not as a developed, at least as an involved faculty capable of development. Or if, instead of speaking thus in the abstract, we will but recollect, that it is to the great Author of life, that man owes the possession, and is responsible for the use, of his innate faculties, education should not only decide what is to be made of a child, but rather inquire, what is a child qualified for? what is his destiny, as a created and responsible being? what are his faculties as a rational and moral being? what are the means pointed out for their perfection, and the end held out as the highest object of their efforts, by the Almighty Father of all, both in creation, and in the page of revelation?

To these questions, the answer must be simple and comprehensive. It must combine all mankind, it must be applicable to all, without distinction of zones, or nations, in which they may be born. It must acknowledge, in the first place, the rights of man in the fullest sense of the word. It must proceed to show, that these rights, far from being confined to those exterior advantages which have from time to time been secured by a successful struggle of the people, embrace a much higher privilege, the nature of which is not yet generally understood or appreciated. They embrace the rightful claims of all classes to a general diffusion of useful knowledge, a careful development of the intellect, and judicious attention to all the faculties of man, physical, intellectual, and moral.

It is in vain to talk of liberty, when man is unnerved, or his mind not stored with knowledge, or his judgment neglected, and above all, when he is left unconscious of his rights and his duties as a moral being.

—*Translated from the German*

SOURCE: Johann Heinrich Pestalozzi. *Letters on Early Education: Addressed to J. P. Greaves, Esq., with a Memoir of Pestalozzi.* London: Sherwood, Gilbert, and Piper. 1827.

CATHARINE E. BEECHER

from *Suggestions Respecting Improvements in Education*
(1829)

Beecher (1800–1878) was an older sister of Harriet Beecher Stowe, the inspired author of the novel that awakened America to the poison of slavery, Uncle Tom's Cabin. Catharine Beecher believed that women were particularly suited to teaching children and advocated for teachers' increased pay and social standing: "Most of the defects which are continually discovered and lamented in present systems of education may be traced, either directly or indirectly to the fact that the formation of the minds of children has not been made a profession securing wealth, influence, or honor, to those who enter it." She addressed this essay to the Trustees of the Hartford Female Seminary, a teacher-training school she founded in 1824 with two of her siblings.

It is believed that much good, which might be accomplished, remains unaffected, from the mere fact that mankind either do not know that it can be done, or are ignorant of the means to accomplish it. This, probably, is particularly true in the department of education.

Were the community only aware of what might be accomplished in those years, which, by the youth of our country, are devoted to education, could it be seen how much expense is vainly thrown away, how much time is painfully spent to no good purpose, how often the young mind is cramped and injured in some of its most noble faculties, by the discipline of the school room; could it be seen how much toil to pupils, vexation to teachers, and expense to parents, a little pecuniary aid, and improved methods of instruction would save, while the advantages of education would be increased a hundred fold, could all this be seen and realized, such effects would follow as it would now be deemed enthusiasm to portray.

It is believed therefore, that teachers, who have the best opportunity for learning and realizing these things, could not do a more essential service to the public, than by communicating the results of their experience and observation on such subjects. For until the community is apprized of the various defects of present systems of education, by those who are appointed to watch over its interests, the efforts cannot be expected which are necessary to correct them, nor that tone of public feeling which will demand such efforts.

This suggestion therefore may serve as an apology for the writer in thus communicating certain views on this subject, which have been deemed, by others, of sufficient importance to allow presenting them to the public.

Most of the defects which are continually discovered and lamented in present systems of education may be traced, either directly or indirectly to the fact that the formation of the minds of children has not been made a profession securing wealth, influence, or honour, to those who enter it.

The three professions of law, divinity, and medicine, present a reasonable prospect of reputation, influence and emolument to active and cultivated minds. The mercantile, manufacturing and mechanical professions, present a hope of gaining at least that wealth which can so readily purchase estimation and influence. But the profession of a teacher has not offered any such stimulus.

It has been looked upon as the resource of poverty, or as a drudgery suited only to inferior minds and far beneath the aims of the intellectual aspirant for fame and influence, or of the active competitor for wealth and distinction. The consequence of this has been, as a general fact, that this profession has never, until very recently, commanded, or secured the effort of gifted minds. These have all forsaken this for a more lucrative or a more honorable avenue; and few have engaged in it except those whose talents would not allow them to rise in other professions, or, those who only made it a temporary resort, till better prospects should offer.

In all other professions, we find bodies of men united by a common professional interest; we find organs of public communication in the form of periodicals, or of official reports; in all other professions the improvement of distinguished minds, and the result of their successful experiments are recorded and transmitted for the benefit of those who may succeed. The duties of all other professions are deemed of so much consequence that years must be spent, even after a liberal education, in preparing for these peculiar duties, and the public are so tenacious lest these professions should be filled by persons not properly prepared, that none may be admitted, but upon an examination before those qualified by study and experience to judge of the acquisitions of each candidate.

Even the simple business of making a shoe is deemed of such importance and difficulty as to demand an apprenticeship for years, and mankind are usually very cautious not to hazard employing even one of this profession who is unprepared for the business he attempts.

But to form the mind of man is deemed so simple and easy an affair, that no such preparation or precautions are required. Any person may become a teacher without any definite preparation, and without any test of skill or experience. Thousands will be found who would consider it ridiculous for a child to have his foot covered by an awkward and inexperienced artisan, who yet without a moment's examination would commit the formation of his mind to almost anyone who will offer to do the business. Were our country suddenly deprived of every artist who could make a shoe, we should immediately witness frequent combination and consultation to supply the loss. The most ingenious would be employed to communicate to others their skill, and thousands of minds would be directing their energies to restoring this useful art to its former advance toward perfection. But the human mind, that spark of immortality, that wonderful origin of knowledge, invention, affection, and moral power, where has been the combined effort, the patient instruction, the collected treasures of experience, the enthusiasm of interest, which should direct in clothing this emanation of Deity with all its expanded powers, its glowing affections, and undying energies? Has it not been the desultory, disunited business of a class of persons, driven to it by necessity, performing it without the enthusiasm which glows in all other professions and leaving it whenever a livelihood could be obtained in any other respectable way?

As this has heretofore been considered a profession so simple and easy as to demand little preparation for its peculiar duties, if these duties are arduous, and difficult, we should naturally expect it to be filled by those who are unprepared to discharge them properly.

It is to mothers, and to teachers, that the world is to look for the character which is to be enstamped on each succeeding generation, for it is to them that the great business of education is almost exclusively committed. And will it not appear by examination that neither mothers nor teachers have ever been properly educated for their profession. What is the profession of a Woman? Is it not to form immortal minds, and to watch, to nurse, and to rear the bodily system, so fearfully and wonderfully made, and upon the order and regulation of which, the health and well-being of the mind so greatly depends?

But let most of our sex upon whom these arduous duties devolve, be asked; have you ever devoted any time and study, in the course of your education, to any preparation for these duties? Have you been taught any thing of the structure, the nature, and the laws of the body, which you inhabit? Were you ever taught to understand the operation of diet, air, exercise and modes of dress upon the human frame? Have the causes which are continually operating to prevent good health, and the modes by which it might be perfected and preserved ever been made the subject of any instruction? Perhaps almost every voice would respond, no; we have attended to almost every thing more than to this; we have been taught more concerning the structure of the earth; the laws of the heavenly bodies; the habits and formation of plants; the philosophy of language; more of almost any thing, than the structure of the human frame and the laws of health and reason. But is it not the business, the profession of a woman to guard the health and form the physical habits of the young? And is not the cradle of infancy and the chamber of sickness sacred to woman alone? And ought she not to know at least some of the general principles of that perfect and wonderful piece of mechanism committed to her preservation and care?

The restoration of health is the physician's profession, but the preservation of it falls to other hands, and it is believed that the time will come, when woman will be taught to understand something respecting the construction of the human frame; the philosophical results which will naturally follow from restricted exercise, unhealthy modes of dress, improper diet, and many other causes, which are continually operating to destroy the health and life of the young.

Again let our sex be asked respecting the instruction they have received in the course of their education, on that still more arduous and difficult department of their profession, which relates to the intellect and the moral susceptibilities. Have you been taught the powers and faculties of the human mind, and the laws by which it is regulated? Have you studied how to direct its several faculties; how to restore those that are overgrown, and strengthen and mature those that are deficient? Have you been taught the best modes of communicating knowledge as well as of acquiring it? Have you learned the best mode of correcting bad moral habits and forming good ones?

Have you made it an object to find how a selfish disposition may be made generous; how a reserved temper may be made open and frank; how pettishness and ill humor may be changed to cheerfulness and kindness? Has any woman studied her profession in this respect? It is feared the same answer must be returned, if not from all, at least from most of our sex. No; we have acquired wisdom from the observation and experience of others, on almost all other subjects, but the philosophy of the direction and control of the human mind, has not been an object of thought or study. And thus it appears that though it is woman's express business to rear the body, and form the mind, there is scarcely anything to which her attention has been less directed.

But this strange and irrational neglect may be considered as the result of an equal neglect as it respects those whose exclusive business it is to form the mind and communicate knowledge. To the parents of a family there are many other cares committed besides the formation of the mental and moral habits of children. Indeed the pecuniary circumstances of most parents will allow them to devote but little time to the discharge of such duties. It is therefore an exceedingly wise and needful arrangement that a class of persons should be devoted exclusively to supplying these deficiencies. And it is the teachers of children who are to thus cooperate with parents, and who in many cases have much the most influence in forming both mental and moral habits. But teachers have never been properly instructed in their professions, and of course they cannot properly teach others to perform the same duties. Year after year has witnessed vast improvements accomplished in all the various departments of arts and sciences, but common school education has gone on in the same beaten track, age after age, as if the acme of perfection had been attained and no improvements were to be desired. Preparation for its duties has by few been considered of any great necessity. The professional skill demanded, has amounted to little more than an ability to restrain by fear, or by emulation the buoyant spirits and activity of youth, daily to furnish a specified lesson to each pupil, and then to find out how many words each has learned without any assistance from a teacher in discovering the meaning of the language, which in most school books is employed to lock up ideas. To perform these duties does not require any great professional knowledge, and did this really include all the duties of a teacher, there would be no cause of complaint, that the profession was not sufficiently honorable and lucrative, nor that its incumbents were not properly qualified. While teachers remain unqualified, it is not to be expected that many pupils will improve upon the modes pursued by those who have had the formation of their own minds, and thus the evil is perpetuated through society in all its various interests both of family and school education.

Many of the most serious evils in education, have arisen from the loan of proper school books. It may yet be found that no art requires so much patient observation, intellectual acumen, and ready invention, as that of communicating by language the various ideas which the youthful mind is to gain in the course of an education. Words are used with so many different meanings, and change so much in their signification by varieties in use; are such an imperfect organ of communication, and there are so many employed by matured minds to which children attach no definite idea, that the task of preparing books for young minds is one demanding no ordinary genius, experience, and nicety of observation. But the profession which makes such demands has until recently been forsaken by most minds of superior endowments, for more lucrative or honorable professions. Of course the books prepared for children are ordinarily made either by persons of only ordinary qualifications, or by men of superior intellect, who having never attempted to teach, know nothing of the difficulties of the art. The last make their school books very intelligible, clear, and well arranged for all who already understand what is to be taught; and they are not unintelligible to most mature minds, who have obtained a general knowledge of language. But school books made by this class of persons are, ordinarily as ill adapted to the wants of children as if they were written with half the words in a foreign tongue; and beside the defects occasioned by the use of language which the young mind does not comprehend, there are other defects of an equally serious nature, which need not now be considered.

The result has been an almost entire destitution of such books as are needed in elementary instruction, and minds of a superior order who are now entered upon the duties of this profession, have had but little time to do more than to discover the mistakes of past systems, and to begin some imperfect remedy. To prepare proper books for common schools must be a work of time, to be accomplished only by the efforts of superior minds, actively engaged in discovering by experiment the most successful methods of communicating ideas to the young mind. None but a teacher can understand the necessities of immature minds or test the suitableness of plans devised for their supply.

[. . .]

The writer holds that it ought to be a maxim in education, that *There Is No Defect In Character, Habits, or Manners, but Is Susceptible of Remedy.* Heretofore it has too often been the case, that teachers and guardians of youth, when they have found bad habits and bad dispositions existing in their pupils, have felt that these were evils that they must learn to bear with and control, rather than peculiarities which must be cured and eradicated. But this is not so. Let a teacher have sufficient time and facilities afforded, let her make this a definite and express object, let her seek to learn from the experience of others the various operations of the human mind, let her study the various methods of controlling the understanding, the conscience, and the natural affections, and there is scarce any thing she may not hope to effect. A selfish disposition can be made generous; a morose temper can be made kind; a reserved character can be made open and frank; an indolent mind can be stimulated to activity; pettishness and ill-humor can be changed to patient cheerfulness; a stubborn and unsubdued spirit can be made docile and tractable; vanity and heedless levity can be subdued; negligence in dress and personal habits can be remedied; uncouth or disagreeable manners or habits can be cured; anything can be effected in a mind endued with reason, conscience, and affection, if proper efforts are made, and proper facilities afforded.

SOURCE: Catharine E. Beecher. *Suggestions Respecting Improvements in Education: Presented to the Trustees of the Hartford Female Seminary and Published at Their Request.* Hartford, Connecticut: Packard and Butler. 1829.

FRIEDRICH FROEBEL

"Account of the German Kindergarten"
(1843)

Froebel (1782–1852) was the founder of the "kindergarten," the first of which he opened in 1840. "This Kindergarten rests on the conviction that the isolated education of children in the family before they are fit for school, as it now is on the whole, and can be under existing relations, no longer satisfies the requirements of the time." As a young man, he studied under Pestalozzi and then developed his own ideas about promoting education through blocks and play. He began training kindergarten teachers in 1849.

Having founded the German Kindergarten three years ago, it seems to us now to be the time to give a public report of its existence and of its continued course. In order to introduce the subject and not to be unintelligible to those who have heard but little about it, it seems to us judicious to recall to memory in a brief sketch, the origin and task of this undertaking.

Owing to the deeply felt need of suitable fostering of the child before its entrance into the school, the German Kindergarten was established as a mutual German educational work, on the Guttenberg festival day in 1840, a day which testifies to the light which has become general.

This Kindergarten rests on the conviction that the isolated education of children in the family before they are fit for school, as it now is on the whole, and can be under existing relations, no longer satisfies the requirements of the time. The aim of the Kindergarten, therefore, is to bring the needed help to the family and to the communities.

In order to afford this help there are needed, first, institutions for the oversight and development of children, and, afterward, capable nurses and educators. The institutions for the care of children in the first respect are established for the lower classes. Important as we must find these, we yet recognize the fact that they are, for the most

49

part, still insufficient. Concerning the second (the training of nursery maids, etc.), there is, as yet, on the whole, very little done for it. Now how is this double need to be met? This is the problem which the German Kindergarten strives to solve.

Its aim is, therefore, on the one side, not only to have an oversight of children before the school age, but to give them means of employment corresponding to their whole nature; to strengthen their bodies; to exercise their senses: to employ the awakening spirit; judiciously to make them familiar with Nature and with man; and especially rightly to guide heart and mind, and to lead them to the original cause of all life, and to union with Him. They should be joyous and versatile in play, exercising and training all their powers, vividly expressing themselves in innocent serenity, harmony and pure childlikeness; and should truly prepare for the school and the coming stages of life, as the plants in a garden thrive under the blessing of Heaven, and the careful tending of the gardener.

On the other side, its aim is to instruct persons, especially young persons of both sexes, in the right guidance and employment of children; to give good helpers to the mothers in the tending of their little ones; to give the families better nurses and educators; and to give skilled mothers[9] and intelligent child-leaders to the institutions for the care of little children, and to Kindergartens in other places.

But, third, in order to make a better fostering of childhood a common good, the German Kindergarten must set for itself the aim of familiarizing and generalizing the suitable material for play (that is, material which is in conformity with the plays and ways of playing and founded on the different stages of development of the child and grounded in the nature of man), for which purpose a general means of communication, a public paper, was required to give utterance to the wishes, needs, endeavors, progress, etc., showing themselves in this circle, as well as to combine the Kindergartens established in different places, with one another and with the general German Kindergarten.

The German Kindergarten is to be, therefore:

A model institution for the fostering of children.

An institution in which child-leaders can practice.

An institution which seeks to generalize suitable plays and ways of playing.

9. The name given to the women who took a mother's place to the children in the institution.— *Translator.*

Finally, an institution with which all who are working in such a spirit—parents, educators, and especially training Kindergartens, can be placed in a connection full of life by means of a paper devoted to that purpose.[10]

In order to provide the Kindergarten with the needful basis for the realization of all this (especially landed property, habitable buildings, and, in general, all that is needed for such an institution, in the course of development), the way of taking contributions up to ten dollars was adopted. This way was chosen with the object stated in the plan, viz., that the educational work to be accomplished by it may be the permanent, constantly and continuously developing property of all subscribers, especially of the German women and girls. Our confidence rested upon the generosity of the intelligent friends of man, who recognize the time with its needs, and regard, in the germ, the future seed-sowing; but above all, on the pious feeling of the women and girls, since the earliest education, the tending of childhood is laid by the Creator at the heart of the feminine sex. The women who find their mutual bond in the fostering of childhood, are thus to found a work from which flows out to them all that they needed for the fulfillment of their holy duties and for the attainment of their high aim. Therefore, the Kindergarten is built upon the deeply religious love of women, trusting on Him who, as the Father, wills that not one of his children shall be lost, in the spirit of him who perceived the kingdom of Heaven in little children, and in the spirit of those who find their peace in protecting and cherishing pure humanity.

—Translated by Josephine Jarvis

SOURCE: *Third and Last Volume of Friedrich Froebel's Pedagogics of the Kindergarten.* St. Louis: Woodward and Tiernan. 1904.

10. This paper was a weekly. It was edited by Froebel, and was called the *Sunday Sheet.—Translator.*

LEV TOLSTOY

"Who Is to Teach Whom to Write, We the Peasant-Children or the Peasant-Children Us?"
(1862)

Best known as the author of two of the most important novels in world litera-
ture, War and Peace *and* Anna Karenina, *Tolstoy (1828–1910) was a*
Russian nobleman who, before marrying in his early thirties, set up a school
on his estate for the local peasant children. He threw himself into this work
and wrote about the school and his experiences and discoveries. He evoked
classroom scenes and episodes with a vividness that has never been surpassed;
in this essay, published in his short-lived education journal Yasnaya Polyana, *he describes the children composing stories based on proverbs.*

In the fifth issue of *Yasnaya Polyana*, in the section of children's compositions, the editor published by mistake "The Story of How a Boy
Was Frightened in Tula." This little story was composed not by a
boy, but by a teacher from a dream the boy told him. Some of the
readers who follow *Yasnaya Polyana* expressed doubt that it was really
a pupil's work. I hasten to apologize to readers for this oversight and
by this occurrence note how impossible counterfeits are in such a
case. This tale was recognized not because it was better but because it
was worse, incomparably worse, than *all* the children's compositions.
All the remaining tales were the children's themselves. Two of them,
"He Feeds with the Spoon but Pokes the Eye with the Handle" and
"The Life of a Soldier's Wife," are printed in this issue[11], and were
put together in the following way.

A teacher's main art in teaching language and his main direction
with the goal of guiding children to write compositions is in providing themes, though not so much in providing them as in presenting
the most choices, in pointing out methods of composition, in showing elementary steps. Many smart and talented pupils wrote non-

11. See Christopher Edgar's translations of these two stories in *Tolstoy as Teacher: Leo
Tolstoy's Writings on Education.* New York: Teachers and Writers Collaborative. 2000.

sense; they wrote: "The fire started, they began dragging things out, and I went outside," and nothing came of it, even though the subject was rich and the event described had left a deep impression on the child. They did not understand the main thing: why write and what was the good of writing? They did not understand art—the beauty of expressing life in words and the attractions of this art. As I already wrote in the second issue, I tried many various methods of giving them subjects. Depending on their mood, I provided specific artistic, touching, amusing, epic themes—none of them worked. Then, just like that, I accidentally stumbled upon the present method.

For quite some time, reading from Snegirev's collected proverbs has been for me not just one of my favorite activities but *passions*. Each proverb conjures up for me individuals from among the people and their actions in the sense of the proverb. Among my unfulfilled day-dreams, I always imagine for myself a series of stories, pictures, illustrating the proverbs. Once, last winter, after supper I began reading Snegirov's book and I brought it with me to the school. There was a Russian language class.

"Hey, now, someone write on a proverb," I said.

The best pupils—Fedka, Semka and others—raised their ears.

"Who's writing on a proverb?" "What's that?" "Tell us," poured forth the questions.

I opened to the proverb "He feeds with the spoon, but pokes the eye with the handle."

"Here, imagine for yourselves," I said, "that a peasant takes in some beggar, and then, after his good deed, he began to reproach him—and that leads to 'He feeds with the spoon, but pokes the eye with the handle.'"

"But how would you write that?" said Fedka, and all the others who had raised their ears suddenly gave up, convinced that this business was beyond their strength, and took up again with their previous work.

"You write it yourself," someone said to me.

Everyone was busy with something; I took the pen and ink and began to write.

"Well," I said, "who will write it best?—I'll do it with you." I began the tale, printed in the fourth issue of *Yasnaya Polyana*, and I wrote down the first page. Any unprejudiced person with a feeling for art and for the people, having read first this writing of mine and the following pages of the tale, written by the pupils themselves, would pick out this page from the others, like a fly from milk: it is so false, artificial and written with such poor language. It must be noted also that in the original it was even uglier and was much corrected thanks to the pupils' suggestions.

Fedka, from beneath his notebook, kept looking at me and, meeting my eyes, he smiled, winked and said, "Write, write, or I'll give it to you!" It amused him, apparently, when a big person also composed. Finishing his own writing worse and more hastily than usual, he crawled up on the back of my armchair and began to read over my shoulder. I could not continue any more; the others came over and I read my writing aloud to them. It did not please them, no one praised it. I was embarrassed, and in order to appease my literary vanity, I began to tell them my plan of what was to come. Gradually as I told it, it grew on me and I liked it, and they began to prompt me.

Somebody said, "The old man should be a magician." Another said, "No, not that—he'll be just a soldier." "No, it's better to let him *rob* them." "No, that wouldn't go with the proverb," and so on.

Everyone became thoroughly interested. It was new and fascinating for them, apparently, to be present during the process of composition and to take part in it. Their judgments were for the most part similar to each other's and faithful to the narrative's construction and even to its very details and characterizations. They almost all took part in the composition; but, from the very beginning, Semka especially distinctly stood out, with his sharp artistic descriptions, and Fedka, with his faithful poetic representations, especially in his glowing and rapid imagination. Their strictures were so purposeful and definite that more than once, when I argued with them, I then had to concede. Fixed in my head were the demands of regular construction and an exact correspondence of the idea of the proverb to the tale; they, on the other hand, only had the demand of artistic truth. For example, I wanted the peasant, having taken the old man into his home, to repent of his good deed, while they considered that impossible and created the cantankerous woman. I said, "At first, the peasant was sorry for the old man, but then later he regretted giving him the bread." Fedka answered that this would be nonsense: "He didn't listen to the woman from the start and he didn't give in afterward either."

"But what kind of person is he, to you?" I asked.

"He's like Uncle Timofey," said Fedka, smiling, "like so, a thin little beard, and he goes to church, and he has beehives."

"He's good yet stubborn?" I said.

"Yes," said Fedka, "so he won't listen to the woman." It was there, when they brought the old man into the cottage, that the spirited work began. For the first time apparently, they felt the charm of casting artistic details in words. In this respect Semka especially distinguished himself: the very truest details poured out one after the other. The sole reproach that one might make to him was that these details described only the present moment, without connection to the overall feeling of the narrative. I could not keep up with the writing and only asked them to wait and not forget what they had said.

Semka, it seemed, saw and described what was appearing before his eyes: the stiff, frozen bast-shoes, and the mud that trickled from them when they thawed, and how they turned into toast after the woman tossed them in the oven.

Fedka, on the other hand, saw only those details that evoked in him those feelings he had for particular characters. Fedka saw the snow that got into the old man's foot-wraps, felt the woe with which the old man said, "Lord, how it falls!" (Fedka even made a face as he imagined how the old man said this, waving his hands and shaking his head.) He saw the ragged overcoat, the torn shirt, under which could be seen the old man's thin body, damp from the melting snow. He thought up the woman who grumbled as, at her husband's command, she removed the old man's bast shoes, and his pitiful moan, through his teeth, saying: "Easy, mother-dear, I have sores there." Semka needed primarily objective images: bast shoes, the overcoat, the old man, the woman, almost without connection among them; Fedka needed to evoke the feelings of sympathy with which he himself was filled.

He dashed on ahead, spoke about how they would feed the old man, how he would fall at night, how then in the field he would teach the boy to read, so that I had to ask him not to rush or forget what he had said. His eyes shone almost in tears; his dark, skinny little hands writhed; he was angry at me and constantly urged me and kept asking: "Did you write it? Did you?" He treated the others despotically and angrily, he wanted to be the only one to speak—and not speak as people talk but as writing, that is, artistically imprint with words the images of the feeling. He did not allow, for example, the transposing of words. If he said: "On my legs I have sores," he did not allow it to be "I have sores on my legs." His soul, softened and moved by the feeling of compassion, that is of love, clothed every image in artistic form and refused everything not corresponding to the idea of eternal beauty and harmony.

As soon as Semka got carried away by an expression of disproportionate details about the lambs near the door, and so on, Fedka got angry and said: "Now look, that's enough!" I had only to hint, for example, about what the peasant did, how his wife ran to the neighbor and right away in Fedka's imagination was called up an image of the lambs baaing near the door, the old man sighing and the delirious boy Serozhka's ravings; I only had to hint at an artificialness or falseness in my picture and he would right away angrily say it was not necessary. I suggested, for example, describing the peasant's looks—he agreed; but at my suggestion to describe what the peasant was thinking when his wife ran to the neighbor, a turn of thought immediately came to him: "Eh, if you came across Savoska-the-corpse, he'd pull out your hair!" And he said this with such weariness and calm customary seriousness, and at the same time with such a good-natured tone, leaning his head on his hand, that the boys rolled with laughter.

The main characteristic in all art—the sense of proportion—was extraordinarily developed in him. All the excessive details prompted by the boys jarred on him. He was so despotic directing the construction of this narrative—and justified in this despotism—that soon the boys went home and the only one left was Semka, who, although he did not give in to him, worked in another role.

We worked from seven to eleven o'clock; they did not feel hunger or weariness, and even became angry with me when I stopped writing. They took up the writing themselves turn by turn, but soon gave it up; it didn't work.

Only then Fedka asked me what my name was. We laughed that he didn't know. He said, "I know what you're called, but what's your last name? Where I live we have the Fokanychevs, Zyabrevs, the Yermilins."

I told him.

"And we'll publish it?" he asked.

"Yes!"

"Then we have to print: 'Work by Makarov, Morozov and Tolstoy.'" For a long time he was agitated and could not fall asleep, and I cannot convey that feeling of agitation, joy, fear and almost regret that I experienced in the course of that evening. I felt that from this day a new world of pleasure and suffering had opened for him—the world of art. It seemed to me that I had seen what nobody ever has the right to see—the conception of the mysterious flower of poetry. It was terrible and joyful for me, like a treasure-seeker who had seen a fern's blooming; it was joyful to me because suddenly, absolutely unexpectedly the philosopher's stone, which I had searched for in vain for two years, was revealed to me—the art of teaching the expression of thoughts; it was terrible because this art called up new demands, a whole world of desires not corresponding to the manner in which the pupils lived, or so it seemed to me at the first moment. There could be no mistaking it. This was not an accident but a conscious act of creation.

I ask the reader to read the first part of the narrative and note the abundant touches of true creative talent scattered throughout; for example, the detail that the woman spitefully complains to the neighbor-man about her husband, and despite this, the woman, with whom the author has a clear lack of sympathy, cries when the man puts her in mind about the ruin of her home.

For an author who writes by intellect and memory alone, the cantankerous woman represents only the peasant's opposite-number. She, from the desire to annoy her husband, would have called in the neighbor. But Fedka's artistic feeling was caught up by the woman as well—and so she also cries, she is afraid and suffers; she, in his eyes, is not to blame. Following this is a secondary detail, when the neighbor puts on the woman's coat. I remember this so struck me that I asked, "Why especially a woman's coat?" None of us suggested to Fedka the idea of saying that the neighbor put on that coat. He said, "That's just how it'd be." When I asked whether he could say he put on a man's coat, he said, "No, it's better a woman's." In fact, this detail is extraordinary. At first you cannot figure why it has to be a woman's coat—yet you feel that it is excellent and that it could not be expressed otherwise.

Every artistic phrase, whether the work of Goethe or Fedka, distinguishes itself from the inartistic in that it calls up countless possible thoughts, imaginings and revelations. The neighbor, in the woman's coat, involuntarily presents to us a puny, narrow-chested peasant, just as he must apparently be. The woman's coat, having been tossed across the bench and the first falling to hand, completely presents to us a winter evening in the life of a peasant. We necessarily imagine, by the occasion of the coat, the evening, a time at which the peasant sits by the little torch, undressed, and the women, who walk in and out for water and to tend the cows, and all that external disorder of peasant living, where no one has clearly determined clothes and nothing has a determined place. With one phrase, "he put on the woman's coat," he impresses the whole character of the environment in which the action takes place, and this phrase is not accidentally but consciously made.

I remember so vividly how the peasant's words were called up in his imagination when the peasant found the paper but could not read it: "Now, if my Serozha knew how to read, he would hop up all lively, grab the paper from my hands and read the whole thing and tell me who this old man is." So can be seen the relationship of a working man to a book he holds in his weathered hands; the worthy man, with his patriarchal, pious inclinations, stands before you. You feel that the author deeply loves and thereby completely understands him, so that he lets him make a digression about how nowadays a soul can perish just like that.

I suggested the idea of the dream, but it was Fedka who came up with the idea of the goat with wounds on its legs, and he especially enjoyed that. The musing of the peasant while his back is itching, and the picture of the quiet night—all this is far from accidental; in all these features one feels so strongly the artist's conscious strength. I remember as well when the peasant was going to sleep, I suggested starting him thinking about his son's future and about the future relationship of his son with the old man, and that the old man could teach Serozhka to read and write and so on. Fedka frowned and said, "Yes, sure, fine," but it was obvious he didn't like my suggestion, and twice he forgot it. The sense of proportion only the rare artist attains by the greatest difficulty lived in all its primal strength in his unspoiled child's soul.

I abandoned the lesson because I was too agitated.

"What's with you? Why are you so pale? Really, are you unwell?" a colleague asked me. Truly, there have been in my life only two or three times that I ever experienced such a strong impression as on that night, and for a long time I wasn't able to give myself an account of what I experienced. It vaguely seemed to me that I had looked through glass at a working beehive hidden before from mortal gaze; it seemed to me I had criminally spied into a peasant-child's pure innocent soul. I vaguely felt something like repentance for sacrilege. It reminded me of those children who idle and dissipated old men used to pose and present sensual pictures for arousing their tired, worn-out imaginations, and yet at the same time I was joyful, as joyful as someone who sees something that no one has ever seen before.

For a long time I couldn't explain to myself the impression I had experienced, even though I felt that this impression was one of those which at a mature age lead a person to a new stage of life and bring him to renounce his old life and fully devote himself to the new. Even the next day I did not believe what I had experienced the day before. It seemed to me so strange that a half-educated peasant-boy suddenly revealed such a conscious artistic power that, in all his immeasurable development, Goethe could not achieve. It seemed to me so strange and insulting that I, the author of *Childhood*, who have achieved some success and been recognized for my artistic talent by the cultivated Russian public, that I, in the matter of art, not only could not direct or help eleven-year-old Semka and Fedka, but could only just barely in a happy moment of excitement follow along and understand them. It seemed so strange to me and I still could not believe what had happened the day before.

The next evening we took up a continuation of the tale. When I asked Fedka whether he had thought about the next part and how to go on, he, not answering, waved his hands and said only, "I know, I know! Who'll write?" We started the continuation and again from the boys was the same sense of artistic truth, proportion and enthusiasm.

Halfway through class I had to leave them. They continued without me and wrote two pages just as good, full of feeling and true as the first. These pages were only a bit less detailed and these details were sometimes not so agilely laid out; there were also two repetitions. All that, obviously, came about from the mechanics of writing that made it difficult for them. The third day was the same. During the lessons other boys would show up, and knowing the tone and grip of the narrative, they often prompted and added their own true details. Semka sometimes came and left. Only Fedka from the beginning to the end carried on the tale and reviewed every suggested alteration.

There could be no doubt or thoughts anymore that this success was accidental; we had happened to stumble across that method which was the more natural and stimulating than all others. But it was so unusual that I did not believe what was right in front of my eyes. As if on purpose, something special occurred that erased all my doubts. I had to leave for a few days and the narrative remained unfinished. The manuscript, three big sheets, covered with writing, remained in the room of the teacher to whom I had shown it. Even before my leaving, at the time of composition, a new pupil showed our boys the art of making "flappers" out of paper, and the whole school, as usually happens, found this a period of flappers, replacing a period of snowballs, replacing, in its turn, a period of whittled sticks. The period of flappers continued during my trip.

Semka and Fedka, who were in the choir, used to go to the teacher's room to sing and spent there whole evenings and sometimes the night. Meanwhile, during singing-time, it seems they made flappers their business, and every possible piece of paper that fell into their hands turned into flappers. The teacher went off to eat, forgetting to say that the papers on the table were important, and so the manuscript of the work by Makarov, Morozov and Tolstoy was turned into flappers. The next day, before class, the flapper-mania was at such a stage that it annoyed these same pupils, and in consequence by general agreement declared a persecution of flappers: with yells and squeals, all the flappers were taken away and with a celebration were put into the burning oven.

The flapper period had ended, but with it perished our manuscript. Never had such a loss been so heavy for me as losing those three sheets of writing; I was in despair. Giving it up as hopeless, I wanted to begin a new tale, but was unable to forget the loss and involuntarily every moment poured reproaches on the teacher and the flapper-makers. (I cannot help noting in this case that only in consequence of our outward lack of order and the pupils' full freedom, for which I was teased by Markov in *The Russian Messenger* and Glebov in *Education* (No. 4), I, without the smallest effort, threats or trickery, found out all the details of the complicated story of the manuscript being made into flappers and their burning. Semka and Fedka saw that I was distressed, and though they sympathized they evidently did not understand why I was. Fedka shyly suggested to me, finally, that they write it out again.

"Alone?" I said. "I won't be able to help this time."

"Semka and I will spend the night," said Fedka. And actually after the lesson, they came to my house at 9 o'clock, locked the door of my study, which provided me not a little pleasure, and they laughed a bit, and then went quiet. Until midnight, whenever I went up to the door, I heard their quiet voices talking things over and the squeakings of the pen. Only once did they argue about what was where before, and they came to me to judge whether the peasant looked for the bag before—and then the woman went to the neighbor—or after. I told them it made no difference.

At 12 I tapped at the door and went in. Fedka, in a new white heavy coat, with black trim, sat deeply in the armchair, crossing one leg over the other, and leaning his bushy head on one hand and playing with scissors with the other. His big, dark eyes, shining with an unnatural but serious mature glint, looked off somewhere in the distance; his twisted lips pressed together as if he were preparing to whistle, apparently held a phrase, which he, having coined in his imagination, wanted to say aloud. Tousle-headed Semka, standing before the big writing desk, with a big white sheepskin over his back (tailors had just passed through the village) and his belt loosened, was writing crooked lines, continually dipping his pen in the ink. I ruffled Semka's hair, and when he, with his broad cheekbones and tangled hair, looked in fright at me with his befuddled and sleepy eyes, it was so funny that I laughed out loud, but the children did not laugh. Fedka, not changing the expression on his face, touched Semka's sleeve for him to continue writing. "Wait," he commanded me, "almost done." (Fedka spoke in the familiar form to me when he was excited and agitated.) And he dictated something again. I took their copy-book.

Five minutes later, when they were sitting near the cupboard, having potatoes and kvass, they looked with wonder at the silver spoons and burst out with ringing childish laughter, they themselves not knowing why. The old housekeeper, hearing them from upstairs, also laughed, not knowing why.

"What are you falling over for?" said Semka to Fedka. "Sit straight or you'll eat only on one side." When they took off their coats and lay down on them under the writing table to sleep, they did not stop spilling over with childish, peasant-like, healthy, charming chortles. I read through what they had written. It was just a new variant. Some things were left out, some were newly added artistic beauties. And again there was that feeling of beauty, truth and proportion.

Later, one sheet of the torn-up manuscript was discovered, and in the published story I used my memory and the recovered sheet to combine both variants. The writing of this tale took place in early spring, before the end of our school year. Because of various ob-

stacles, I was not able to conduct new experiments. Only one story
on a proverb was written, and that by two very mediocre and spoiled
boys ("He who is joyful for a holiday is drunk by sunrise"), published
in the third issue. All the same explanation was repeated with these
boys that had been done with Semka and Fedka and their first tale,
only with the differences of talent level, degree of enthusiasm, and
the encouragement on my part.

In summer we do not have classes, did not have classes and will
not have classes. Why holding classes in the summer is not possible,
we will explain in a separate article.

For one part of the summer Fedka and other boys lived with me.
After they swam and played, they thought up ways to keep busy. I
proposed they write stories and suggested a few themes. I told them
a very entertaining story of a robbery, a story of a murder, an account
of the miraculous conversion of a Molokan to orthodoxy and then
I suggested writing, in the form of an autobiography, an account
by a boy whose poor and dissipated father is enlisted as a soldier
and to whom the father returns from service a reformed and good
person.

I said, "I would write it like so: 'I remember when I was a boy, I
had a mother, a father, and some relatives,' and what they were like.
Then I would write how I remembered that my father would go
carousing, my mother was always crying, and that he used to beat
her; then how they sent him to be a soldier, how she wailed about
that, how we began to live worse; and then how my father came
back, and how I wouldn't have known him if he hadn't asked me
whether Matrena—that is, his wife—lived there; and how then we
became happy and began to live well." This is all that I said at the
beginning. Fedka thoroughly liked this theme. He right away seized
a pen and paper and began to write. While he was writing, I led
him only to the ideas about the sister and the soldier's mother's
death. All the rest he wrote himself and did not even show it to me,
besides the first chapter, until it was all done. When he showed me
the first chapter and I began to read it, I sensed that he was strongly
agitated and holding his breath. He looked at the manuscript, following along my reading, then at my face, wanting to guess by my
expression my approval or disapproval. When I told him it was very
good he blushed but said nothing to me and agitatedly, with a quiet
step, went back with his notebook to the table, set the story down
and slowly walked out into the yard. In the yard he was crazily frisky

with his pals that day, and when our eyes met he looked at me with such grateful tender eyes. By the next day he had forgotten what he had written.

I only thought up the title, divided the story into chapters and here and there corrected his mistakes made by oversight. This tale, in its original form, is being published in a booklet as "The Life of a Soldier's Wife."

I am not speaking about the first chapter, although there are inimitable beauties in it and in his presentation the heedless Gordey is thoroughly true and alive—Gordey, who seems ashamed to admit his remorse but considers it only right to ask the commune about his son—I only say that this chapter is incomparably weaker than all that follow.

I am the one to blame for this because I was unable to hold back during the writing of this chapter from prompting him and telling him how I would write it. If there is a triteness in the introduction, in the descriptions of the characters and home-situation, I am the only one to blame. If I had left him alone, I am convinced he would have written the same action, but instinctively, more artistically, without our mannered and impossible method of writing logically set out descriptions; that is, at the beginning describing the principal characters, even their biographies, and then the description of the scene and surroundings, and only then beginning the action.

Strangely enough, all these descriptions, sometimes on tens of pages, less familiarizes the reader with the characters than abruptly throwing in artistic details at the beginning of the action amid absolutely undescribed characters. So it is in the first chapter, with one phrase of Gordey's: "That's all I need!" He, waving his hand, makes up for his debt by becoming a soldier and only asks the commune not to abandon his son—this phrase more familiarizes the reader with the character than several repetitions and my explanatory description of his clothes, figure, and habitual trips to the tavern. In the same way as the impression produced by the words of the old woman, who had forever quarreled with her son, when in her grief says with envy to her daughter-in-law: "That's enough, Matrena! What's to be done? So, it's God's will! And you're still quite young, and maybe God may grant you seeing him again. But me, so old . . . I'm always sick . . . so you see—I'll be dead."

In the second chapter is still noticeable my influence of sentimentality and corruption, but again the profoundly artistic features in the description of pictures and the boy's death redeem it all. I prompted the detail that the boy had thin legs, I prompted the sentimental detail about Uncle Nefedya, who dug the grave; but the mother's lamentation, expressed with one phrase, "Lord, when will this life of bondage end?," presents to the reader the whole essence of the situation; and afterward that night, when the older brother wakes up to his mother's tears and her answer to the grandmother's question, "What's with her?," the simple phrase: "My son has died"—and this old woman, getting up and lighting the fire and washing off the little body—all this was his idea, all this is so compressed, so simple and so strong—not one word could be excised, not one changed or added. In all just five lines, and in these five lines are painted for the reader the whole picture of this sad night, the picture reflected in the imagination of a six- or seven-year-old boy. "At midnight the mother started crying about something. The old woman got up and said, 'What is it? Christ be with you.' The mother said, 'My son has died.' The old woman lit the fire, washed off the child, dressed him in his shirt, fastened a belt on him, and laid him under the icons. When dawn broke . . ." You see this very boy, he wakes up to the familiar crying of the mother; from under the kaftan on the bed, his frightened shining eyes follow after what is going on in the cottage; you see the haggard soldier's wife, who said, just the day before: "Is this life of bondage soon to end?" She is so repentant and beaten down by the thought of the end of this mortal bondage that she can only say, "My son has died." She doesn't know what she is to do, and she calls the old woman for help; this old woman, weary from the suffering of life, bent, thin, with bony limbs, who with hands accustomed to work unhurriedly, calmly goes about her business. She lights the kindling, fetches the water and washes off the child. She puts everything in its place and lays the washed and dressed child under the icons. You see images of that whole sleepless night until sunrise, as if you yourself have lived through it, as her boy has lived through it, looking out from under his kaftan. That night, with all its details, comes into sight and remains in your imagination.

In the third chapter there is even less of my influence. All the individuality of the older sister belongs to him. In the very first chapter he characterizes in one line the relation of the girl to her family: "She worked for her own dowry; she was preparing to marry." This one line paints the complete girl; she cannot take part and actually does not take part in the joy and misery of her family. She has lawful interests, her single goal, decreed by Providence, establishing her future marriage, her own future family. Our fellow authors, especially ones who desire to instruct the people, would have treated the sister in regard to her interest in the family's common need and sorrow. We would have made her either a shameful example of indifference or a model of love and self-sacrifice, and she would be an idea but not a living character—not this very girl. Only a person deeply educated and knowing life would be able to understand that for the sister the question of the family's misery and the father's military service is lawfully a second-stage question: she is to be married. Although a child, the artist in the simplicity of his soul sees this.

If we were to describe the sister as the most touching and self-sacrificing girl, we would absolutely not be able to imagine or love her as we love her now. Now to me she seems so sweet and lively, this fat-cheeked, blushing girl, running in the evening to a dance in the shoes and dress she has bought with her own money. She loves her family, although distressed by that poverty and gloominess that contrast so much with her heartfelt mood. I feel that she is a good girl, because her mother never complains about her or suffers any grief from her. On the contrary, I feel that she, with her cares about clothes, her pipings of songs, her stories of village gossip, picked up from summer work or on the wintry streets, is the only one during the sad time of the soldier's wife's loneliness who represents joy, youth and hope. Purposefully he says that the only joy is when the maiden is given to be married; purposefully he describes the happy wedding with such love and kindness; purposefully after the wedding he has the mother say: "Now we're ruined." Apparently, having given away the sister, they have lost the joy and merriment that she brought into their home. All this description of the wedding is unusually good.

There are details before which you cannot help feeling perplexed. Remembering that this was written by an eleven-year-old boy, you ask yourself, "Isn't this an accident, really?" You see before you this compressed and strong description of a seven-year-old boy, no taller than a table, with intelligent and observant little eyes on whom no one turns attention, but who remembers and notices everything. When he wanted some bread, for example, he didn't say that he asked his mother but that he bent his mother down, and this is said not by accident but because it reminded him of what his relationship was like when he was at that height to his mother's, of how shy they were before others and how close they were when alone. Another of the many observations that he could have made during the wedding ceremony was one he remembered and that exactly describes for him and for every one of us the complete character of these ceremonies. When the people called out "Bitter!", the sister grabbed Kondrashka by the ears and they began to kiss "sweet." Then the grandmother's death, her memories of her son before her death and the special character of the mother's grief—all this is so firm and compressed, and all this is his conception.

I told him more about the father's return than anything else when I gave them the theme of the tale. I liked this scene, and I told it with mushy-sentimentality, but this scene he very much liked as well, and he told me, "Don't say anything! I know, I know!" He began to write and on the spot he finished the whole narrative in one sitting. It will interest me very much to know the opinion of other judges, but I consider it my duty to express my opinion frankly: *There is nothing like this page I have met in Russian literature.* In all this reunion there is not one hint that it is touching; it's told only as fact; and what is told is only as much as is necessary for the reader to understand the situation of all the characters. The soldier in his own home said only three words. At first he even held back and said, "Hello." When he began to forget the role he was taking on, he said, "So is this all the family you've got?" And then everything was expressed with the words, "But where's my mother?" What completely simple and essential words, and in this scene not one of the characters is forgotten! The boy is joyful and even cried, but he is a boy and so, even though his father is crying, he keeps searching his bag and in his pockets. The sister is not forgotten. You see this blushing young woman, who in her fine shoes and clothes shyly enters past the people into the cottage, and, not saying anything, kisses her father. You see the long-lost and happy soldier, who kisses everyone in a row, not knowing whom, and then, learning that the young woman is his daughter, again calls her to himself and kisses her, this time not simply as any young woman but as his daughter, whom he left way back when, as if without regret.

The father has been reformed. How many false and awkward phrases we would have used about this event! But Fedka simply tells how the sister brings the vodka, and the soldier does not begin drinking. And here you see the soldier's wife who, in the pantry, taking out of her bag her last twenty-three kopecks, sighing, with a whisper sends her daughter for the vodka and passes into her hand some copper coins. You see this young woman, raising her apron over her arm with a bottle in hand, stamping along in her shoes, swinging her elbows, as she runs to the tavern. You see how she, all flushed, enters the cottage, takes the bottle out from under her apron, and you see the mother, self-contented and happy as she sets it on the table, and how she is at first offended but then becomes joyful that her husband is not starting to drink, and you see that if he has not started drinking at that moment, that he is already completely reformed. You feel that all these other people have become complete members of the family. "My father prayed to God and sat down at the table. I sat right beside him; Sissy sat on the bench, but Mother stood by the table and looked at Father and said, 'You look so young!—No beard now,' and everyone laughed."

And only when everyone has left begins the genuine family conversations. Only now is revealed that the soldier has become rich and become rich in a very simple and natural way—just like almost all people on earth become rich, that is, the money belongs to others, the treasury, the community, but in consequence of fortunate events, it comes to him. Some of the readers of the tale remarked that this detail is immoral and the idea of the treasury as a milch-cow should be stamped out and not encouraged in the people. For me this detail, not even speaking about its artistic truth, is especially valuable. Apparently there is always left-over treasury money—why shouldn't it end up sometimes in the possession of the homeless soldier Gordey?

Concerning honesty, we find that the people and the upper class have completely opposite ideas. For example, the demands of the people are very serious and severe in its relation to the family, the village, the commune. In relation to outsiders—the public, the government, and especially foreigners and the treasury, the application of the common laws of honesty are dim. A peasant who would never lie to his brother, who would endure all possible privation for his family, who would never take an excess or unworked for kopeck from fellow villagers or neighbors, this very peasant will fleece a foreigner or city-dweller. He will lie with every word to a nobleman or official; if he becomes a soldier, he will, without the smallest compunction, stab a captured Frenchman, and if treasury money falls into his hands, he counts it a crime in relation to his family not to use it. In the upper class, it happens exactly the opposite. One of us sooner deceives his wife, his brother, a merchant with whom he has done business for years, his servants, his peasants, his neighbors, and yet the same fellow of our class while abroad is consumed by a constant terror lest he accidentally cheat someone, and always asks to have it pointed out to him who it is he needs to pay. Our brother noble will fleece his company or regiment for the money for champagne and gloves and will shower attention on a captured Frenchman. This same person, in relation to the treasury money, counts it the greatest crime to use when he is broke, but for the most part, if the opportunity comes, he takes it, though he regards it as disgraceful.

I am not saying that one is better, I am only saying how it seems to me. I note, however, that honesty is not a conviction, that the expression "honest convictions" is nonsense. Honesty is a moral habit; in order to acquire it, it is impossible to proceed by any other way than by starting with one's closest relations. The expression "honest convictions" in my opinion is completely meaningless. There are honest habits but not honest convictions. The words "honest convictions" are only a phrase; the consequence of this is these so-called honest convictions, applied to remote life, demands by the treasury, the government, Europe, humankind—and which are not based on customary honesty, not applied to those people closest to us—these honest convictions or, truer, these expressions of honesty, prove not to correspond to real life.

I return to the tale. While it may seem immoral at first, the mention of taking the official money, in our opinion, on the contrary, has the sweetest, most touching character. How often a literary figure of our circle, desiring in the simplicity of his soul to represent his hero as an ideal of honesty, demonstrates to us the completely vile and dissipated interior of his imagination. Here, on the other hand, the author needs to make his hero happy; for his happiness the return to his family might be enough, but it's necessary to relieve his poverty that for so many years has touched this family; from where is he to take his wealth? From the impersonal treasury; if wealth is to be given, it is necessary to get it from someone—it's impossible to find it in a more legitimate way.

When the money is mentioned in this scene, there is a small detail, one word, which every time I read it, strikes me anew. It lights up the whole picture, paints all the characters and their relations and it is only one word, and the word, incorrectly used, is syntacticaly incor-

rect—this word is "hastened." The teacher of syntax has to say that
this is incorrect. "Hastened" requires a complement—"hastened to
do what?" the teacher has to ask. It is simply said, "Mother took the
money and hastened, carried it away to bury . . ." and this is charming. I would like to say such a word, would desire that language
teachers would say or write such a sentence: "When we had eaten,
Sissy kissed Father again and went home. Then Father rummaged
in the bag and Mother and I looked on. Here Mother saw there a
little book and said, 'Ah, you've learned how to read.' Father said,
'Yes, I've learned.' Then Father took out a big bundle and gave it
to Mother. Mother said, 'What's this?' Father said, 'Money.' Mother
got all happy and hastened and carried it off to bury. Then Mother
came back and said, 'Where did you get this from?' Father said, 'I was
the under-officer and I had the official money; I distributed it to the
soldiers and I was left with the rest, and I took it.' My mother was so
glad and ran around like crazy. Day had already passed and night fell.
They lit the fire. My father took up the little book and began to read.
I sat by him and listened, and Mother held a torch and my father read
the little book for a long while. Then we lay down to sleep. I lay on
the bench with my father and Mother lay down at our feet and for a
long time they chatted, almost until midnight. Then we fell asleep."

Again, a detail just barely noticeable, not at all surprising you but
establishing a deep impression, the detail about how they lie down
to sleep; the father lies down with his son, the mother lies at their
feet, and for a long time they talk. I think of how warmly the son
presses himself to his father's chest and how miraculous it is and how
overjoyed he is as half-sleeping and in dreaminess he keeps hearing
these two voices, one of which he has not heard for so long.

It might seem that everything is concluded: the father has returned,
there is no more poverty. But Fedka had not satisfied himself with
this (so fully alive, apparently, had these imagined people settled in his
imagination), it was necessary for him to even more vividly imagine
the picture of their changed life, to imagine for himself even more
clearly what there is now for this woman, no longer alone, the miserable soldier's wife with little children and what it is like to be in
the home of a strong man, who has lifted off from his wife's tired
shoulders the whole burden of oppressive grief and poverty and will
independently, firmly and cheerfully bring in a a new life. And for
this purpose he pictures for you only one scene: how with a nicked
ax the healthy soldier chops the wood and brings it into the cottage.

You see how the keen-eyed little boy, accustomed to the groaning weak mother and grandmother, admires with awe, respect and pride the muscular arms of his father, the energetic swinging of the ax, the chesty exhalations of muscular work, and the block of wood, split like kindling under the nicked ax. You look on this and are completely put at ease about the future life of the soldier's wife. Now she will no longer lose heart, I think.

"In the morning, Mother got up, walked up to Father and said, 'Gordey! Get up! We need wood to heat the oven.' Daddy got up, put on his boots, put on his cap, and said, 'There's an ax?' Mother said, 'It's nicked—forgive me, maybe it won't chop anything.' My father firmly took the ax with both hands, went up to the block, stood it upright and hit it with all his might and split the block. He chopped the wood and carried it into the cottage. Mother made a fire and the cottage heated up and dawn came on."

But to the artist this is not enough. He wants to show you another side of their life, the poetic, cheerful, family life, and so he paints for you the following picture:

"When the sky was bright, my father said, 'Matrena!' Mother came over and said, 'Well, what is it?' Father said, 'I'm thinking about buying a cow, five lambs, and two horses and a cottage—this one's about to collapse. . . . So it'll be about a hundred and fifty rubles in all.' Mother thought it over and then said, 'But then we'll have completely spent it all.' Father said, 'We'll keep working.' Mother said, 'Well, all right, but where are we going to find the lumber?' Father said, 'Kiryuk, maybe?' Mother said, 'That's the trouble. The Fontanychevs snatched it up.' Father thought and said, 'Well, we'll get it from Bryantsev.' Mother said, 'It's not likely he's got any.' Father said, 'Well, how can't he? He's got a forest.' Mother said, 'As if he won't ask too much—he's such a beast.' Father said, 'I'll go, I'll bring vodka and talk it over with him. You bake an egg in the ashes for dinner.' Mother made dinner—she borrowed from friends. Then Father took the vodka and left for Bryantsev's, but we stayed back and sat around a long time. I got lonely without Father. I began asking Mother to let me go there, where Father had gone. Mother said, 'You'd get lost.' I began to cry and wanted to go, but Mother slapped me and I sat on the oven and started crying more than ever. Then I saw Father come in the cottage and he said, 'What are you crying for?' Mother said, 'Fedyushka wanted to run after you, so I smacked him.' Father came up to me and said, 'What are you crying about?'

I began complaining about Mother. Father went up to mother and began pretending to beat her and saying, 'Don't beat Fedya! Don't beat Fedya!' Mother pretended to cry. And I sat on my father's knee and was happy. Then Father sat at the table, sat me beside him, and called out, 'Feed me and Fedya some supper, Mother—we want to eat.' Mother served us some beef and we dug in. After we ate, Mother said, 'Well, what does the lumber cost?' Father said, 'Fifty silver rubles.' Mother said, 'That's almost nothing.' Father said, 'Yeah, I'll say—the lumber's excellent.'"

It seems so simple, so little is said, but it gives you the perspective of their complete family life. You see that the boy is still a child, who cries and then in a minute will be happy. You see that the boy no longer values the love of his mother and has thrown her over for the virile father who has chopped the wood; you see that the mother knows that this is as it ought to be and does not get jealous; you see this marvelous Gordey, whose happiness fills his heart. You notice that they ate beef, and this charming comedy, which they all play, and they all know that it is a comedy, and they play it from an overflowing of happiness. "Don't beat Fedya, don't beat Fedya!" says the father, gesturing at her. And accustomed to unpretended tears, the mother pretends to cry, joyously smiling at the father and son, and this boy, who crawls up on his father's knees, is proud and happy, not even knowing himself why—proud and happy, maybe, that they are happy now.

"Then Father sat at the table, sat me beside him and called out, 'Feed me and Fedya some supper, Mother—we want to eat.'"

"We want to eat" and he sat him beside him! What love and happy pride of love inspires these words! So charming, and there is nothing more heartfelt than this scene in all the rest of the charming story.

But what do we want to say by all this? What meaning does this story, written by an exceptional boy, have in relation to pedagogy? I will be told, "You, the teacher, unconsciously helped, perhaps in composing these and other stories, and to mark the boundaries of what was yours and what is original is far too difficult." I will be told, "Let's grant it's a good tale. But this is only one of the genres of literature." I will be told, "Fedka and the other boys, whose work you published, are happy exceptions." I will be told, "You yourself are a writer, you unconsciously helped the pupils in such ways that are impossible to be prescribed to other teachers—who aren't, as a rule, writers." I will be told, "From all this it is impossible to derive a general rule or theory. It is partly an interesting phenomenon but nothing more."

I will try to communicate my deductions so that they answer all these suggested objections.

The feelings of truth, beauty and goodness are independent of the degree of development. Beauty, truth and goodness are concepts that express only the harmony of their relations to the sense of truth, beauty and goodness. A lie is only an uncorresponding relationship to a sense of truth; there is no absolute truth. I am not lying when I say that the table is turning from the touch of my fingers if I believe that is the truth; but I do lie saying that I don't have money when, as I understand it, I do have money. No type of large nose is ugly, but it is ugly on a small face. Ugliness is only disharmony in relation to beauty. To give away one's meal to a beggar or to eat it oneself does not have in itself anything bad; but to give it away or to eat this meal when my mother is dying of hunger—that is disharmony in relation to the sense of goodness.

Raising, educating, developing or however you want to influence a child, we have to have and unconsciously do have one goal: to attain as far as possible the greatest harmony in the sense of truth, beauty and goodness. If time did not pass, if a child did not live with all his sides active, we might calmly attain this harmony by adding where there is not enough and by subtracting where it seems to us there is too much. But a child lives, each side of his being extending itself in development, one outstripping another, and for the most part the progress of these sides we take for the goal, and we bring about only development but not *harmonious* development. This is the eternal mistake of all pedagogical theories. We see the ideal ahead when it is behind us. The unavoidable development of a person is not the means for attaining that ideal of harmony, which we bear within us; on the contrary, but it is an obstacle placed there by our Creator against our attaining the highest ideal of harmony. This unavoidable law of forward motion includes the idea of the fruit of the tree of knowledge of good and evil, which our ancestors tasted.

A healthy child is born into the world, fully satisfying the demands of absolute harmony in relation to truth, beauty, and goodness, which we bear in ourselves; he is closer to the inanimate existence—to plants, animals, Nature—that constantly presents to us the very truth, beauty and goodness that we search for and desire. In all times and for all people, the child represents a model of guiltlessness,

sinlessness, goodness, truth and beauty. A person is born complete—
that is the great phrase pronounced by Rousseau, a phrase that stands
like a stone, hard and true. But each hour in life, each minute of time
increases the space and quantity and the time of those relations that
at the time of a person's birth is found in complete harmony, and
each consequent step and each consequent hour threatens a new
transgression and gives less hope of reestablishing the transgressed
harmony.

For the most part, educators lose sight of the fact that childhood
is the original harmony that independently proceeds by unchang-
ing laws toward its goal. The development is mistaken for the goal
because what happens with teachers happens with bad sculptors.
Instead of trying to halt at the place of over-development, or to
establish a common development, instead of waiting for a new opportunity to diminish the previous irregularity, they act like a bad
sculptor who, instead of scraping off the extra, sticks on ever more
and more. So the teachers do, as if they are concerned only to not
stop the process of development; if they think about harmony it is
always to try to achieve it through an as yet unknown model in the
future, going away from the model in the present and past. No matter how irregular a child's development, those original features of
harmony still remain. By moderating or as little as possible pushing
along the development, we might attain a proximity to regularity
and harmony. But we are so sure of ourselves in this, so dreamily
given over to the lie of a mature ideal, so impatient are we with those
anomolies close to us, and so firmly sure of our ability to correct
them, so little do we understand and value the original beauty of a
child, that we soon, as soon as possible, exaggerate and putty over
all the irregularities that strike our sight; we correct and educate the
child. First one side has to be evened out with the other, then the
other has to be evened out with the first. The child is developed ever
further and further, and keeps moving further away from the highest but suppressed original; it becomes less and less possible to attain
the imagined model of a perfect complete grown-up. Our ideal is
behind us, not in front of us. Education spoils and does not improve
people. The more spoiled the child, the less necessary it is to educate
him; he needs more freedom.

To teach and educate a child is impossible and senseless for the
simple reason that the child stands closer than I, closer than any
grown-up, to that ideal harmony of truth, beauty and goodness, to

that which I in my pride want to guide him. The consciousness of this ideal lies stronger in him than in me. He needs from me only the material for him to achieve harmony and well-roundedness. As soon as I gave him full freedom and I stopped teaching him, he wrote such a poetic production that there is nothing like it in Russian literature. Therefore, I am convinced that we cannot teach children, and particularly not peasant-children, to write and compose, especially poetical works. All that we can do is to teach them how to take up the act of composition.

If what I did might be called methods for attaining this goal, these methods would be these:

1. Suggest the largest and most various choice of topics, not making them up especially for children, but proposing the most serious and interesting for the teacher himself.
2. Give the children children's compositions to read and only children's compositions to suggest those forms, because children's compositions are always more correct, graceful and moral than grown-ups' compositions.
3. (Especially important.) Never at any time in reviewing a child's compositions make remarks about the tidiness of the notebook, or about penmanship, or on the spelling, or, above all, on the grammar of the sentence or the logic.
4. The difficulty of a composition is not in its size or content or its artistic themes or language, but in the mechanics of the work, which in the first place consist of selecting one of a large number of ideas and images; in the second place, choosing words for it and fashioning them; in the third place, remembering it and finding its place; in the fourth place, remembering it in order and not repeating the words, and not leaving things out, and being able to combine the later details with the earlier ones; in the fifth place, finally, thinking and writing at the same time, with one not confusing the other.

From this goal I did the following: some of the phases of work I took on myself the first time; by stages I transferred them all to their care. At first, I chose for them from the thoughts and images that seemed to me best, and I remembered and pointed out the places and corrected the writing, preventing them from repetitions, and I myself wrote, leaving it to them only to describe the images and thoughts in words; then I gave them full choice and then they corrected the writing, and finally, as in the piece "The Life of a Soldier's Wife," they took the whole process of writing on themselves.

— *Translated from the Russian by Bob Blaisdell*

Lev Tolstoy. *Yasnaya Polyana*. 1862. (See also Leo Wiener's translation in *Leo Tolstoy: On Education*. University of Chicago Press. 1968.)

MATTHEW ARNOLD

from "General Report for the Year 1880"
(1880)

*The renowned English poet, scholar, and essayist (1822–1888) was, in ad-
dition, one of "Her Majesty's inspectors of schools." (He approved of Tolstoy's
visits to London schools when Tolstoy, whom Arnold knew only as a Russian
nobleman, made a study-tour of European schools in 1861.) The son of the
headmaster at Rugby, Arnold won distinctions at Oxford University. Arnold
here comments upon the effective teaching of poetry.*

I find that of the specific subjects English literature, as it is too ambi-
tiously called—in plain truth the learning by heart and reciting of a
hundred lines or two of standard English poetry—continues to be
by far the most popular. I rejoice to find it so; there is no fact coming under my observation in the working of our elementary schools
which gives me so much satisfaction. The acquisition of good poetry
is a discipline which works deeper than any other discipline in the
range of work of our schools; more than any other, too, it works of
itself, is independent of the school teacher, and cannot be spoiled by
pedantry and injudiciousness on his part.

Some people regard this my high estimate of the value of poetry
in education with suspicion and displeasure. Perhaps they may accept
the testimony of Wordsworth with less suspicion than mine. Wordsworth says, "To be incapable of a feeling of poetry, in my sense of
the word, is to be without love of human nature and reverence for
God." And it is only through acquaintance with poetry, and with
good poetry, that this "feeling of poetry" can be given . . .

The choice of passages to be learnt is of the utmost importance,
and requires close and intelligent observing of the children. Some
years ago it was the fashion to make them learn Goldsmith's *Deserted
Village*, at the recommendation, I believe, of the late Lord Lyndhurst;
or rather, he had given high praise to this poem, and recommended it
as a poem to be got by heart, and so it was supposed that the children

in our elementary schools might with advantage learn it. Nothing could be more completely unsuitable for them, and this being soon proved by the event, the use of the poem for the purpose in question has happily almost ceased. That the poetry chosen should have real beauties of expression and feeling, that these beauties should be such as the children's hearts and minds can lay hold of, and that a distinct point or centre of beauty and interest should occur within the limits of the passage learnt, all these are conditions to be insisted upon. Some of the short pieces by Mrs. Hemans, such as "The Graves of a Household," "The Homes of England," "The Better Land," are to be recommended, because they fulfill all three conditions; they have real merits of expression and sentiment, the merits are such as the children can feel, and the centre of interest, these pieces being so short, necessarily occurs within the limits of what is learnt.

On the other hand, in extracts taken from Scott and Shakespeare, the point of interest is often not reached within the hundred lines which is all that children in the Fourth Standard learn. The judgment scene in *The Merchant of Venice* affords me a good example of what I mean. Taken as a whole, this famous scene has, I need not say, great power; it is dramatic poetry of the first order, it is also well within our school children's comprehension, and very interesting to them. Teachers are fond of selecting it to be learnt by heart, and they are quite right. But what happens is this. The children in the Fourth Standard begin at the beginning, and stop at the end of a hundred lines; now, the children in the Fourth Standard are often a majority of the children learning poetry, and this is all their poetry for the year. But within these hundred lines the real interest of the situation is not reached, neither do they contain any poetry of signal beauty and effectiveness. How little, therefore, has the poetry exercise been made to do for these children, many of whom will leave school at once, and learn no more poetry!

The conclusion I wish to draw is, that the teacher should always take care that the year's poetry of a class shall contain the best poetry in the piece chosen for them, and the central point of interest in it; not be mere prelude and introduction to this centre of interest. To secure this, the teacher may without scruple plunge into the middle of a scene or a passage, and make his children take their hundred lines there explaining to them, of course, the situation at the point where they begin. If they remain another year, they can take a new passage or scene under the same conditions. This is a far better course than to throw a year away, as is frequently done now, upon comparatively ineffective poetry, with the intention that the child, if he remains at school, may next year continue the same passage and reach the point of interest.

I insist at such length upon this poetry exercise, because of the increasing use of it, and because of its extreme importance. Stress is laid upon the necessity of the children knowing thoroughly the meaning of what they recite, and it is assumed that to secure their knowing this is the simplest matter in the world, and that not to secure it proves inexcusable negligence in the teacher. I am more and more refusing to pass children who do not know the meaning of words which occur in what they recite, but I proceed gradually and with caution. If I had begun by rigidly rejecting every child ignorant of the meaning of every word in what he recited, I should never have got the poetry exercise established in my schools at all. The scanty vocabulary of our school children, and their correspondent narrow range of ideas, must be known and allowed for if one is to guide their instruction usefully.

I have found in London schools children of twelve years old, able to pass well in reading, writing, and arithmetic, who yet did not know what "a steed" was. I found in a good school the other day a head class of some thirty, only one of whom knew what "a ford" was. "Steed" is a literary word, "ford" is a word of country life, not of town life; still they are words, one is apt to think, universally understood by everyone above five years old. But even common words of this kind are not universally understood by the children with whom we deal. Very many words are in their reading lessons passed over as certainly known to them, to which they attach no meaning at all, or a wrong one. The poetry exercise is invaluable by causing words to be dwelt upon and canvassed, by leading the children to grasp the meaning of new words, and by thus extending the range of their ideas. But the slowness and difficulty of the process, which are as incontestable as its high value, must be borne in mind, and we must have patience with that slowness and difficulty. . . .

Source: Matthew Arnold. *Reports on Elementary Schools: 1852–1882*. London: Macmillan and Company. 1889.

RALPH WALDO EMERSON

"Education"
(1883)

The Concord poet and essayist (1803–1882) was, as were many of his fellow Transcendentalists, brimming over with ideas about education, how freedom of thought leads to discovery: "The great object of Education should be commensurate with the object of life. It should be a moral one; to teach self-trust: to inspire the youthful man with an interest in himself; with a curiosity touching his own nature; to acquaint him with the resources of his mind, and to teach him that there is all his strength, and to inflame him with a piety towards the Grand Mind in which he lives." Emerson's editor, James E. Cabot, compiled this essay from various commencement addresses.

A new degree of intellectual power seems cheap at any price. The use of the world is that man may learn its laws. And the human race have wisely signified their sense of this, by calling wealth, means,—Man being the end. Language is always wise.

Therefore I praise New England because it is the country in the world where is the freest expenditure for education. We have already taken, at the planting of the Colonies (for aught I know for the first time in the world), the initial step, which for its importance might have been resisted as the most radical of revolutions, thus deciding at the start the destiny of this country,—this, namely, that the poor man, whom the law does not allow to take an ear of corn when starving, nor a pair of shoes for his freezing feet, is allowed to put his hand into the pocket of the rich, and say, You shall educate me, not as you will, but as I will: not alone in the elements, but, by further provision, in the languages, in sciences, in the useful and in elegant arts. The child shall be taken up by the State, and taught, at the public cost, the rudiments of knowledge, and at last, the ripest results of art and science.

Humanly speaking, the school, the college, society, make the difference between men. All the fairy tales of Aladdin or the invisible

Gyges or the talisman that opens kings' palaces or the enchanted halls underground or in the sea, are only fictions to indicate the one miracle of intellectual enlargement. When a man stupid becomes a man inspired, when one and the same man passes out of the torpid into the perceiving state, leaves the din of trifles, the stupor of the senses, to enter into the quasi-omniscience of high thought,—up and down, around, all limits disappear. No horizon shuts down. He sees things in their causes, all facts in their connection.

[. . .]

As every wind draws music out of the Aeolian harp, so doth every object in Nature draw music out of his mind. Is it not true that every landscape I behold, every friend I meet, every act I perform, every pain I suffer, leaves me a different being from that they found me? That poverty, love, authority, anger, sickness, sorrow, success, all work actively upon our being and unlock for us the concealed faculties of the mind? Whatever private or petty ends are frustrated, this end is always answered. Whatever the man does, or whatever befalls him, opens another chamber in his soul,—that is, he has got a new feeling, a new thought, a new organ. Do we not see how amazingly for this end man is fitted to the world?

What leads him to science? Why does he track in the midnight heaven a pure spark, a luminous patch wandering from age to age, but because he acquires thereby a majestic sense of power; learning that in his own constitution he can set the shining maze in order, and finding and carrying their law in his mind, can, as it were, see his simple idea realized up yonder in giddy distances and frightful periods of duration. If Newton come and first of men perceive that not alone certain bodies fall to the ground at a certain rate, but that all bodies in the Universe, the universe of bodies, fall always, and at one rate; that every atom in Nature draws to every other atom,—he extends the power of his mind not only over every cubic atom of his native planet, but he reports the condition of millions of worlds which his eye never saw. And what is the charm which every ore, every new plant, every new fact touching winds, clouds, ocean currents, the secrets of chemical composition and decomposition possess for Humboldt? What but that much revolving of similar facts in his mind has shown him that always the mind contains in its transparent chambers the means of classifying the most refractory phenomena, of depriving them of all casual and chaotic aspect, and subordinating them to a bright reason of its own, and so giving to man a sort of property,—yea, the very highest property in every district and particle of the globe.

By the permanence of Nature, minds are trained alike, and made intelligible to each other. In our condition are the roots of language and communication, and these instructions we never exhaust.

In some sort the end of life is that the man should take up the universe into himself, or out of that quarry leave nothing unrepresented. Yonder mountain must migrate into his mind. Yonder magnificent astronomy he is at last to import, fetching away moon, and planet, solstice, period, comet and binal star, by comprehending their relation and law. Instead of the timid stripling he was, he is to be the stalwart Archimedes, Pythagoras, Columbus, Newton, of the physic, metaphysic and ethics of the design of the world.

For truly the population of the globe has its origin in the aims which their existence is to serve; and so with every portion of them. The truth takes flesh in forms that can express it; and thus in history an idea always overhangs, like the moon, and rules the tide which rises simultaneously in all the souls of a generation.

Whilst thus the world exists for the mind; whilst thus the man is ever invited inward into shining realms of knowledge and power by the shows of the world, which interpret to him the infinitude of his own consciousness,—it becomes the office of a just education to awaken him to the knowledge of this fact.

We learn nothing rightly until we learn the symbolical character of life. Day creeps after day, each full of facts, dull, strange, despised things, that we cannot enough despise,—call heavy, prosaic and desert. The time we seek to kill: the attention it is elegant to divert from things around us. And presently the aroused intellect finds gold and gems in one of these scorned facts,—then finds that the day of facts is a rock of diamonds; that a fact is an Epiphany of God.

We have our theory of life, our religion, our philosophy; and the event of each moment, the shower, the steamboat disaster, the passing of a beautiful face, the apoplexy of our neighbor, are all tests to try our theory, the approximate result we call truth, and reveal its defects. If I have renounced the search of truth, if I have come into the port of some pretending dogmatism, some new church or old church, some Schelling or Cousin, I have died to all use of these new events that are born out of prolific time into multitude of life every hour. I am as a bankrupt to whom brilliant opportunities offer in vain. He has just foreclosed his freedom, tied his hands, locked himself up and given the key to another to keep.

When I see the doors by which God enters into the mind; that there is no sot or fop, ruffian or pedant into whom thoughts do not enter by passages which the individual never left open, I can expect any revolution in character. "I have hope," said the great Leibnitz, "that society may be reformed, when I see how much education may be reformed."

It is ominous, a presumption of crime, that this word Education has so cold, so hopeless a sound. A treatise on education, a convention for education, a lecture, a system, affects us with slight paralysis and a certain yawning of the jaws. We are not encouraged when the law touches it with its fingers. Education should be as broad as man. Whatever elements are in him that should foster and demonstrate. If he be dexterous, his tuition should make it appear; if he be capable of dividing men by the trenchant sword of his thought, education should unsheathe and sharpen it; if he is one to cement society by his all-reconciling affinities, oh! hasten their action! If he is jovial, if he is mercurial, if he is great-hearted, a cunning artificer, a strong commander, a potent ally, ingenious, useful, elegant, witty, prophet, diviner,—society has need of all these. The imagination must be addressed. Why always coast on the surface and never open the interior of Nature, not by science, which is surface still, but by poetry? Is not the Vast an element of the mind? Yet what teaching, what book of this day appeals to the Vast?

Our culture has truckled to the times,—to the senses. It is not man worthy. If the vast and the spiritual are omitted, so are the practical and the moral. It does not make us brave or free. We teach boys to be such men as we are. We do not teach them to aspire to be all they can. We do not give them a training as if we believed in their noble nature. We scarce educate their bodies. We do not train the eye and the hand. We exercise their understandings to the apprehension and comparison of some facts, to a skill in numbers, in words; we aim to make accountants, attorneys, engineers; but not to make able, earnest, great-hearted men. The great object of Education should be commensurate with the object of life. It should be a moral one; to teach self-trust: to inspire the youthful man with an interest in himself; with a curiosity touching his own nature; to acquaint him with the resources of his mind, and to teach him that there is all his strength, and to inflame him with a piety towards the Grand Mind in which he lives. Thus would education conspire with the Divine Providence. A man is a little thing whilst he works by and for himself, but, when he gives voice to the rules of love and justice, is godlike, his word is current in all countries; and all men, though his enemies, are made his friends and obey it as their own.

In affirming that the moral nature of man is the predominant element and should therefore be mainly consulted in the arrangements of a school, I am very far from wishing that it should swallow up all the other instincts and faculties of man. It should be enthroned in his mind, but if it monopolize the man he is not yet sound, he does not yet know his wealth. He is in danger of becoming merely devout, and wearisome through the monotony of his thought. It is not less necessary that the intellectual and the active faculties should be nourished and matured. Let us apply to this subject the light of the same torch by which we have looked at all the phenomena of the time; the infinitude, namely, of every man. Everything teaches that.

One fact constitutes all my satisfaction, inspires all my trust, viz., this perpetual youth, which, as long as there is any good in us, we cannot get rid of. It is very certain that the coming age and the departing age seldom understand each other. The old man thinks the young man has no distinct purpose, for he could never get anything intelligible and earnest out of him. Perhaps the young man does not think it worth his while to explain himself to so hard and inapprehensive a confessor. Let him be led up with a long-sighted forbearance, and let not the sallies of his petulance or folly be checked with disgust or indignation or despair.

I call our system a system of despair, and I find all the correction, all the revolution that is needed and that the best spirits of this age promise, in one word, in Hope. Nature, when she sends a new mind into the world, fills it beforehand with a desire for that which she wishes it to know and do. Let us wait and see what is this new creation, of what new organ the great Spirit had need when it incarnated this new Will. A new Adam in the garden, he is to name all the beasts in the field, all the gods in the sky. And jealous provision seems to have been made in his constitution that you shall not invade and contaminate him with the worn weeds of your language and opinions. The charm of life is this variety of genius, these contrasts and flavors by which Heaven has modulated the identity of truth, and there is a perpetual hankering to violate this individuality, to warp his ways of thinking and behavior to resemble or reflect your thinking and behavior. A low self-love in the parent desires that his child should repeat his character and fortune; an expectation which the child, if justice is done him, will nobly disappoint. By working on the theory that this resemblance exists, we shall do what in us lies to defeat his proper promise and produce the ordinary and mediocre. I suffer whenever I see that common sight of a parent or senior imposing his opinion and way of thinking and being on a young soul to which they are totally unfit. Cannot we let people be themselves, and enjoy life in their own way? You are trying to make that man another you. One's enough.

Or we sacrifice the genius of the pupil, the unknown possibilities of his nature, to a neat and safe uniformity, as the Turks whitewash the costly mosaics of ancient art which the Greeks left on their temple walls. Rather let us have men whose manhood is only the continuation of their boyhood, natural characters still; such are able and fertile for heroic action; and not that sad spectacle with which we are too familiar, educated eyes in uneducated bodies.

I like boys, the masters of the playground and of the street,—boys, who have the same liberal ticket of admission to all shops, factories, armories, town-meetings, caucuses, mobs, target-shootings, as flies have; quite unsuspected, coming in as naturally as the janitor,—known to have no money in their pockets, and themselves not suspecting the value of this poverty; putting nobody on his guard, but seeing the inside of the show,—hearing all the asides. There are no secrets from them, they know everything that befalls in the fire-company, the merits of every engine and of every man at the brakes, how to work it, and are swift to try their hand at every part; so too the merits of every locomotive on the rails, and will coax the engineer to let them ride with him and pull the handles when it goes to the engine-house. They are there only for fun, and not knowing that they are at school, in the courthouse, or the cattle-show, quite as much and more than they were, an hour ago, in the arithmetic class.

They know truth from counterfeit as quick as the chemist does. They detect weakness in your eye and behavior a week before you open your mouth, and have given you the benefit of their opinion quick as a wink. They make no mistakes, have no pedantry, but entire belief on experience. Their elections at baseball or cricket are founded on merit, and are right. They don't pass for swimmers until they can swim, nor for stroke-oar until they can row: and I desire to be saved from their contempt. If I can pass with them, I can manage well enough with their fathers.

Everybody delights in the energy with which boys deal and talk with each other; the mixture of fun and earnest, reproach and coaxing, love and wrath, with which the game is played;—the good-natured yet defiant independence of a leading boy's behavior in the school-yard. How we envy in later life the happy youths to whom their boisterous games and rough exercise furnish the precise element which frames and sets off their school and college tasks, and teaches them, when least they think it, the use and meaning of these. In their fun and extreme freak they hit on the topmost sense of Horace. The young giant, brown from his hunting-tramp, tells his story well, interlarded with lucky allusions to Homer, to Virgil, to college-songs, to Walter Scott; and Jove and Achilles, partridge and trout, opera and binomial theorem, Caesar in Gaul, Sherman in Savannah, and hazing in Holworthy, dance through the narrative in merry confusion, yet the logic is good. If he can turn his books to such picturesque account in his fishing and hunting, it is easy to see how his reading and experience, as he has more of both, will interpenetrate each other. And everyone desires that this pure vigor of action and wealth of narrative, cheered with so much humor and street rhetoric, should be carried into the habit of the young man, purged of its uproar and rudeness, but with all its vivacity entire. His hunting and campings-out have given him an indispensable base: I wish to add a taste for good company through his impatience of bad.

That stormy genius of his needs a little direction to games, charades, verses of society, song, and a correspondence year by year with his wisest and best friends. Friendship is an order of nobility; from its revelations we come more worthily into nature. Society he must have or he is poor indeed; he gladly enters a school which forbids conceit, affectation, emphasis and dullness, and requires of each only the flower of his nature and experience; requires good will, beauty, wit and select information; teaches by practice the law of conversation, namely, to hear as well as to speak.

Meantime, if circumstances do not permit the high social advantages, solitude has also its lessons. The obscure youth learns there the practice instead of the literature of his virtues; and, because of the disturbing effect of passion and sense, which by a multitude of trifles impede the mind's eye from the quiet search of that fine horizon-line which truth keeps,—the way to knowledge and power has ever been an escape from too much engagement with affairs and possessions; a way, not through plenty and superfluity, but by denial and renunciation, into solitude and privation; and, the more is taken away, the more real and inevitable wealth of being is made known to us. The solitary knows the essence of the thought, the scholar in society only its fair face. There is no want of example of great men, great benefactors, who have been monks and hermits in habit. The bias of mind is sometimes irresistible in that direction. The man is, as it were, born deaf and dumb, and dedicated to a narrow and lonely life. Let him study the art of solitude, yield as gracefully as he can to his destiny. Why cannot he get the good of his doom, and if it is from eternity a settled fact that he and society shall be nothing to each other, why need he blush so, and make wry faces to keep up a freshman's seat in the fine world? Heaven often protects valuable souls charged with great secrets, great ideas, by long shutting them up with their own thoughts. And the most genial and amiable of men must alternate society with solitude, and learn its severe lessons.

There comes the period of the imagination to each, a later youth; the power of beauty, the power of books, of poetry. Culture makes his books realities to him, their characters more brilliant, more effective on his mind, than his actual mates. Do not spare to put novels into the hands of young people as an occasional holiday and experiment; but, above all, good poetry in all kinds, epic, tragedy, lyric. If we can touch the imagination, we serve them, they will never forget it. Let him read *Tom Brown at Rugby*, read *Tom Brown at Oxford*,—better yet, read *Hodson's Life*—Hodson who took prisoner the king of Delhi. They teach the same truth,—a trust, against all appearances, against all privations, in your own worth, and not in tricks, plotting, or patronage.

I believe that our own experience instructs us that the secret of Education lies in respecting the pupil. It is not for you to choose what he shall know, what he shall do. It is chosen and foreordained, and he only holds the key to his own secret. By your tampering and thwarting and too much governing he may be hindered from his end and kept out of his own. Respect the child. Wait and see the new product of Nature. Nature loves analogies, but not repetitions. Respect the child. Be not too much his parent. Trespass not on his solitude.

But I hear the outcry which replies to this suggestion:—Would you verily throw up the reins of public and private discipline; would you leave the young child to the mad career of his own passions and whimsies, and call this anarchy a respect for the child's nature? I answer,—Respect the child, respect him to the end, but also respect yourself. Be the companion of his thought, the friend of his friendship, the lover of his virtue,—but no kinsman of his sin. Let him find you so true to yourself that you are the irreconcilable hater of his vice and the imperturbable slighter of his trifling.

The two points in a boy's training are, to keep his nature and train off all but that:—to keep his nature, but stop off his uproar, fooling and horse-play;—keep his nature and arm it with knowledge in the very direction in which it points. Here are the two capital facts, Genius and Drill. The first is the inspiration in the well-born healthy child, the new perception he has of nature. Somewhat he sees in forms or hears in music or apprehends in mathematics, or believes practicable in mechanics or possible in political society, which no one else sees or hears or believes. This is the perpetual romance of new life, the invasion of God into the old dead world, when he sends into quiet houses a young soul with a thought which is not met, looking for something which is not there, but which ought to be there: the thought is dim but it is sure, and he casts about restless for means and masters to verify it; he makes wild attempts to explain himself and invoke the aid and consent of the bystanders. Baffled for want of language and methods to convey his meaning, not yet clear to himself, he conceives that though not in this house or town, yet in some other house or town is the wise master who can put him in possession of the rules and instruments to execute his will. Happy this child with a bias, with a thought which entrances him, leads him, how into deserts now into cities, the fool of an idea. Let him follow it in good and in evil report, in good or bad company; it will justify itself; it will lead him at last into the illustrious society of the lovers of truth.

In London, in a private company, I became acquainted with a gentleman, Sir Charles Fellowes, who, being at Xanthus, in the Aegean Sea, had seen a Turk point with his staff to some carved work on the corner of a stone almost buried in the soil. Fellowes scraped away the dirt, was struck with the beauty of the sculptured ornaments, and, looking about him, observed more blocks and fragments like this. He returned to the spot, procured laborers and uncovered many blocks. He went back to England, bought a Greek grammar and learned the language; he read history and

studied ancient art to explain his stones; he interested Gibson the
sculptor; he invoked the assistance of the English Government; he
called in the succor of Sir Humphry Davy to analyze the pigments;
of experts in coins, of scholars and connoisseurs; and at last in his
third visit brought home to England such statues and marble re-
liefs and such careful plans that he was able to reconstruct, in the
British Museum, where it now stands, the perfect model of the
Ionic trophy-monument, fifty years older than the Parthenon of
Athens, and which had been destroyed by earthquakes, then by
iconoclast Christians, then by savage Turks. But mark that in the
task he had achieved an excellent education, and become associated
with distinguished scholars whom he had interested in his pursuit; in
short, had formed a college for himself; the enthusiast had found the
master, the masters, whom he sought. Always genius seeks genius,
desires nothing so much as to be a pupil and to find those who can
lend it aid to perfect itself.

Nor are the two elements, enthusiasm and drill, incompatible.
Accuracy is essential to beauty. The very definition of the intellect
is Aristotle's: "that by which we know terms or boundaries." Give a
boy accurate perceptions. Teach him the difference between the similar and the same. Make him call things by their right names. Pardon
in him no blunder. Then he will give you solid satisfaction as long as
he lives. It is better to teach the child arithmetic and Latin grammar
than rhetoric or moral philosophy, because they require exactitude
of performance; it is made certain that the lesson is mastered, and
that power of performance is worth more than the knowledge. He
can learn anything which is important to him now that the power
to learn is secured: as mechanics say, when one has learned the use
of tools, it is easy to work at a new craft.

Letter by letter, syllable by syllable, the child learns to read, and
in good time can convey to all the domestic circle the sense of
Shakespeare. By many steps each just as short, the stammering boy
and the hesitating collegian, in the school debate, in college clubs,
in mock court, comes at last to full, secure, triumphant unfolding
of his thought in the popular assembly, with a fullness of power that
makes all the steps forgotten.

But this function of opening and feeding the human mind is not
to be fulfilled by any mechanical or military method; is not to be
trusted to any skill less large than Nature itself. You must not neglect the form, but you must secure the essentials. It is curious how

perverse and intermeddling we are, and what vast pains and cost we incur to do wrong. Whilst we all know in our own experience and apply natural methods in our own business,—in education our common sense fails us, and we are continually trying costly machinery against nature, in patent schools and academies and in great colleges and universities.

The natural method forever confutes our experiments, and we must still come back to it. The whole theory of the school is on the nurse's or mother's knee. The child is as hot to learn as the mother is to impart. There is mutual delight. The joy of our childhood in hearing beautiful stories from some skilful aunt who loves to tell them, must be repeated in youth. The boy wishes to learn to skate, to coast, to catch a fish in the brook, to hit a mark with a snowball or a stone; and a boy a little older is just as well pleased to teach him these sciences. Not less delightful is the mutual pleasure of teaching and learning the secret of algebra, or of chemistry, or of good reading and good recitation of poetry or of prose, or of chosen facts in history or in biography.

Nature provided for the communication of thought, by planting with it in the receiving mind a fury to impart it. 'Tis so in every art, in every science. One burns to tell the new fact, the other burns to hear it. See how far a young doctor will ride or walk to witness a new surgical operation. I have seen a carriage-maker's shop emptied of all its workmen into the street, to scrutinize a new pattern from New York. So in literature, the young man who has taste for poetry, for fine images, for noble thoughts, is insatiable for this nourishment, and forgets all the world for the more learned friend,—who finds equal joy in dealing out his treasures.

Happy the natural college thus self-instituted around every natural teacher; the young men of Athens around Socrates; of Alexandria around Plotinus; of Paris around Abelard; of Germany around Fichte, or Niebuhr, or Goethe: in short the natural sphere of every leading mind. But the moment this is organized, difficulties begin. The college was to be the nurse and home of genius; but, though every young man is born with some determination in his nature, and is a potential genius; is at last to be one; it is, in the most, obstructed and delayed, and, whatever they may hereafter be, their senses are now opened in advance of their minds. They are more sensual than intellectual. Appetite and indolence they have, but no enthusiasm. These come in numbers to the college: few geniuses: and the teaching comes to be arranged for these many, and not for those few. Hence the instruction seems to require skilful tutors, of accurate and systematic mind, rather than ardent and inventive masters. Besides, the youth of genius are eccentric, won't drill, are irritable, uncertain, explosive, solitary, not men of the world, not good for everyday association. You have to work for large classes instead of individuals; you must lower your flag and reef your sails to wait for the dull sailors; you grow departmental, routinary, military almost with your discipline and college police. But what doth such a school to form a great and heroic character? What abiding Hope can it inspire? What Reformer will it nurse? What poet will it breed to sing to the human race? What discoverer of Nature's laws will it prompt to enrich us by disclosing in the mind the statute which all matter must obey? What fiery soul will it send out to warm a nation with his charity? What tranquil mind will it have fortified to walk with meekness in private and obscure duties, to wait and to suffer? Is it not manifest that our academic institutions should have a wider scope; that they should not be timid and keep the ruts of the last generation, but that wise men thinking for themselves and heartily seeking the good of mankind, and counting the cost of innovation, should dare to arouse the young to a just and heroic life; that the moral nature should be addressed in the school-room, and children should be treated as the high-born candidates of truth and virtue?

So to regard the young child, the young man, requires, no doubt, rare patience: a patience that nothing but faith in the remedial forces of the soul can give. You see his sensualism; you see his want of those tastes and perceptions which make the power and safety of your character. Very likely. But he has something else. If he has his own vice, he has its correlative virtue. Every mind should be allowed to make its own statement in action, and its balance will appear. In these judgments one needs that foresight which was attributed to an eminent reformer, of whom it was said, "his patience could see in the bud of the aloe the blossom at the end of a hundred years." Alas for the cripple Practice when it seeks to come up with the bird Theory, which flies before it. Try your design on the best school. The scholars are of all ages and temperaments and capacities. It is difficult to class them; some are too young, some are slow, some perverse. Each requires so much consideration, that the morning hope of the teacher, of a day of love and progress, is often closed at evening by despair.

Each single case, the more it is considered, shows more to be done; and the strict conditions of the hours, on one side, and the number of tasks, on the other. Whatever becomes of our method, the conditions stand fast,—six hours, and thirty, fifty, or a hundred and fifty pupils. Something must be done, and done speedily, and in this distress the wisest are tempted to adopt violent means, to proclaim martial law, corporal punishment, mechanical arrangement, bribes, spies, wrath, main strength and ignorance, in lieu of that wise genial providential influence they had hoped, and yet hope at some future day to adopt. Of course the devotion to details reacts injuriously on the teacher. He cannot indulge his genius, he cannot delight in personal relations with young friends, when his eye is always on the clock, and twenty classes are to be dealt with before the day is done. Besides, how can he please himself with genius, and foster modest virtue? A sure proportion of rogue and dunce finds its way into every school and requires a cruel share of time, and the gentle teacher, who wished to be a Providence to youth, is grown a martinet, sore with suspicions; knows as much vice as the judge of a police court, and his love of learning is lost in the routine of grammars and books of elements.

A rule is so easy that it does not need a man to apply it; an automaton, a machine, can be made to keep a school so. It facilitates labor and thought so much that there is always the temptation in large schools to omit the endless task of meeting the wants of each single mind, and to govern by steam. But it is at frightful cost. Our modes of Education aim to expedite, to save labor; to do for masses what cannot be done for masses, what must be done reverently, one by one: say rather, the whole world is needed for the tuition of each pupil. The advantages of this system of emulation and display are so prompt and obvious, it is such a timesaver, it is so energetic on slow and on bad natures, and is of so easy application, needing no sage or poet, but any tutor or schoolmaster in his first term can apply it,—that it is not strange that this calomel of culture should be a popular medicine. On the other hand, total abstinence from this drug, and the adoption of simple discipline and the following of nature, involves at once immense claims on the time, the thoughts, on the life of the teacher. It requires time, use, insight, event, all the great lessons and assistances of God; and only to think of using it implies character and profoundness; to enter on this course of discipline is to be good and great. It is precisely analogous to the difference

between the use of corporal punishment and the methods of love.
It is so easy to bestow on a bad boy a blow, overpower him, and get
obedience without words, that in this world of hurry and distraction,
who can wait for the returns of reason and the conquest of self; in the
uncertainty too whether that will ever come? And yet the familiar
observation of the universal compensations might suggest the fear
that so summary a stop of a bad humor was more jeopardous than
its continuance.

Now the correction of this quack practice is to import into Education the wisdom of life. Leave this military hurry and adopt the
pace of Nature. Her secret is patience. Do you know how the natu-
ralist learns all the secrets of the forest, of plants, of birds, of beasts,
of reptiles, of fishes, of the rivers and the sea? When he goes into
the woods the birds fly before him and he finds none; when he goes
to the river-bank, the fish and the reptile swim away and leave him
alone. His secret is patience; he sits down, and sits still; he is a statue;
he is a log. These creatures have no value for their time, and he must
put as low a rate on his. By dint of obstinate sitting still, reptile, fish,
bird and beast, which all wish to return to their haunts, begin to
return. He sits still; if they approach, he remains passive as the stone
he sits upon. They lose their fear. They have curiosity too about him.
By and by the curiosity masters the fear, and they come swimming,
creeping and flying towards him; and as he is still immovable, they
not only resume their haunts and their ordinary labors and manners,
show themselves to him in their work-day trim, but also volunteer
some degree of advances towards fellowship and good understanding
with a biped who behaves so civilly and well. Can you not baffle the
impatience and passion of the child by your tranquility? Can you
not wait for him, as Nature and Providence do? Can you not keep
for his mind and ways, for his secret, the same curiosity you give to
the squirrel, snake, rabbit, and the sheldrake and the deer? He has
a secret; wonderful methods in him; he is,—every child,—a new
style of man; give him time and opportunity. Talk of Columbus and
Newton! I tell you the child just born in yonder hovel is the beginning of a revolution as great as theirs. But you must have the believing and prophetic eye. Have the self-command you wish to inspire.
Your teaching and discipline must have the reserve and taciturnity
of Nature. Teach them to hold their tongues by holding your own.
Say little; do not snarl; do not chide; but govern by the eye. See what
they need, and that the right thing is done.

I confess myself utterly at a loss in suggesting particular reforms in our ways of teaching. No discretion that can be lodged with a school-committee, with the overseers or visitors of an academy, of a college, can at all avail to reach these difficulties and perplexities, but they solve themselves when we leave institutions and address individuals. The will, the male power, organizes, imposes its own thought and wish on others, and makes that military eye which controls boys as it controls men; admirable in its results, a fortune to him who has it, and only dangerous when it leads the workman to overvalue and overuse it and precludes him from finer means. Sympathy, the female force,—which they must use who have not the first,—deficient in instant control and the breaking down of resistance, is more subtle and lasting and creative. I advise teachers to cherish mother-wit. I assume that you will keep the grammar, reading, writing and arithmetic in order; 't is easy and of course you will. But smuggle in a little contraband wit, fancy, imagination, thought. If you have a taste which you have suppressed because it is not shared by those about you, tell them that. Set this law up, whatever becomes of the rules of the school: they must not whisper, much less talk; but if one of the young people says a wise thing, greet it, and let all the children clap their hands. They shall have no book but schoolbooks in the room; but if one has brought in a Plutarch or Shakespeare or *Don Quixote* or Goldsmith or any other good book, and understands what he reads, put him at once at the head of the class. Nobody shall be disorderly, or leave his desk without permission, but if a boy runs from his bench, or a girl, because the fire falls, or to check some injury that a little dastard is inflicting behind his desk on some helpless sufferer, take away the medal from the head of the class and give it on the instant to the brave rescuer. If a child happens to show that he knows any fact about astronomy, or plants, or birds, or rocks, or history, that interests him and you, hush all the classes and encourage him to tell it so that all may hear. Then you have made your school-room like the world. Of course you will insist on modesty in the children, and respect to their teachers, but if the boy stops you in your speech, cries out that you are wrong and sets you right, hug him!

To whatsoever upright mind, to whatsoever beating heart I speak, to you it is committed to educate men. By simple living, by an illimitable soul, you inspire, you correct, you instruct, you raise, you embellish all. By your own act you teach the beholder how to do the practicable. According to the depth from which you draw your life, such is the depth not only of your strenuous effort, but of your manners and presence.

The beautiful nature of the world has here blended your happiness with your power. Work straight on in absolute duty, and you lend an arm and an encouragement to all the youth of the universe. Consent yourself to be an organ of your highest thought, and lo! suddenly you put all men in your debt, and are the fountain of an energy that goes pulsing on with waves of benefit to the borders of society, to the circumference of things.

SOURCE: Ralph Waldo Emerson. *Lectures and Biographical Sketches*. Boston: Houghton Mifflin. 1883.

JOHN DEWEY

"My Pedagogic Creed"
(1897)

The American philosopher John Dewey (1859–1952) is America's most famous theorist on education. He did not describe particular teachers or students, schools or classrooms, but he did synthesize and clarify fundamental principles of education for practitioners and policy-makers: "If education is life, all life has, from the outset, a scientific aspect; an aspect of art and culture and an aspect of communication. It cannot, therefore, be true that the proper studies for one grade are mere reading and writing, and that at a later grade, reading, or literature, or science, may be introduced. The progress is not in the succession of studies but in the development of new attitudes towards, and new interests in, experience." While teaching at the University of Chicago he formulated this manifesto, which challenged his anti-progressive contemporaries.

Article I: What Education Is

I believe that all education proceeds by the participation of the individual in the social consciousness of the race. This process begins unconsciously almost at birth, and is continually shaping the individual's powers, saturating his consciousness, forming his habits, training his ideas, and arousing his feelings and emotions. Through this unconscious education the individual gradually comes to share in the intellectual and moral resources which humanity has succeeded in getting together. He becomes an inheritor of the funded capital of civilization. The most formal and technical education in the world cannot safely depart from this general process. It can only organize it; or differentiate it in some particular direction.

I believe that the only true education comes through the stimulation of the child's powers by the demands of the social situations in which he finds himself. Through these demands he is stimulated to act as a member of a unity, to emerge from his original narrowness of action and feeling and to conceive of himself from the standpoint of the welfare of the group to which he belongs. Through the responses which others make to his own activities he comes to know what these mean in social terms. The value which they have is reflected back into them. For instance, through the response which is made to the child's instinctive babblings the child comes to know what those babblings mean; they are transformed into articulate language and thus the child is introduced into the consolidated wealth of ideas and emotions which are now summed up in language.

I believe that this educational process has two sides—one psychological and one sociological; and that neither can be subordinated to the other or neglected without evil results following. Of these two sides, the psychological is the basis. The child's own instincts and powers furnish the material and give the starting point for all education. Save as the efforts of the educator connect with some activity which the child is carrying on of his own initiative independent of the educator, education becomes reduced to a pressure from without. It may, indeed, give certain external results but cannot truly be called educative. Without insight into the psychological structure and activities of the individual, the educative process will, therefore, be haphazard and arbitrary. If it chances to coincide with the child's activity it will get a leverage; if it does not, it will result in friction, or disintegration, or arrest of the child's nature.

I believe that knowledge of social conditions, of the present state of civilization, is necessary in order properly to interpret the child's powers. The child has his own instincts and tendencies, but we do not know what these mean until we can translate them into their social equivalents. We must be able to carry them back into a social past and see them as the inheritance of previous race activities. We must also be able to project them into the future to see what their outcome and end will be. In the illustration just used, it is the ability to see in the child's babblings the promise and potency of a future social intercourse and conversation which enables one to deal in the proper way with that instinct.

I believe that the psychological and social sides are organically related and that education cannot be regarded as a compromise between the two, or a superimposition of one upon the other. We are told that the psychological definition of education is barren and formal—that it gives us only the idea of a development of all the mental powers without giving us any idea of the use to which these powers are put. On the other hand, it is urged that the social definition of education, as getting adjusted to civilization, makes of it a forced and external process, and results in subordinating the freedom of the individual to a preconceived social and political status.

I believe each of these objections is true when urged against one side isolated from the other. In order to know what a power really is we must know what its end, use, or function is; and this we cannot know save as we conceive of the individual as active in social relationships. But, on the other hand, the only possible adjustment which we can give to the child under existing conditions, is that which arises through putting him in complete possession of all his powers. With the advent of democracy and modern industrial conditions, it is impossible to foretell definitely just what civilization will be twenty years from now. Hence it is impossible to prepare the child for any precise set of conditions. To prepare him for the future life means to give him command of himself; it means so to train him that he will have the full and ready use of all his capacities; that his eye and ear and hand may be tools ready to command, that his judgment may be capable of grasping the conditions under which it has to work, and the executive forces be trained to act economically and efficiently. It is impossible to reach this sort of adjustment save as constant regard is had to the individual's own powers, tastes, and interests—say, that is, as education is continually converted into psychological terms. In sum, I believe that the individual who is to be educated is a social individual and that society is an organic union of individuals. If we eliminate the social factor from the child we are left only with an abstraction; if we eliminate the individual factor from society, we are left only with an inert and lifeless mass. Education, therefore, must begin with a psychological insight into the child's capacities, interests, and habits. It must be controlled at every point by reference to these same considerations. These powers, interests, and habits must be continually interpreted—we must know what they mean. They must be translated into terms of their social equivalents—into terms of what they are capable of in the way of social service.

Article II: What the School Is

I believe that the school is primarily a social institution. Education being a social process, the school is simply that form of community life in which all those agencies are concentrated that will be most effective in bringing the child to share in the inherited resources of the race, and to use his own powers for social ends.

I believe that education, therefore, is a process of living and not a preparation for future living.

I believe that the school must represent present life—life as real and vital to the child as that which he carries on in the home, in the neighborhood, or on the play-ground.

I believe that education which does not occur through forms of life, forms that are worth living for their own sake, is always a poor substitute for the genuine reality and tends to cramp and to deaden.

I believe that the school, as an institution, should simplify existing social life; should reduce it, as it were, to an embryonic form. Existing life is so complex that the child cannot be brought into contact with it without either confusion or distraction; he is either overwhelmed by multiplicity of activities which are going on, so that he loses his own power of orderly reaction, or he is so stimulated by these various activities that his powers are prematurely called into play and he becomes either unduly specialized or else disintegrated.

I believe that, as such simplified social life, the school life should grow gradually out of the home life; that it should take up and continue the activities with which the child is already familiar in the home.

I believe that it should exhibit these activities to the child, and reproduce them in such ways that the child will gradually learn the meaning of them, and be capable of playing his own part in relation to them.

I believe that this is a psychological necessity, because it is the only way of securing continuity in the child's growth, the only way of giving a background of past experience to the new ideas given in school.

I believe it is also a social necessity because the home is the form of social life in which the child has been nurtured and in connection with which he has had his moral training. It is the business of the school to deepen and extend his sense of the values bound up in his home life.

I believe that much of present education fails because it neglects this fundamental principle of the school as a form of community life. It conceives the school as a place where certain information is to be given, where certain lessons are to be learned, or where certain habits are to be formed. The value of these is conceived as lying largely in the remote future; the child must do these things for the sake of something else he is to do; they are mere preparation. As a result they do not become a part of the life experience of the child and so are not truly educative.

I believe that moral education centers about this conception of the school as a mode of social life, that the best and deepest moral training is precisely that which one gets through having to enter into proper relations with others in a unity of work and thought. The present educational systems, so far as they destroy or neglect this unity, render it difficult or impossible to get any genuine, regular moral training.

I believe that the child should be stimulated and controlled in his work through the life of the community.

I believe that under existing conditions far too much of the stimulus and control proceeds from the teacher, because of neglect of the idea of the school as a form of social life.

I believe that the teacher's place and work in the school is to be interpreted from this same basis. The teacher is not in the school to impose certain ideas or to form certain habits in the child, but is there as a member of the community to select the influences which shall affect the child and to assist him in properly responding to these influences.

I believe that the discipline of the school should proceed from the life of the school as a whole and not directly from the teacher.

I believe that the teacher's business is simply to determine on the basis of larger experience and riper wisdom, how the discipline of life shall come to the child.

I believe that all questions of the grading of the child and his promotion should be determined by reference to the same standard. Examinations are of use only so far as they test the child's fitness for social life and reveal the place in which he can be of most service and where he can receive the most help.

Article III: The Subject-Matter of Education

I believe that the social life of the child is the basis of concentration, or correlation, in all his training or growth. The social life gives the unconscious unity and the background of all his efforts and of all his attainments.

I believe that the subject-matter of the school curriculum should mark a gradual differentiation out of the primitive unconscious unity of social life.

I believe that we violate the child's nature and render difficult the best ethical results, by introducing the child too abruptly to a number of special studies, of reading, writing, geography, etc., out of relation to this social life.

I believe, therefore, that the true center of correlation of the school subjects is not science, nor literature, nor history, nor geography, but the child's own social activities.

I believe that education cannot be unified in the study of science, or so-called nature study, because apart from human activity, nature itself is not a unity; nature in itself is a number of diverse objects in space and time, and to attempt to make it the center of work by itself, is to introduce a principle of radiation rather than one of concentration.

I believe that literature is the reflex expression and interpretation of social experience; that hence it must follow upon and not precede such experience. It, therefore, cannot be made the basis, although it may be made the summary of unification.

I believe once more that history is of educative value in so far as it presents phases of social life and growth. It must be controlled by reference to social life. When taken simply as history it is thrown into the distant past and becomes dead and inert. Taken as the record of man's social life and progress it becomes full of meaning. I believe, however, that it cannot be so taken excepting as the child is also introduced directly into social life.

I believe accordingly that the primary basis of education is in the child's powers at work along the same general constructive lines as those which have brought civilization into being.

I believe that the only way to make the child conscious of his social heritage is to enable him to perform those fundamental types of activity which makes civilization what it is.

I believe, therefore, in the so-called expressive or constructive activities as the center of correlation.

I believe that this gives the standard for the place of cooking, sewing, manual training, etc., in the school.

I believe that they are not special studies which are to be introduced over and above a lot of others in the way of relaxation or relief, or as additional accomplishments. I believe rather that they represent, as types, fundamental forms of social activity; and that it is possible and desirable that the child's introduction into the more formal subjects of the curriculum be through the medium of these activities.

I believe that the study of science is educational in so far as it brings out the materials and processes which make social life what it is.

I believe that one of the greatest difficulties in the present teaching of science is that the material is presented in purely objective form, or is treated as a new peculiar kind of experience which the child can add to that which he has already had. In reality, science is of value because it gives the ability to interpret and control the experience already had. It should be introduced, not as so much new subject-matter, but as showing the factors already involved in previous experience and as furnishing tools by which that experience can be more easily and effectively regulated.

I believe that at present we lose much of the value of literature and language studies because of our elimination of the social element. Language is almost always treated in the books of pedagogy simply as the expression of thought. It is true that language is a logical instrument, but it is fundamentally and primarily a social instrument. Language is the device for communication; it is the tool through which one individual comes to share the ideas and feelings of others. When treated simply as a way of getting individual information, or as a means of showing off what one has learned, it loses its social motive and end.

I believe that there is, therefore, no succession of studies in the ideal school curriculum. If education is life, all life has, from the outset, a scientific aspect; an aspect of art and culture and an aspect of communication. It cannot, therefore, be true that the proper studies for one grade are mere reading and writing, and that at a later grade, reading, or literature, or science, may be introduced. The progress is not in the succession of studies but in the development of new attitudes towards, and new interests in, experience.

I believe finally, that education must be conceived as a continuing reconstruction of experience; that the process and the goal of education are one and the same thing.

I believe that to set up any end outside of education, as furnishing its goal and standard, is to deprive the educational process of much of its meaning and tends to make us rely upon false and external stimuli in dealing with the child.

Article IV: The Nature of Method

I believe that the question of method is ultimately reducible to the question of the order of development of the child's powers and interests. The law for presenting and treating material is the law implicit within the child's own nature. Because this is so I believe the following statements are of supreme importance as determining the spirit in which education is carried on:

(1.) I believe that the active side precedes the passive in the development of the child nature; that expression comes before conscious impression; that the muscular development precedes the sensory; that movements come before conscious sensations; I believe that consciousness is essentially motor or impulsive; that conscious states tend to project themselves in action.

I believe that the neglect of this principle is the cause of a large part of the waste of time and strength in school work. The child is thrown into a passive, receptive or absorbing attitude. The conditions are such that he is not permitted to follow the law of his nature; the result is friction and waste.

I believe that ideas (intellectual and rational processes) also result from action and devolve for the sake of the better control of action. What we term reason is primarily the law of orderly or effective action. To attempt to develop the reasoning powers, the powers of judgment, without reference to the selection and arrangement of means in action, is the fundamental fallacy in our present methods of dealing with this matter. As a result we present the child with arbitrary symbols. Symbols are a necessity in mental development, but they have their place as tools for economizing effort; presented by themselves they are a mass of meaningless and arbitrary ideas imposed from without.

(2.) I believe that the image is the great instrument of instruction. What a child gets out of any subject presented to him is simply the images which he himself forms with regard to it.

I believe that if nine-tenths of the energy at present directed towards making the child learn certain things, were spent in seeing to it that the child was forming proper images, the work of instruction would be indefinitely facilitated.

I believe that much of the time and attention now given to the preparation and presentation of lessons might be more wisely and profitably expended in training the child's power of imagery and in seeing to it that he was continually forming definite, vivid, and growing images of the various subjects with which he comes in contact in his experience.

(3.) I believe that interests are the signs and symptoms of growing power. I believe that they represent dawning capacities. Accordingly the constant and careful observation of interests is of the utmost importance for the educator.

I believe that these interests are to be observed as showing the state of development which the child has reached.

I believe that they prophesy the stage upon which he is about to enter.

I believe that only through the continual and sympathetic observation of childhood's interests can the adult enter into the child's life and see what it is ready for, and upon what material it could work most readily and fruitfully.

I believe that these interests are neither to be humored nor repressed. To repress interest is to substitute the adult for the child, and so to weaken intellectual curiosity and alertness, to suppress initiative, and to deaden interest. To humor the interests is to substitute the transient for the permanent. The interest is always the sign of some power below; the important thing is to discover this power. To humor the interest is to fail to penetrate below the surface and its sure result is to substitute caprice and whim for genuine interest.

(4.) I believe that the emotions are the reflex of actions.

I believe that to endeavor to stimulate or arouse the emotions apart from their corresponding activities, is to introduce an unhealthy and morbid state of mind.

I believe that if we can only secure right habits of action and thought, with reference to the good, the true, and the beautiful, the emotions will for the most part take care of themselves.

I believe that next to deadness and dullness, formalism and routine, our education is threatened with no greater evil than sentimentalism.

I believe that this sentimentalism is the necessary result of the attempt to divorce feeling from action.

Article V: The School and Social Progress

I believe that education is the fundamental method of social progress and reform.

I believe that all reforms which rest simply upon the enactment of law, or the threatening of certain penalties, or upon changes in mechanical or outward arrangements, are transitory and futile.

I believe that education is a regulation of the process of coming to share in the social consciousness; and that the adjustment of individual activity on the basis of this social consciousness is the only sure method of social reconstruction.

I believe that this conception has due regard for both the individualistic and socialistic ideals. It is duly individual because it recognizes the formation of a certain character as the only genuine basis of right living. It is socialistic because it recognizes that this right character is not to be formed by merely individual precept, example, or exhortation, but rather by the influence of a certain form of institutional or community life upon the individual, and that the social organism through the school, as its organ, may determine ethical results.

I believe that in the ideal school we have the reconciliation of the individualistic and the institutional ideals.

I believe that the community's duty to education is, therefore, its paramount moral duty. By law and punishment, by social agitation and discussion, society can regulate and form itself in a more or less haphazard and chance way. But through education society can formulate its own purposes, can organize its own means and resources, and thus shape itself with definiteness and economy in the direction in which it wishes to move.

I believe that when society once recognizes the possibilities in this direction, and the obligations which these possibilities impose, it is impossible to conceive of the resources of time, attention, and money which will be put at the disposal of the educator.

I believe it is the business of every one interested in education to insist upon the school as the primary and most effective instrument of social progress and reform in order that society may be awakened to realize what the school stands for, and aroused to the necessity of endowing the educator with sufficient equipment properly to perform his task.

I believe that education thus conceived marks the most perfect and intimate union of science and art conceivable in human experience.

I believe that the art of thus giving shape to human powers and adapting them to social service, is the supreme art; one calling into its service the best of artists; that no insight, sympathy, tact, executive power is too great for such service.

I believe that with the growth of psychological science, giving added insight into individual structure and laws of growth; and with growth of social science, adding to our knowledge of the right organization of individuals, all scientific resources can be utilized for the purposes of education.

I believe that when science and art thus join hands the most commanding motive for human action will be reached; the most genuine springs of human conduct aroused and the best service that human nature is capable of guaranteed.

I believe, finally, that the teacher is engaged, not simply in the training of individuals, but in the formation of the proper social life.

I believe that every teacher should realize the dignity of his calling; that he is a social servant set apart for the maintenance of proper social order and the securing of the right social growth.

I believe that in this way the teacher always is the prophet of the true God and the usherer in of the true kingdom of God.

SOURCE: *The School Journal*. Volume 54, No. 3. January 16, 1897.

ARTHUR CHRISTOPHER BENSON

"Training of Teachers"
(1902)

The son of a headmaster, Benson (1862–1925), taught for many years at England's Eton, one of the oldest boys' schools in the world. He was a dedicated diary-keeper, and his reflections on education are always based on particular experiences. He observes of one of his teaching strategies: ". . . the only way to interest boys is to treat frankly of what has interested myself, without any reference as to whether it ought to have interested me. The result is not invariably successful—a man must have sufficient tact to see that a hobby of his own is not always attractive to immature minds—but it is generally so; whereas to regulate one's teaching by a standard of dignity is generally to succeed in depriving it of the last shred of interest. One must be sincere in teaching above all things, and it is impossible to be convincing if one is perpetually endeavoring to enforce things in which one does not believe."

I confess that I am somewhat skeptical about the training of teachers; it seems to me like training people to become good conversationalists. The receipt is to know the subject you are teaching, and to have a lively, genial, and effective personality. It seems to me that it is an art which cannot be learnt by demonstration. Even a profound knowledge of the subject is comparatively unimportant except in advanced work; a brisk, idle man with a knack of exposition and the art of clear statement can be a scandalously effective teacher. In fact, the more profound the knowledge of the teacher is, the more risk there is of his being unable to sympathise with the difficulties of boys, and of his being incapable of conceiving the possible depths of their ignorance. The perfect combination is sound knowledge, endless patience, and inexhaustible sympathy.

A man who can keep the boys interested and amused, who can appreciate the slender nuances which differentiate the work of a boy who has tried to learn his lesson from the work of a boy who has just done enough to pass muster, will have a much greater effect on a class than a man whose knowledge is far deeper, but who has not the art of commanding attention, or of sympathising with the unformed mind. The real difficulty is the question of discipline, and no one can possibly be an effective teacher who has to be always looking about for signs of inattention and misbehaviour.

And here lies the root of the matter. A man may have conducted classes satisfactorily at a training college where the disciplinary difficulty is nonexistent, he may have seen and heard a lesson brilliantly conducted by an effective teacher, but when he is face to face with a class of his own, he may find that he has no real control, and that he cannot command the attention of the boys sufficiently to allow him to imitate the method he has seen successfully pursued. Moreover, in teaching, which is above all things a spontaneous, a dramatic process, the method of conducting a lesson must be to a great extent a matter of idiosyncrasy. No one can form himself upon a model. Some masters have the art of rapid questioning, some the art of exposition, and it matters little which is employed, so long as the result is alertness and interest in the boys. The best training of all would be to be able to observe through a loophole the conducting of a lesson by a first-rate teacher—I say through a loophole, because there are many first-rate teachers the edge of whose teaching would be dulled if the lesson had to be conducted in the presence of a critical observer.

I have myself known a master whose teaching greatly impressed the headmaster whenever he visited the schoolroom. The teacher in question was learned, accurate, and clear-headed; his questions were to the point, his explanations lucid; but the headmaster did not know that it was only his own presence that kept the class in a submissive frame of mind, and that on ordinary occasions the time of the master was so fully occupied by an entirely unsuccessful attempt to keep the boys in order that he never had an opportunity of indulging in the lucid exposition of the lesson which had seemed so impressive.

The fact is that the boys who have been through a public school themselves have practically been trained as teachers as far as training can be given. They have seen innumerable lessons given, and they can to a certain extent discriminate methods.

The teacher's aim is, after all, to make the boys think—to put them into such a frame of mind that they will take in and assimilate knowledge and make it their own, not to drive facts in like a row of nails. The best teacher I have ever heard is one who deals very little with questions, but lectures with a zest and with a certain air of bringing out facts of incredible importance, which could not be obtained in any other place and in any other circumstances. The result is that the boys are kept in a state of pleased expectancy. And this knowledge is not only such as stands the test of examinations; it attracts the boys to the subject, it makes them enthusiastic.

I do not say that it is not an advantage to a man to have passed through a certain period of training, but I do maintain that such training can never make a man an effective teacher. It may just give him an inkling of how to set to work; but a sensible man, with a gift for discipline, who can realise that the small boys, whom he will almost certainly have to begin by teaching, are sure to be almost entirely ignorant and very slow of comprehension, but that if their interest can once be aroused they will make rapid progress,—such a man will learn more in a week from teaching a division of his own, where he has no one to depend on but himself, than in months spent at a training college.

What I believe would be a still better system would be to attach a young master, on first going to a public school, to some competent senior—to get the senior master to be present when he takes a lesson, and occasionally to take a lesson before him. But as far as mere methods are concerned, I am sure I could tell a young man in half an hour the simple dodges which have proved in my own case useful and effective.

The best training that a teacher can get is the training that he can give himself. If he has found an illustration or a story effective, let him note it down for future use; let him read widely rather than profoundly, so that he has a large stock-in-trade of anecdote and illustration. Let him try experiments; let him grasp that monotony is the one thing that alienates the attention of boys sooner than anything else; let him contrive to get brisk periods of intense work rather than long tracts of dreary work. These are facts which can only be learnt by practice and among the boys. I declare I believe that one of the most useful qualities that I have found myself to possess from the point of view of teaching is the capacity for being rapidly and easily bored myself. If the tedium of a long and dull lesson is insupportable to myself, I have enough imagination to know that it must be far worse for the boys.

Education is not and cannot be a wholly scientific thing. It is the contact of one mind with another, and it is governed by the same laws that the intercourse of men in ordinary life is governed by. A teacher must keep himself fresh in mind and body alike, and a dreary, tired, and dispirited man is not likely to produce any profound impression on the tender mind, except that the subjects which he endeavours to instill are in themselves a tedious and uninspiring business.

One last mistake I may touch upon here. I have known very worthy teachers who have insisted with conscientious perseverance in only imparting knowledge of a kind that ought to interest the well-regulated mind. Now very few minds are well-regulated, and I have found myself that the only way to interest boys is to treat frankly of what has interested myself, without any reference as to whether it ought to have interested me. The result is not invariably successful—a man must have sufficient tact to see that a hobby of his own is not always attractive to immature minds—but it is generally so; whereas to regulate one's teaching by a standard of dignity is generally to succeed in depriving it of the last shred of interest. One must be sincere in teaching above all things, and it is impossible to be convincing if one is perpetually endeavouring to enforce things in which one does not believe.

Lastly, I am inclined to think that the best system of all, if it were feasible, would be to send a young man for a few weeks to a training college after he has had say a year's experience of teaching in a school. He will have learnt by that time what his weak points are, he will have some idea of what the difficulties are. He will be alert to see how to deal with a lesson, how to explain, what kind of questions to put and how to put them. He will probably have acquired some enthusiasm for his art; he will realise that what seemed so simple in the hands of a skilled teacher, before he had any experience of difficulties, is not an easy matter after all.

SOURCE: Arthur Christoper Benson. *The Schoolmaster; A Commentary upon the Aims and Methods of an Assistant-Master in a Public School.* London: John Murray. 1902.

ANNE MANSFIELD SULLIVAN

"The Education of Helen Keller"
(1903)

Anne Mansfield Sullivan (1866–1936) was the teacher from Massachusetts whose success with the deaf and blind girl Helen Keller (1880–1968) helped make the both of them world famous. More importantly, Sullivan's ingenious work and Keller's brilliance helped publicize the possibilities of teaching all people, no matter the disabilities. The editor of Keller's 1903 work The Story of My Life, *John Albert Macy, describes the amazing teacher-student connection: "There is, then, a good deal that Miss Sullivan has done for Miss Keller which no other teacher can do in just the same way for any one else. To have another Helen Keller there must be another Miss Sullivan. To have another, well-educated deaf and blind child, there need only be another teacher, living under favorable conditions, among plenty of external interests, unseparated from her pupil, allowed to have a free hand, and using as many as she needs of the principles which Miss Sullivan has saved her the trouble of finding out for herself, modifying and adding as she finds it necessary . . ." Sullivan's account of educating Keller is presented through her letters from her first month in Tuscumbia, Alabama; the excerpts conclude with Keller's vital realization that "everything has a name, and that the manual alphabet is the key to everything she wants to know."*

March 6, 1887

It was 6:30 when I reached Tuscumbia. I found Mrs. Keller and Mr. James Keller waiting for me. They said somebody had met every train for two days. The drive from the station to the house, a distance of one mile, was very lovely and restful. I was surprised to find Mrs. Keller a very young-looking woman, not much older than myself, I should think. Captain Keller met us in the yard and gave me a cheery welcome and a hearty handshake. My first question was, "Where is Helen?" I tried with all my might to control the eagerness that made me tremble so that I could hardly walk. As we approached the house I saw a child standing in the doorway, and Captain Keller said, "There she is. She has known all day that some one was expected, and she has been wild ever since her mother went to the station for you."

I had scarcely put my foot on the steps, when she rushed toward me with such force that she would have thrown me backward if Captain Keller had not been behind me. She felt my face and dress and my bag, which she took out of my hand and tried to open. It did not open easily, and she felt carefully to see if there was a keyhole. Finding that there was, she turned to me, making the sign of turning a key and pointing to the bag. Her mother interfered at this point and showed Helen by signs that she must not touch the bag. Her face flushed, and when her mother attempted to take the bag from her, she grew very angry. I attracted her attention by showing her my watch and letting her hold it in her hand. Instantly the tempest subsided, and we went upstairs together. Here I opened the bag, and she went through it eagerly, probably expecting to find something to eat. Friends had probably brought her candy in their bags, and she expected to find some in mine.

I made her understand, by pointing to a trunk in the hall and to myself and nodding my head, that I had a trunk, and then made the sign that she had used for eating, and nodded again. She understood in a flash and ran downstairs to tell her mother, by means of emphatic signs, that there was some candy in a trunk for her. She returned in a few minutes and helped me put away my things. It was too comical to see her put on my bonnet and cock her head first on one side, then on the other, and look in the mirror, just as if she could see.

Somehow I had expected to see a pale, delicate child—I suppose I got the idea from Dr. Howe's description of Laura Bridgman when she came to the Institution. But there's nothing pale or delicate about Helen. She is large, strong, and ruddy, and as unrestrained in her movements as a young colt. She has none of those nervous habits that are so noticeable and so distressing in blind children. Her body is well formed and vigorous, and Mrs. Keller says she has not been ill a day since the illness that deprived her of her sight and hearing.

She has a fine head, and it is set on her shoulders just right. Her face is hard to describe. It is intelligent, but lacks mobility, or soul, or something. Her mouth is large and finely shaped. You see at a glance that she is blind. One eye is larger than the other, and protrudes noticeably. She rarely smiles; indeed, I have seen her smile only once or twice since I came. She is unresponsive and even impatient of caresses from any one except her mother. She is very quick-tempered and wilful, and nobody, except her brother James, has attempted to control her. The greatest problem I shall have to solve is how to discipline and control her without breaking her spirit. I shall go rather slowly at first and try to win her love. I shall not attempt to conquer her by force alone; but I shall insist on reasonable obedience from the start. One thing that impresses everybody is Helen's tireless activity. She is never still a moment. She is here, there, and everywhere. Her hands are in everything; but nothing holds her attention for long. Dear child, her restless spirit gropes in the dark. Her untaught, unsatisfied hands destroy whatever they touch because they do not know what else to do with things.

She helped me unpack my trunk when it came, and was delighted when she found the doll the little girls sent her. I thought it a good opportunity to teach her her first word. I spelled "d-o-l-l" slowly in her hand and pointed to the doll and nodded my head, which seems to be her sign for possession. Whenever anybody gives her anything, she points to it, then to herself, and nods her head. She looked puzzled and felt my hand, and I repeated the letters. She imitated them very well and pointed to the doll. Then I took the doll, meaning to give it back to her when she had made the letters; but she thought I meant to take it from her, and in an instant she was in a temper, and tried to seize the doll. I shook my head and tried to form the letters with her fingers; but she got more and more angry. I forced her into a chair and held her there until I was nearly exhausted. Then it occurred to me that it was useless to continue the struggle—I must do something to turn the current of her thoughts. I let her go, but refused to give up the doll.

I went downstairs and got some cake (she is very fond of sweets). I showed Helen the cake and spelled "c-a-k-e" in her hand, holding the cake toward her. Of course she wanted it and tried to take it; but I spelled the word again and patted her hand. She made the letters rapidly, and I gave her the cake, which she ate in a great hurry, thinking, I suppose, that I might take it from her.

Then I showed her the doll and spelled the word again, holding the doll toward her as I held the cake. She made the letters "d-o-l'" and I made the other "l" and gave her the doll. She ran downstairs with it and could not be induced to return to my room all day.

Yesterday I gave her a sewing-card to do. I made the first row of vertical lines and let her feel it and notice that there were several rows of little holes. She began to work delightedly and finished the card in a few minutes, and did it very neatly indeed. I thought I would try another word; so I spelled "c-a-r-d." She made the "c-a," then stopped and thought, and making the sign for eating and pointing downward she pushed me toward the door, meaning that I must go downstairs for some cake. The two letters "c-a," you see, had reminded her of Friday's "lesson"—not that she had any idea that cake was the name of the thing, but it was simply a matter of association, I suppose. I finished the word "c-a-k-e" and obeyed her command. She was delighted. Then I spelled "d-o-l-l" and began to hunt for it.

She follows with her hands every motion you make, and she knew that I was looking for the doll. She pointed down, meaning that the doll was downstairs. I made the signs that she had used when she wished me to go for the cake, and pushed her toward the door. She started forward, then hesitated a moment, evidently debating within herself whether she would go or not. She decided to send me instead. I shook my head and spelled "d-o-l-l" more emphatically, and opened the door for her; but she obstinately refused to obey. She had not finished the cake she was eating, and I took it away, indicating that if she brought the doll I would give her back the cake. She stood perfectly still for one long moment, her face crimson; then her desire for the cake triumphed, and she ran downstairs and brought the doll, and of course I gave her the cake, but could not persuade her to enter the room again.

She was very troublesome when I began to write this morning. She kept coming up behind me and putting her hand on the paper and into the ink-bottle. These blots are her handiwork.

Finally I remembered the kindergarten beads, and set her to work stringing them. First I put on two wooden beads and one glass bead, then made her feel of the string and the two boxes of beads. She nodded and began at once to fill the string with wooden beads. I shook my head and took them all off and made her feel of the two wooden beads and the one glass bead. She examined them thoughtfully and began again. This time she put on the glass bead first and the two wooden ones next. I took them off and showed her that the two wooden ones must go on first, then the glass bead. She had no further trouble and filled the string quickly, too quickly, in fact. She tied the ends together when she had finished the string, and put the beads round her neck. I did not make the knot large enough in the next string, and the beads came off as fast as she put them on; but she solved the difficulty herself by putting the string through a bead and tying it. I thought this very clever. She amused herself with the beads until dinner-time, bringing the strings to me now and then for my approval.

My eyes are very much inflamed. I know this letter is very carelessly written. I had a lot to say, and couldn't stop to think how to express things neatly. Please do not show my letter to any one. If you want to, you may read it to my friends.

March 7

I had a battle royal with Helen this morning. Although I try very hard not to force issues, I find it very difficult to avoid them. Helen's table manners are appalling. She puts her hands in our plates and helps herself, and when the dishes are passed, she grabs them and takes out whatever she wants.

This morning I would not let her put her hand in my plate. She persisted, and a contest of wills followed. Naturally the family was much disturbed, and left the room. I locked the dining-room door, and proceeded to eat my breakfast, though the food almost choked me. Helen was lying on the floor, kicking and screaming and trying to pull my chair from under me. She kept this up for half an hour, then she got up to see what I was doing. I let her see that I was eating, but did not let her put her hand in the plate. She pinched me, and I slapped her every time she did it. Then she went all round the table to see who was there, and finding no one but me, she seemed bewildered.

After a few minutes she came back to her place and began to eat her breakfast with her fingers. I gave her a spoon, which she threw on the floor. I forced her out of the chair and made her pick it up. Finally I succeeded in getting her back in her chair again, and held the spoon in her hand, compelling her to take up the food with it and put it in her mouth. In a few minutes she yielded and finished her breakfast peaceably. Then we had another tussle over folding her napkin. When she had finished, she threw it on the floor and ran toward the door. Finding it locked, she began to kick and scream all over again.

It was another hour before I succeeded in getting her napkin folded. Then I let her out into the warm sunshine and went up to my room and threw myself on the bed exhausted. I had a good cry and felt better. I suppose I shall have many such battles with the little woman before she learns the only two essential things I can teach her, obedience and love.

Good-by, dear. Don't worry; I'll do my best and leave the rest to whatever power manages that which we cannot. I like Mrs. Keller very much.

March 11

Since I wrote you, Helen and I have gone to live all by ourselves in a little garden-house about a quarter of a mile from her home, only a short distance from Ivy Green, the Keller homestead. I very soon made up my mind that I could do nothing with Helen in the midst of the family, who have always allowed her to do exactly as she pleased. She has tyrannized over everybody, her mother, her father, the servants, the little darkies who play with her, and nobody had ever seriously disputed her will, except occasionally her brother James, until I came; and like all tyrants she holds tenaciously to her divine right to do as she pleases. If she ever failed to get what she wanted, it was because of her inability to make the vassals of her household understand what it was. Every thwarted desire was the signal for a passionate outburst, and as she grew older and stronger, these tempests became more violent.

As I began to teach her, I was beset by many difficulties. She wouldn't yield a point without contesting it to the bitter end. I couldn't coax her or compromise with her. To get her to do the simplest thing, such as combing her hair or washing her hands or buttoning her boots, it was necessary to use force, and, of course, a distressing scene followed. The family naturally felt inclined to interfere, especially her father, who cannot bear to see her cry. So they were all willing to give in for the sake of peace. Besides, her past experiences and associations were all against me. I saw clearly that it was useless to try to teach her language or anything else until she learned to obey me. I have thought about it a great deal, and the more I think, the more certain I am that obedience is the gateway through which knowledge, yes, and love, too, enter the mind of the child.

As I wrote you, I meant to go slowly at first. I had an idea that I could win the love and confidence of my little pupil by the same means that I should use if she could see and hear. But I soon found that I was cut off from all the usual approaches to the child's heart. She accepted everything I did for her as a matter of course, and re-

fused to be caressed, and there was no way of appealing to her affection or sympathy or childish love of approbation. She would or she
wouldn't, and there was an end of it. Thus it is, we study, plan and
prepare ourselves for a task, and when the hour for action arrives,
we find that the system we have followed with such labor and pride
does not fit the occasion; and then there's nothing for us to do but
rely on something within us, some innate capacity for knowing and
doing, which we did not know we possessed until the hour of our
great need brought it to light.

I had a good, frank talk with Mrs. Keller, and explained to her
how difficult it was going to be to do anything with Helen under
the existing circumstances. I told her that in my opinion the child
ought to be separated from the family for a few weeks at least—that
she must learn to depend on and obey me before I could make any
headway.

After a long time Mrs. Keller said that she would think the matter
over and see what Captain Keller thought of sending Helen away
with me. Captain Keller fell in with the scheme most readily and
suggested that the little garden-house at the "old place" be got ready
for us. He said that Helen might recognize the place, as she had often
been there, but she would have no idea of her surroundings, and they
could come every day to see that all was going well, with the understanding, of course, that she was to know nothing of their visits. I hurried the preparations for our departure as much as possible, and here
we are.

The little house is a genuine bit of paradise. It consists of one large
square room with a great fireplace, a spacious bay-window, and a
small room where our servant, a little negro boy, sleeps. There is a
piazza in front, covered with vines that grow so luxuriantly that you
have to part them to see the garden beyond. Our meals are brought
from the house, and we usually eat on the piazza. The little negro
boy takes care of the fire when we need one, so I can give my whole
attention to Helen. She was greatly excited at first, and kicked and
screamed herself into a sort of stupor, but when supper was brought
she ate heartily and seemed brighter, although she refused to let me
touch her. She devoted herself to her dolls the first evening, and
when it was bedtime she undressed very quietly, but when she felt
me get into bed with her, she jumped out on the other side, and
nothing that I could do would induce her to get in again. But I was
afraid she would take cold, and I insisted that she must go to bed. We

had a terrific tussle, I can tell you. The struggle lasted for nearly two hours. I never saw such strength and endurance in a child. But fortunately for us both, I am a little stronger, and quite as obstinate when I set out. I finally succeeded in getting her on the bed and covered her up, and she lay curled up as near the edge of the bed as possible.

The next morning she was very docile, but evidently homesick. She kept going to the door, as if she expected some one, and every now and then she would touch her cheek, which is her sign for her mother, and shake her head sadly. She played with her dolls more than usual, and would have nothing to do with me. It is amusing and pathetic to see Helen with her dolls. I don't think she has any special tenderness for them—I have never seen her caress them; but she dresses and undresses them many times during the day and handles them exactly as she has seen her mother and the nurse handle her baby sister. This morning Nancy, her favorite doll, seemed to have some difficulty about swallowing the milk that was being administered to her in large spoonfuls; for Helen suddenly put down the cup and began to slap her on the back and turn her over on her knees, trotting her gently and patting her softly all the time. This lasted for several minutes; then this mood passed, and Nancy was thrown ruthlessly on the floor and pushed to one side, while a large, pink-cheeked, fuzzy-haired member of the family received the little mother's undivided attention.

Helen knows several words now, but has no idea how to use them, or that everything has a name. I think, however, she will learn quickly enough by and by. As I have said before, she is wonderfully bright and active and as quick as lightning in her movements.

March 13

You will be glad to hear that my experiment is working out finely. I have not had any trouble at all with Helen, either yesterday or today. She has learned three new words, and when I give her the objects, the names of which she has learned, she spells them unhesitatingly; but she seems glad when the lesson is over.

We had a good frolic this morning out in the garden. Helen evidently knew where she was as soon as she touched the boxwood hedges, and made many signs which I did not understand. No doubt they were signs for the different members of the family at Ivy Green.

I have just heard something that surprised me very much. It seems that Mr. Anagnos had heard of Helen before he received Captain

Keller's letter last summer. Mr. Wilson, a teacher at Florence, and a friend of the Kellers', studied at Harvard the summer before and went to the Perkins Institution to learn if anything could be done for his friend's child. He saw a gentleman whom he presumed to be the director, and told him about Helen. He says the gentleman was not particularly interested, but said he would see if anything could be done. Doesn't it seem strange that Mr. Anagnos never referred to this interview?

March 20

My heart is singing for joy this morning. A miracle has happened! The light of understanding has shone upon my little pupil's mind, and behold, all things are changed! The wild little creature of two weeks ago has been transformed into a gentle child. She is sitting by me as I write, her face serene and happy, crocheting a long red chain of Scotch wool. She learned the stitch this week, and is very proud of the achievement. When she succeeded in making a chain that would reach across the room, she patted herself on the arm and put the first work of her hands lovingly against her cheek. She lets me kiss her now, and when she is in a particularly gentle mood, she will sit in my lap for a minute or two; but she does not return my caresses. The great step—the step that counts—has been taken.

The little savage has learned her first lesson in obedience, and finds the yoke easy. It now remains my pleasant task to direct and mould the beautiful intelligence that is beginning to stir in the child-soul. Already people remark the change in Helen. Her father looks in at us morning and evening as he goes to and from his office, and sees her contentedly stringing her beads or making horizontal lines on her sewing-card, and exclaims, "How quiet she is!"

When I came, her movements were so insistent that one always felt there was something unnatural and almost weird about her. I have noticed also that she eats much less, a fact which troubles her father so much that he is anxious to get her home. He says she is homesick. I don't agree with him; but I suppose we shall have to leave our little bower very soon.

Helen has learned several nouns this week. "M-u-g" and "m-i-l-k," have given her more trouble than other words. When she spells "milk," she points to the mug, and when she spells "mug," she makes the sign for pouring or drinking, which shows that she has confused the words. She has no idea yet that everything has a name.

Yesterday I had the little negro boy come in when Helen was having her lesson, and learn the letters, too. This pleased her very much and stimulated her ambition to excel Percy. She was delighted if he made a mistake, and made him form the letter over several times. When he succeeded in forming it to suit her, she patted him on his woolly head so vigorously that I thought some of his slips were intentional.

One day this week Captain Keller brought Belle, a setter of which he is very proud, to see us. He wondered if Helen would recognize her old playmate. Helen was giving Nancy a bath, and didn't notice the dog at first. She usually feels the softest step and throws out her arms to ascertain if any one is near her. Belle didn't seem very anxious to attract her attention. I imagine she has been rather roughly handled sometimes by her little mistress. The dog hadn't been in the room more than half a minute, however, before Helen began to sniff, and dumped the doll into the washbowl and felt about the room. She stumbled upon Belle, who was crouching near the window where Captain Keller was standing. It was evident that she recognized the dog; for she put her arms round her neck and squeezed her. Then Helen sat down by her and began to manipulate her claws. We couldn't think for a second what she was doing; but when we saw her make the letters "d-o-l-l" on her own fingers, we knew that she was trying to teach Belle to spell.

March 28

Helen and I came home yesterday. I am sorry they wouldn't let us stay another week; but I think I have made the most I could of the opportunities that were mine the past two weeks, and I don't expect that I shall have any serious trouble with Helen in the future. The back of the greatest obstacle in the path of progress is broken. I think "no" and "yes," conveyed by a shake or a nod of my head, have become facts as apparent to her as hot and cold or as the difference between pain and pleasure. And I don't intend that the lesson she has learned at the cost of so much pain and trouble shall be unlearned. I shall stand between her and the over-indulgence of her parents. I have told Captain and Mrs. Keller that they must not interfere with me in any way. I have done my best to make them see the terrible injustice to Helen of allowing her to have her way in everything, and I have pointed out that the processes of teaching the child that everything cannot be as he wills it, are apt to be painful both to him and to his teacher. They have promised to let me have a free hand and help me as much as possible. The improvement they cannot help seeing in their child has given them more confidence in me. Of course, it is hard for them. I realize that it hurts to see their afflicted little child punished and made to do things against her will.

Only a few hours after my talk with Captain and Mrs. Keller (and they had agreed to everything), Helen took a notion that she wouldn't use her napkin at table. I think she wanted to see what would happen. I attempted several times to put the napkin round her neck; but each time she tore it off and threw it on the floor and finally began to kick the table. I took her plate away and started to take her out of the room. Her father objected and said that no child of his should be deprived of his food on any account. Helen didn't come up to my room after supper, and I didn't see her again until breakfast-time. She was at her place when I came down. She had put the napkin under her chin, instead of pinning it at the back, as was her custom. She called my attention to the new arrangement, and when I did not object she seemed pleased and patted herself. When she left the dining-room, she took my hand and patted it. I wondered if she was trying to "make up." I thought I would try the effect of a little belated discipline. I went back to the dining-room and got a napkin.

When Helen came upstairs for her lesson, I arranged the objects on the table as usual, except that the cake, which I always give her in bits as a reward when she spells a word quickly and correctly, was not there. She noticed this at once and made the sign for it. I showed her the napkin and pinned it round her neck, then tore it off and threw it on the floor and shook my head. I repeated this performance several times. I think she understood perfectly well; for she slapped her hand two or three times and shook her head. We began the lesson as usual. I gave her an object, and she spelled the name (she knows twelve now). After spelling half the words, she stopped suddenly, as if a thought had flashed into her mind, and felt for the napkin. She pinned it round her neck and made the sign for cake (it didn't occur to her to spell the word, you see). I took this for a promise that if I gave her some cake she would be a good girl. I gave her a larger piece than usual, and she chuckled and patted herself.

April 3

We almost live in the garden, where everything is growing and blooming and glowing. After breakfast we go out and watch the men at work. Helen loves to dig and play in the dirt like any other child. This morning she planted her doll and showed me that she expected her to grow as tall as I. You must see that she is very bright, but you have no idea how cunning she is. At ten we come in and string beads for a few minutes. She can make a great many combinations now, and often invents new ones herself. Then I let her decide whether she will sew or knit or crochet. She learned to knit very quickly, and is making a wash-cloth for her mother. Last week she made her doll an apron, and it was done as well as any child of her age could do it. But I am always glad when this work is over for the day. Sewing and crocheting are inventions of the devil, I think. I'd rather break stones on the king's highway than hem a handkerchief. At eleven we have gymnastics. She knows all the free-hand movements and the "Anvil Chorus" with the dumb-bells. Her father says he is going to fit up a gymnasium for her in the pump-house; but we both like a good romp better than set exercises. The hour from twelve to one is devoted to the learning of new words. *But you mustn't think this is the only time I spell to Helen; for I spell in her hand everything we do all day long, although she has no idea as yet what the spelling means.*

After dinner I rest for an hour, and Helen plays with her dolls or frolics in the yard with the little darkies, who were her constant companions before I came.

Later I join them, and we make the rounds of the outhouses. We visit the horses and mules in their stalls and hunt for eggs and feed the turkeys. Often, when the weather is fine, we drive from four to six, or go to see her aunt at Ivy Green or her cousins in the town. Helen's instincts are decidedly social; she likes to have people about her and to visit her friends, partly, I think, because they always have things she likes to eat. After supper we go to my room and do all sorts of things until eight, when I undress the little woman and put her to bed. She sleeps with me now. . . . I like to have Helen depend on me for everything, *and I find it much easier to teach her things at odd moments than at set times.*

On March 31st I found that Helen knew eighteen nouns and three verbs. Here is a list of the words. Those with a cross after them are words she asked for herself: DOLL, MUG, PIN, KEY,

DOG, HAT, CUP, BOX, WATER, MILK, CANDY, EYE (X), FINGER (X), TOE (X), HEAD (X), CAKE, BABY, MOTHER, SIT, STAND, WALK. On April 1st she learned the nouns KNIFE, FORK, SPOON, SAUCER, TEA, PAPA, BED, and the verb RUN.

April 5

I must write you a line this morning because something very important has happened. Helen has taken the second great step in her education. She has learned that *everything has a name, and that the manual alphabet is the key to everything she wants to know.*

In a previous letter I think I wrote you that "mug" and "milk" had given Helen more trouble than all the rest. She confused the nouns with the verb "drink." She didn't know the word for "drink," but went through the pantomime of drinking whenever she spelled "mug" or "milk." This morning, while she was washing, she wanted to know the name for "water." When she wants to know the name of anything, she points to it and pats my hand. I spelled "w-a-t-e-r" and thought no more about it until after breakfast. Then it occurred to me that with the help of this new word I might succeed in straightening out the "mug-milk" difficulty.

We went out to the pump-house, and I made Helen hold her mug under the spout while I pumped. As the cold water gushed forth, filling the mug, I spelled "w-a-t-e-r" in Helen's free hand. The word coming so close upon the sensation of cold water rushing over her hand seemed to startle her. She dropped the mug and stood as one transfixed. A new light came into her face. She spelled "water" several times.

Then she dropped on the ground and asked for its name and pointed to the pump and the trellis, and suddenly turning round she asked for my name. I spelled "Teacher." Just then the nurse brought Helen's little sister into the pump-house, and Helen spelled "baby" and pointed to the nurse. All the way back to the house she was highly excited, and learned the name of every object she touched, so that in a few hours she had *added thirty words to her vocabulary. Here are some of them:* DOOR, OPEN, SHUT, GIVE, GO, COME, and a great many more.

P.S.—I didn't finish my letter in time to get it posted last night; so I shall add a line. Helen got up this morning like a radiant fairy. She has flitted from object to object, asking the name of everything and kissing me for very gladness. Last night when I got in bed, she stole into my arms of her own accord and kissed me for the first time, and I thought my heart would burst, so full was it of joy.

SOURCE: John Albert Macy. *The Story of My Life by Helen Keller: With Her Letters (1887-1901) and a Supplementary Account of Her Education, Including Passages from the Reports and Letters of Her Teacher, Anne Mansfield Sullivan.* New York: Doubleday, Page and Company. 1903.

GEORGE HERBERT PALMER

from *The Ideal Teacher*
(1908)

Palmer (1842–1933) was a philosophy professor at Harvard for forty years. The ideal teacher, he explains, must have imagination: "At every instant of the teacher's life he must be controlled by this mighty power. . . . We incessantly go outside ourselves and enter into the many lives about us,—lives dull, dark, and unintelligible to any but an eye like ours. And this is imagination, the sympathetic creation in ourselves of conditions which belong to others."

The teacher's art takes its rise in what I call an aptitude for vicariousness. As year by year my college boys prepare to go forth into life, some laggard is sure to come to me and say, "I want a little advice. Most of my classmates have their minds made up about what they are going to do. I am still uncertain. I rather incline to be a teacher, because I am fond of books and suspect that in any other profession I can give them but little time. Business men do not read. Lawyers only consult books. And I am by no means sure that ministers have read all the books they quote. On the whole it seems safest to choose a profession in which books will be my daily companions. So I turn toward teaching. But before settling the matter I thought I would ask how you regard the profession." "A noble profession," I answer, "but quite unfit for you. I would advise you to become a lawyer, a car conductor, or something equally harmless. Do not turn to anything so perilous as teaching. You would ruin both it and yourself; for you are looking in exactly the wrong direction."

Such an inquirer is under a common misconception. The teacher's task is not primarily the acquisition of knowledge, but the impartation of it,—an entirely different matter. We teachers are forever taking thoughts out of our minds and putting them elsewhere. So long as we are content to keep them in our possession, we are not teachers at all. One who is interested in laying hold on wisdom is likely to become a scholar. And while no doubt it is well for a teacher to be a fair scholar,—I have known several such,—that is not the main thing. What constitutes the teacher is the passion to make scholars; and again and again it happens that the great scholar has no such passion whatever.

But even that passion is useless without aid from imagination. At every instant of the teacher's life he must be controlled by this mighty power. Most human beings are contented with living one life and delighted if they can pass that agreeably. But this is far from enough for us teachers. We incessantly go outside ourselves and enter into the many lives about us,—lives dull, dark, and unintelligible to any but an eye like ours. And this is imagination, the sympathetic creation in ourselves of conditions which belong to others. Our profession is therefore a double-ended one. We inspect truth as it rises fresh and interesting before our eager sight. But that is only the beginning of our task. Swiftly we then seize the lines of least intellectual resistance in alien minds and, with perpetual reference to these, follow our truth till it is safely lodged beyond ourselves. Each mind has its peculiar set of frictions. Those of our pupils can never be the same as ours. We have passed far on and know all about our subject. For us it wears an altogether different look from that which it has for beginners. It is their perplexities which we must reproduce and—as if a rose should shut and be a bud again—we must reassume in our developed and accustomed souls something of the innocence of childhood. Such is the exquisite business of the teacher, to carry himself back with all his wealth of knowledge and understand how his subject should appear to the meager mind of one glancing at it for the first time.

And what absurd blunders we make in the process! Becoming immersed in our own side of the affair, we blind ourselves and read-ily attribute to our pupils modes of thought which are not in the least theirs. I remember a lesson I had on this point, I who had been teaching ethics half a lifetime. My nephew, five years old, was fond of stories from the Odyssey. He would creep into bed with me in the morning and beg for them. One Sunday, after I had given him a pretty stiff bit of adventure, it occurred to me that it was an appro-priate day for a moral. "Ulysses was a very brave man," I remarked. "Yes," he said, "and I am very brave." I saw my opportunity and seized it. "That is true," said I. "You have been gaining courage lately. You used to cry easily, but you don't do that nowadays. When you want to cry now, you think how like a baby it would be to cry, or how you would disturb mother and upset the house; and so you conclude not to cry." The little fellow seemed hopelessly puzzled. He lay silent a minute or two and then said, "Well no, Uncle, I don't do that. I just go *sh-sh-sh,* and I don't." There the moral crisis is stated in its simplicity; and I had been putting off on that holy little nature sophistications borrowed from my own battered life.

But while I am explaining the blunders caused by self-engrossment and lack of imagination, let me show what slight adjustments will sometimes carry us past depressing difficulties. One year when I was lecturing on some intricate problems of obligation, I began to doubt whether my class was following me, and I determined that I would make them talk. So the next day I constructed an ingenious ethical case and, after stating it to the class, I said, "Supposing now the state of affairs were thus and thus, and the interests of the persons involved were such and such, how would you decide the question of right,— Mr. Jones." Poor Jones rose in confusion. "You mean," he said, "if the case were as you have stated it? Well, hm, hm, hm,—yes,—I don't think I know, sir." And he sat down. I called on one and another with the same result. A panic was upon them, and all their minds were alike empty. I went home disgusted, wondering whether they had comprehended anything I had said during the previous fortnight, and hoping I might never have such a stupid lot of students again. Suddenly it flashed upon me that it was I who was stupid. That is usually the case when a class fails; it is the teacher's fault. The next day I went back prepared to begin at the right end. I began, "Oh, Mr. Jones." He rose, and I proceeded to state the situation as before. By the time I paused he had collected his wits, had worked off his superfluous flurry, and was ready to give me an admirable answer. Indeed in a few minutes the whole class was engaged in an eager discussion. My previous error had been in not remembering that they, I, and everybody, when suddenly attacked with a big question, are not in the best condition for answering. Occupied as I was with my end of the story, the questioning end, I had not worked in that double-ended fashion which alone can bring the teacher success; in short, I was deficient in vicariousness,—in swiftly putting myself in the weak one's place and bearing his burden.

Now it is in this chief business of the artistic teacher, to labor imaginatively himself in order to diminish the labors of his slender pupil, that most of our failures occur. Instead of lamenting the imperviousness of our pupils, we had better ask ourselves more frequently whether we have neatly adjusted our teachings to the conditions of their minds. We have no right to tumble out in a mass whatever comes into our heads, leaving to that feeble folk the work of finding in it what order they may. Ours it should be to see that every beginning, middle, and end of what we say is helpfully shaped for readiest access to those less intelligent and interested than we. But this is vicariousness. Noblesse oblige. In this profession any one who will be great must be a nimble servant, his head full of others' needs.

Some discouraged teacher, glad to discover that his past failures have been due to the absence of sympathetic imagination, may resolve that he will not commit that blunder again. On going to his class tomorrow he will look out upon his subject with his pupils' eyes, not with his own. Let him attempt it, and his pupils will surely say to one another, "What is the matter to-day with teacher?" They will get nothing from that exercise. No, what is wanted is not a resolve, but an aptitude. The time for using vicariousness is not the time for acquiring it. Rather it is the time for dismissing all thoughts of it from the mind. On entering the classroom we should leave every consideration of method outside the door, and talk simply as interested men and women in whatever way comes most natural to us. But into that nature vicariousness should long ago have been wrought. It should be already on hand. Fortunate we if our great-grandmother supplied us with it before we were born. There are persons who, with all good will, can never be teachers. They are not made in that way. Their business it is to pry into knowledge, to engage in action, to make money, or to pursue whatever other aim their powers dictate; but they do not readily think in terms of the other person. They should not, then, be teachers.

Source: George Herbert Palmer. *The Ideal Teacher*. Boston: Houghton Mifflin. 1910.

D. H. LAWRENCE

"A Lesson on a Tortoise"
(1909)

David Herbert Lawrence (1885–1930), the greatest British writer of the twentieth century, worked as a grade-school teacher for several years before giving it up and making writing his full-time career. His poems and essays about teaching illuminate and dramatize a set-upon teacher's psychology. This essay was left in manuscript and not published until after his death.

It was the last lesson on Friday afternoon, and this, with Standard VI, was Nature Study from half-past three till half-past four. The last lesson of the week is a weariness to teachers and scholars. It is the end; there is no need to keep up the tension of discipline and effort any longer, and yielding to weariness, a teacher is spent.

But Nature Study is a pleasant lesson. I had got a big old tortoise, who had not yet gone to sleep, though November was darkening the early afternoon, and I knew the boys would enjoy sketching him. I put him under the radiator to warm while I went for a large empty shell that I had sawn in two to show the ribs of some ancient tortoise absorbed in his bony coat. When I came back I found Joe, the old reptile, stretching slowly his skinny neck, and looking with indifferent eyes at the two intruding boys who were kneeling beside him. I was too good-tempered to send them out again into the playground, too slack with the great relief of Friday afternoon. So I bade them put out the Nature books ready. I crouched to look at Joey, and stroked his horny, blunt head with my finger. He was quite lively. He spread out his legs and gripped the floor with his flat hand-like paws, then he slackened again as if from a yawn, drooping his head meditatively.

I felt pleased with myself, knowing that the boys would be delighted with the lesson. "He will not want to walk," I said to myself, "and if he takes a sleepy stride, they'll be just in ecstasy, and I can eas-

128

ily calm him down to his old position." So I anticipated their entry. At the end of playtime I went to bring them in. They were a small class of about thirty—my own boys. A difficult, mixed class, they were, consisting of six London Home boys, five boys from a fairly well-to-do Home for the children of actors, and a set of commoners varying from poor lads who hobbled to school, crippled by broken enormous boots, to boys who brought soft, light shoes to wear in school on snowy days. The Gordons were a difficult set; you could pick them out: crop-haired, coarsely dressed lads, distrustful, always ready to assume the defensive. They would lie till it made my heart sick, if they were charged with offence, but they were willing, and would respond beautifully to an appeal. The actors were of different fibre: some gentle, a pleasure even to look at; others polite and obedient, but indifferent, covertly insolent and vulgar; all of them more or less gentlemanly.

The boys crowded round the table noisily as soon as they discovered Joe. "Is he alive?—Look, his head's coming out! He'll bite you?—He *won't!*"—with much scorn—"Please, Sir, do tortoises bite?" I hurried them off to their seats in a little group in front, and pulled the table up to the desks. Joe kept fairly still. The boys nudged each other excitedly, making half-audible remarks concerning the poor reptile, looking quickly from me to Joe and then to their neighbours. I set them sketching, but in their pleasure at the novelty they could not be still:

"Please, Sir—shall we draw the marks on the shell? Please, Sir, has he only got four toes?"—"Toes!" echoes somebody, covertly delighted at the absurdity of calling the grains of claws "toes." "Please, Sir, he's moving—Please, Sir!"

I stroked his neck and calmed him down:

"Now don't make me wish I hadn't brought him. That's enough. Miles—you shall go to the back and draw twigs if I hear you again! Enough now—be still, get on with the drawing, it's hard!"

I wanted peace for myself. They began to sketch diligently. I stood and looked across at the sunset, which I could see facing me through my window, a great gold sunset, very large and magnificent, rising up in immense gold beauty beyond the town, that was become a low dark strip of nothingness under the wonderful up-building of the western sky. The light, the thick, heavy golden sunlight which is only seen in its full dripping splendour in town, spread on the desks and the floor like gold lacquer. I lifted my hands, to take the sunlight on then, smiling faintly to myself trying to shut my fingers over its tangible richness.

"Please, Sir!"—I was interrupted—"Please, Sir, can we have rubbers?"[12]

The question was rather plaintive. I had said they should have rubbers no more. I could not keep my stock, I could not detect the thief among them, and I was weary of the continual degradation of bullying them to try to recover what was lost among them. But it was Friday afternoon, very peaceful and happy. Like a bad teacher, I went back on my word:

"Well—!" I said, indulgently.

My monitor, a pale, bright, erratic boy, went to the cupboard and took out a red box.

"Please, Sir!" he cried, then he stopped and counted again in the box. "Eleven! There's only eleven, Sir, and there were fifteen when I put them away on Wednesday—!"

The class stopped, every face upturned. Joe sunk, and lay flat on his shell, his legs limp. Another of the hateful moments had come. The sunset was smeared out, the charm of the afternoon was smashed like a fair glass that falls to the floor. My nerves seemed to tighten, and to vibrate with sudden tension.

"Again!" I cried, turning to the class in passion, to the upturned faces, and the sixty watchful eyes.

"Again! I am sick of it, sick of it, I am! A thieving, wretched set!—a skulking, mean lot!" I was quivering with anger and distress.

"Who is it? You must know! You are all as bad as one another, you hide it—a miserable—!" I looked round the class in great agitation. The "Gordons" with their distrustful faces, were noticeable:

"Marples!" I cried to one of them, "where are those rubbers?"

"I don't know where they are—I've never 'ad no rubbers"—he almost shouted back, with the usual insolence of his set. I was more angry:

"You must know! They're gone—they don't melt into air, they don't fly—who took them then? Rawson, do you know anything of them?"

"No, Sir!" he cried, with impudent insolence.

"Come here!" I cried, "come here! Fetch the cane, Burton. We'll make an end, insolence and thieving and all."

12. "rubbers": pencil-erasers.

The boy dragged himself to the front of the class, and stood slackly, almost crouching, glaring at me. The rest of the "Gordons" sat upright in their desks, like animals of a pack ready to spring. There was tense silence for a moment. Burton handed me the cane and I turned from the class to Wood. I liked him best among the Gordons.

"Now, my lad!" I said. "I'll cane you for impudence first."

He turned swiftly to me; tears sprang to his eyes.

"Well," he shouted at me, "you always pick on the Gordons—you're always on us—!" This was so manifestly untrue that my anger fell like a bird shot in a mid-flight.

"Why!" I exclaimed, "what a disgraceful untruth! I am always excusing you, letting you off—!"

"But you pick on us—you start on us—you pick on Marples, an' Rawson, an' on me. You always begin with the Gordons."

"Well," I answered, justifying myself, "isn't it natural? Haven't you boys stolen—haven't these boys stolen—several times—and been caught?"

"That doesn't say as we do now," he replied.

"How am I to know? You don't help me. How do I know? Isn't it natural to suspect you—?"

"Well, it's not us. We know who it is. Everybody knows who it is—only they won't tell."

"Who know?" I asked.

"Why Rawson, and Maddock, and Newling, and all of 'em."

I asked these boys if they could tell me. Each one shook his head, and said, "No, sir." I went round the class. It was the same. They lied to me every one.

"You see," I said to Wood.

"Well—they won't own up," he said. "I shouldn't 'a done if you hadn't 'a been goin' to cane me."

This frankness was painful, but I preferred it. I made them all sit down. I asked Wood to write his knowledge on a piece of paper, and I promised not to divulge. He would not. I asked the boys he had named, all of them. They refused. I asked them again—I appealed to them.

"Let them all do it then!" said Wood. I tore up scraps of paper, and gave each boy one.

"Write on it the name of the boy you suspect. He is a thief and a sneak. He gives endless pain and trouble to us all. It is your duty."

They wrote furtively, and quickly doubled up the papers. I collected them in the lid of the rubber box, and sat at the table to examine them. There was dead silence, they all watched me. Joe had withdrawn into his shell, forgotten.

A few papers were blank; several had "I suspect nobody"—these I threw in the paper basket; two had the name of an old thief, and these I tore up; eleven bore the name of my assistant monitor, a splendid, handsome boy, one of the oldest of the actors. I remembered how deferential and polite he had been when I had asked him, how ready to make barren suggestions; I remembered his shifty, anxious look during the questioning; I remembered how eager he had been to do things for me before the monitor came in the room. I knew it was he—without remembering.

"Well!" I said, feeling very wretched when I was convinced that the papers were right. "Go on with the drawing."

They were very uneasy and restless, but quiet. From time to time they watched me. Very shortly, the bell rang. I told the two monitors to collect up the things, and I sent the class home. We did not go into prayers. I, and they, were in no mood for hymns and the evening prayer of gratitude.

When the monitors had finished, and I had turned out all the lights but one, I sent home Curwen, and kept my assistant-monitor a moment.

"Segar, do you know anything of my rubbers?"

"No, Sir"—he had a deep, manly voice, and he spoke with earnest protestation—flushing.

"No? Nor my pencils?—nor my two books?"

"No, Sir! I know nothing about the books."

"No? The pencils then—?"

"No, Sir! Nothing! I don't know anything about them."

"Nothing, Segar?"

"No, Sir."

He hung his head, and looked so humiliated, a fine, handsome lad, that I gave it up. Yet I knew he would be dishonest again, when the opportunity arrived.

"Very well! You will not help as monitor any more. You will not come into the classroom until the class comes in—any more. You understand?"

"Yes, Sir"—he was very quiet.

"Go along then."

He went out and silently closed the door. I turned out the last light, tried the cupboards and went home.

I felt very tired and very sick. The night had come up, the clouds were moving darkly, and the sordid streets near the school felt like disease in the lamplight.

SOURCE: *Phoenix II: Uncollected, Unpublished, and Other Prose Works by D. H. Lawrence.* Edited by Warren Roberts and Harry T. Moore. New York: Viking Press. 1968.

MARIA MONTESSORI

"History of Methods"
(1912)

Maria Montessori (1870–1952) was the first woman in Italy to earn a medical degree. Her pedagogical insights began, she writes, when she worked with "deficient" children in Rome from 1898 to 1900 (her translator uses the term "idiot" to describe a student with learning disabilities, which, while offensive today, was the accepted psychological term of the period.): "I felt that the methods which I used had in them nothing peculiarly limited to the instruction of idiots. I believed that they contained educational principles more rational than those in use, so much more so, indeed, that through their means an inferior mentality would be able to grow and develop. This feeling, so deep as to be in the nature of an intuition, became my controlling idea after I had left the school for deficients, and, little by little, I became convinced that similar methods applied to normal children would develop or set free their personality in a marvelous and surprising way." Schools applying Montessori's methods exist today in countries all over the world. As educators continue to discover, methods and programs developed for the instruction of students with learning disabilities often come to have wide application in conventional pedagogy.

[. . .] About fifteen years ago, being assistant doctor at the Psychiatric Clinic of the University of Rome, I had occasion to frequent the insane asylums to study the sick and to select subjects for the clinics. In this way I became interested in the idiot children who were at that time housed in the general insane asylums. In those days thyroid organotherapy was in full development, and this drew the attention of physicians to deficient children. I myself, having completed my regular hospital services, had already turned my attention to the study of children's diseases.

It was thus that, being interested in the idiot children, I became conversant with the special method of education devised for these unhappy little ones by Edward Seguin, and was led to study thor-

oughly the idea, then beginning to be prevalent among the physicians, of the efficacy of "pedagogical treatment" for various morbid
forms of disease such as deafness, paralysis, idiocy, rickets, etc. The
fact that pedagogy must join with medicine in the treatment of
disease was the practical outcome of the thought of the time. And
because of this tendency the method of treating disease by gymnastics became widely popular. I, however, differed from my colleagues
in that I felt that mental deficiency presented chiefly a pedagogical,
rather than mainly a medical, problem. Much was said in the medical
congresses of the medico-pedagogic method for the treatment and
education of the feeble-minded, and I expressed my differing opinion in an address on Moral Education at the Pedagogical Congress of
Turin in 1898. I believe that I touched a chord already vibrant, because the idea, making its way among the physicians and elementary
teachers, spread in a flash as presenting a question of lively interest
to the school.

In fact I was called upon by my master, Guido Baccelli, the great
Minister of Education, to deliver to the teachers of Rome a course
of lectures on the education of feeble-minded children. This course
soon developed into the State Orthophrenic School, which I directed for more than two years.

In this school we had an all-day class of children composed of
those who in the elementary schools were considered hopelessly
deficient. Later on, through the help of a philanthropic organization,
there was founded a Medical Pedagogic Institute where, besides the
children from the public schools, we brought together all of the idiot
children from the insane asylums in Rome.

I spent these two years with the help of my colleagues in preparing the teachers of Rome for a special method of observation and
education of feeble-minded children. Not only did I train teachers,
but what was much more important, after I had been in London and
Paris for the purpose of studying in a practical way the education of
deficients, I gave myself over completely to the actual teaching of the
children, directing at the same time the work of the other teachers
in our institute.

I was more than an elementary teacher, for I was present, or directly taught the children, from eight in the morning to seven in the
evening without interruption. These two years of practice are my
first and indeed my true degree in pedagogy. From the very beginning of my work with deficient children (1898 to 1900) I felt that the

methods which I used had in them nothing peculiarly limited to the instruction of idiots. I believed that they contained educational principles more rational than those in use, so much more so, indeed, that through their means an inferior mentality would be able to grow and develop. This feeling, so deep as to be in the nature of an intuition, became my controlling idea after I had left the school for deficients, and, little by little, I became convinced that similar methods applied to normal children would develop or set free their personality in a marvelous and surprising way.

It was then that I began a genuine and thorough study of what is known as remedial pedagogy, and, then, wishing to undertake the study of normal pedagogy and of the principles upon which it is based, I registered as a student of philosophy at the University. A great faith animated me, and although I did not know that I should ever be able to test the truth of my idea, I gave up every other occupation to deepen and broaden its conception. It was almost as if I prepared myself for an unknown mission.

The methods for the education of deficients had their origin at the time of the French Revolution in the work of a physician whose achievements occupy a prominent place in the history of medicine, as he was the founder of that branch of medical science which today is known as Otiatria (diseases of the ear).

He was the first to attempt a methodical education of the sense of hearing. He made these experiments in the institute for deaf mutes founded in Paris by Pereire, and actually succeeded in making the semi-deaf hear clearly. Later on, having in charge for eight years the idiot boy known as "the wild boy of Aveyron," he extended to the treatment of all the senses those educational methods which had already given such excellent results in the treatment of the sense of hearing. A student of Pinel, Itard was the first educator to practice the observation of the pupil in the way in which the sick are observed in the hospitals, especially those suffering from diseases of the nervous system.

The pedagogic writings of Itard are most interesting and minute descriptions of educational efforts and experiences, and anyone reading them today must admit that they were practically the first attempts at experimental psychology. But the merit of having completed a genuine educational system for deficient children was due to Edward Seguin, first a teacher and then a physician. He took the experiences of Itard as his starting point, applying these methods, modifying and completing them during a period of ten years' experience with children taken from the insane asylums and placed in a little school in Rue Pigalle in Paris. This method was described for the first time in a volume of more than six hundred pages, published in Paris in 1846, with the title *Traitement Moral, Hygiene et Education des Idiots*. Later Seguin emigrated to the United States of America where he founded many institutions for deficients, and where, after another twenty years of experience, he published the second edition of his method, under a very different title: *Idiocy and Its Treatment by the Physiological Method*. This volume was published in New York in 1866, and in it Seguin had carefully defined his method of education, calling it the physiological method. He no longer referred in the title to a method for the "education of idiots" as if the method were special to them, but spoke now of idiocy treated by a physiological method. If we consider that pedagogy always had psychology as its base, and that Wundt defines a "physiological psychology," the coincidence of these ideas must strike us, and lead us to suspect in the physiological method some connection with physiological psychology.

While I was assistant at the Psychiatric Clinic, I had read Edward Seguin's French book, with great interest. But the English book which was published in New York twenty years later, although it was quoted in the works about special education by Bourneville, was not to be found in any library. I made a vain quest for it, going from house to house of nearly all the English physicians, who were known to be specially interested in deficient children, or who were superintendents of special schools. The fact that this book was unknown in England, although it had been published in the English language, made me think that the Seguin system had never been understood. In fact, although Seguin was constantly quoted in all the publications dealing with institutions for deficients, the educational applications described were quite different from the applications of Seguin's system.

Almost everywhere the methods applied to deficients are more or less the same as those in use for normal children. In Germany, especially, a friend who had gone there in order to help me in my researches, noticed that although special materials existed here and there in the pedagogical museums of the schools for deficients, these materials were rarely used. Indeed, the German educators hold the principle that it is well to adapt to the teaching of backward children, the same method used for normal ones; but these methods are much more objective in Germany than with us.

At the Bicetre, where I spent some time, I saw that it was the didactic apparatus of Seguin far more than his method which was being used, although the French text was in the hands of the educators. The teaching there was purely mechanical, each teacher following the rules according to the letter. I found, however, wherever I went, in London as well as in Paris, a desire for fresh counsel and for new experiences, since far too often Seguin's claim that with his methods the education of idiots was actually possible, had proved only a delusion.

After this study of the methods in use throughout Europe I concluded my experiments upon the deficients of Rome, and taught them throughout two years. I followed Seguin's book, and also derived much help from the remarkable experiments of Itard.

Guided by the work of these two men, I had manufactured a great variety of didactic material. These materials, which I have never seen complete in any institution, became in the hands of those who knew how to apply them, a most remarkable and efficient means, but unless rightly presented, they failed to attract the attention of the deficients.

I felt that I understood the discouragement of those working with feeble-minded children, and could see why they had, in so many cases, abandoned the method. The prejudice that the educator must place himself on a level with the one to be educated, sinks the teacher of deficients into a species of apathy. He accepts the fact that he is educating an inferior personality, and for that very reason he does not succeed. Even so those who teach little children too often have the idea that they are educating babies and seek to place themselves on the child's level by approaching him with games, and often with foolish stories. Instead of all this, we must know how to call to the man which lies dormant within the soul of the child. I felt this, intuitively, and believed that not the didactic material, but my voice which called to them, awakened the children, and encouraged them to use the didactic material, and through it, to educate themselves. I was guided in my work by the deep respect which I felt for their misfortune, and by the love which these unhappy children know how to awaken in those who are near them.

Seguin, too, expressed himself in the same way on this subject. Reading his patient attempts, I understand clearly that the first didactic material used by him was spiritual. Indeed, at the close of the French volume, the author, giving a resume of his work, concludes by saying rather sadly, that all he has established will be lost or useless, if the teachers are not prepared for their work. He holds rather original views concerning the preparation of teachers of deficients. He would have them good to look upon, pleasant-voiced, careful in every detail of their personal appearance, doing everything possible to make themselves attractive. They must, he says, render themselves attractive in voice and manner, since it is their task to awaken souls which are frail and weary, and to lead them forth to lay hold upon the beauty and strength of life.

This belief that we must act upon the spirit, served as a sort of secret key, opening to me the long series of didactic experiments so wonderfully analyzed by Edward Seguin—experiments which, properly understood, are really most efficacious in the education of idiots. I myself obtained most surprising results through their application, but I must confess that, while my efforts showed themselves in the intellectual progress of my pupils, a peculiar form of exhaustion prostrated me. It was as if I gave to them some vital force from within me. Those things which we call encouragement, comfort, love, respect, are drawn from the soul of man, and the more freely we give of them, the more do we renew and reinvigorate the life about us.

Without such inspiration the most perfect external stimulus may pass unobserved. Thus the blind Saul, before the glory of the sun, exclaimed, "This?—It is the dense fog!"

Thus prepared, I was able to proceed to new experiments on my own account. This is not the place for a report of these experiments, and I will only note that at this time I attempted an original method for the teaching of reading and writing, a part of the education of the child which was most imperfectly treated in the works of both Itard and Seguin.

I succeeded in teaching a number of the idiots from the asylums both to read and to write so well that I was able to present them at a public school for an examination together with normal children. And they passed the examination successfully.

These results seemed almost miraculous to those who saw them. To me, however, the boys from the asylums had been able to compete with the normal children only because they had been taught in a different way. They had been helped in their psychic development, and the normal children had, instead, been suffocated, held back. I found myself thinking that if, some day, the special education which had developed these idiot children in such a marvelous fashion, could be applied to the development of normal children, the "miracle" of which my friends talked would no longer be possible. The abyss between the inferior mentality of the idiot and that of the normal brain can never be bridged if the normal child has reached his full development.

While everyone was admiring the progress of my idiots, I was searching for the reasons which could keep the happy healthy children of the common schools on so low a plane that they could be equaled in tests of intelligence by my unfortunate pupils! . . .

—*Translated from the Italian by Anne E. George*

SOURCE: Maria Montessori. *The Montessori Method: Scientific Pedagogy as Applied to Child Education.* New York: Frederick A. Stokes. 1912.

WILLIAM LYON PHELPS

"Imagination in Teaching"
(1912)

Phelps (1865–1943) was an English professor at Yale for forty years and a popular magazine writer. While humorous and self-deprecating in his presentation, Phelps allows us humanities teachers little leeway: "the teacher who teaches History or Literature, and does not set fire to the imagination of his pupils, is a failure." He's right. At the same time, Phelps wonders where teachers are to find the inner resources when they are so hard-pressed: "How can men and women teach vigorously day after day when their bodies are tired, their nerves overstrained, and their salaries insufficient to support them decently? . . . If only the money that is squandered on the building of battle ships and firing off expensive powder into the air could be spent on teachers!"

If a teacher wishes success with pupils, he must inflame their imagination. The lesson should put the classroom under the spell of an illusion, like a great drama. Everything abstract, so far as possible, must be avoided, and there must be a sedulous cultivation of the concrete. If a pupil feels the reality of any subject, feels its relation to actual life, half the battle is gained. Terms must be clothed in flesh and blood. When I was a very small boy, my mother told me that every night when I went to bed I must surely not leave out the stopple in the fixed water basin; to neglect this was dangerous to health, she said. But she insisted that it was still more important—I don't yet know why—not to leave any standing water in the basin. These two things she impressed on my mind. I immediately invented names for the two dangers. I called them "Captain Stoppleout" and "General Standing Water," thus indicating not only that they were formidable military foes to be overcome, but indicating also the difference in their rank.

It is much easier to teach History and Literature with imagination than it is Mathematics; yet there are great teachers of Mathematics who have made the subject actually alive. They are rare. One reason why I was a dunce in Mathematics was because I could not get an imaginative hold of it. Propositions in Geometry interested me not in the least. Suppose ABC did equal DEF, what of it? Parallel lines do not meet—who cares? If I could only have seen them as two dear and intimate friends, doing their best to get together, struggling with all their might to touch each other, and yet in vain—with the empty assurance that they would meet in infinity, a kind of comfortless Nirvana! Professor Andrew W. Phillips of Yale, an admirable teacher of Mathematics, taught the subject with poetic imagination and irresistible humor and obtained good results from most of his pupils. I read in a German play that the mathematician is like a man who lives in a glass room at the top of a mountain covered with eternal snow—he sees eternity and infinity all about him, but not much humanity.

There is something fundamentally wrong about the teaching of foreign languages in our American schools. I cannot give the remedy, because, if I were to teach these subjects, even supposing that I had the necessary training and knowledge, I fear I should not get any better results. I studied Latin six years, four at school and two at college; I studied Greek five years, three at school and two at college. Both subjects have always been a great inspiration to me, and I would not be without this foundation for anything. Yet here is the wretched truth. Although I always did well in both studies, and received as high marks in Latin and Greek as I obtained low ones in Mathematics, at the end of all these years of patient and continuous study I could not for the life of me read a page of easy Latin or Greek at sight. As Upton Sinclair has said, the lines were full of words whose appearance was familiar, but whose meaning I did not know. And the teaching of French and German in schools and colleges is singularly barren of practical results. I had secured a comfortable seat in a railway carriage at Nuremberg, the carriage on the outside having an enormous sign, "Nach Munchen." At the last moment two men, father and son, sprang in breathlessly, placed their bags in the racks, and then suddenly the young gentleman cried, "Father, does *nach* mean not?" "Yes," said the parental authority. "Then we are in the wrong train!" and they both began feverishly to drag down their baggage. I quieted their fears, by telling them that the train was going to Munich, their desired haven. Apart from the fact that it would be a curious railway policy to mark the name of a town whither a train was not going, I was a little surprised that so familiar a word as *nach* was unknown to Americans traveling in Germany. I said to the handsome youth, "I suppose you have never studied German?" "Oh, yes, I have," and he told me that very June he had successfully passed the entrance requirement in German at a great Eastern university!

Faithful, minute grammatical training is an absolute essential when one begins to study a dead or living tongue. But the letter killeth. Grammar without immediate and specific application is simply an unrelated exercise of memory. How faithfully I learned the pages of the Latin and Greek grammar, without knowing in the least what to do with my store of facts! Once, when I repeated like a parrot the endings of all Latin feminine nouns—of the third declension, was it?—I rebelled, and remarked in the schoolroom, immediately after my triumphant rapid-fire performance, "I don't see the use of all this." The teacher gave me a stinging rebuke, saying it was my business to learn what I was told, and not to question methods that I knew nothing about. I can remember even now the prepositions that are followed by the subjunctive, and while dressing in the morning I used to sing, to an improvised tune, those that govern the ablative case. The ablative case, God save the mark!

When we studied Caesar's *Commentaries* on the Gallic War, a wonderful book, written by one of the most interesting men that ever lived, I had no idea that Caesar wrote sense: I thought he wrote only sentences. Once more, the grammar is essential; but has it importance in itself, or only as a help to the understanding? "All Gaul is divided into three parts." What is the most important fact in that sentence? Why, the most important fact is just what it says, that the country is divided into three parts. It would be a tremendously important fact if the United States were divided into three parts. Yet our teachers seemed to think the important fact in that striking first sentence was that Gaul was the subject, and, therefore, nominative. The grammatical construction of the phrase rather than its living meaning was the thing invariably insisted on, although we were reading a book full of history and human nature.

Some time later, when we were studying the Civil War with Mr. Bernadotte Perrin, he recommended us to read Froude's *Sketch of Caesar*. I read this with extraordinary delight, almost with shouts of joy. What a man! Later I saw the situation clearly. Here was Caesar, a brilliant statesman; Cassius, a professional politician; Brutus, a Mugwump. Brutus was the type of sincere reformer, whose ideals were greater than his practical judgment. Wishing to reform the state, he unconsciously played into the hands of a skilful and unscrupulous professional politician, Cassius, and between them they succeeded in killing the most useful man in the world.

The Latin language must be taught: the teacher cannot spend the time needed for drill, in telling interesting and entertaining historical anecdotes. But a word in season, how good is it! How it makes the whole subject alive and real, and with what energy a student will study when his imagination is deeply touched! When we were in college one of our Latin teachers was Mr. Ambrose Tighe, now a lawyer in St. Paul. Besides teaching us Latin, he told us about Roman history, Roman institutions, Roman politics, Roman personalities. It was a delight to enter his classroom, for he was a living inspiration. But in doing all this, he incurred the displeasure of higher powers, and had to leave. They felt he was too "popular," too superficial, and that he shirked the hard work of teaching Latin in order to give interesting talks.

But the teacher who teaches History or Literature, and does not set fire to the imagination of his pupils, is a failure. Mr. James Whitcomb Riley says that, when a boy at school, he especially hated History.

"It was a dull and juiceless thing." Such a pupil must have had a desperately bad teacher to entertain such a view of History. The teacher is an active force, not a telephone receiver. In the high school, I remember only too well our lessons in Greek History. We filed into the room: the accomplished lady at the desk touched a bell. She called my name. I rose confidently, for I loved History, and especially Greek History. She said, "Well, begin." I thought I had not heard aright. "What did you say?" "I said, Begin"; and she got her marking-book ready. To the next pupil, she said, "Go on." These were the only comments she ever made. Seeing what was wanted, I thereafter learned that Aristides got his come-uppance six lines from the bottom of the left-hand page; that the battle of Marathon began in the second paragraph of page so-and-so; and I obtained eventually a good mark. Fortunately, she could not kill my love of History, for I have read it as child and man with sympathetic imagination. I wept bitterly over the downfall of the Athenian expedition to Syracuse. How I admired Perikles, how I loved Athens, how I hated Sparta! With what raptures of delight I followed the career of Epaminondas! To this day, I cannot think of the battle of the Metaurus in Roman history, and Hannibal's awful disappointment, without a sad sinking of the heart. And although I have not seen for thirty years the school history of Rome we studied, I remember word for word the rather rhetorical flourish with which the historian described Hannibal's last hopeless years in Italy. "For four long years, in that wild and mountainous country, with unabated courage and astounding tenacity, the dying lion clung to the land that had been so long the theater of his glory."

What I regret is, that, owing to stupid and incompetent teaching, my schoolmates hated History with all their might.

Take the sentence, "Hannibal crossed the Alps, and descended into Italy." Here are eight words, and how shall we teach them so that the pupil will never forget this extraordinary feat? There are some minds to whom the most important facts in this sentence are that Hannibal is the subject, the Alps the object, and so on. But the ordinary boy or girl cannot get into a state of violent excitement over such valuable details. Who was Hannibal, anyhow, and what business had he in the Alps? He was a man from Africa, from a hot climate: such a person does not seem qualified for membership in the Alpine Club. But he not only crossed the Mediterranean, without the assistance of the Hamburg-American or Norddeutscher-Lloyd, but somehow induced a large number of his countrymen to come with him—no mean undertaking in itself. Then he finally reached the Alps, and they all began to climb. There are tourists even today who complain of difficulties; although the roads are magnificent, there are tunnels and rack-and-pinions, there is the faithful and omniscient Baedeker, there are everywhere, high and low, hotels so luxurious that they cost you ten dollars a day, board and room extra. But Hannibal had no railways, no inns, no tunnels, no roads, and no guides, and was among treacherous seas of ice and snow, with an army accustomed to a quite different climate and environment. Somehow or other, he persuaded them; he led them up, and led them down, and brought them into Italy in such good condition that they gave a terrific thrashing to the best-trained soldiers in the world, who were all ready to receive them. When the eye of the imagination follows Hannibal on this expedition, those eight words, "Hannibal crossed the Alps, and descended into Italy," are full of pictures. We are forced to the conviction that Mommsen was right, when he wrote, "Hannibal was a great man."

English Literature above all must be taught with the imagination. Is it not unfortunate that many mature lovers of literature are afraid to have the great English classics taught in the schools, simply because the boys and girls may acquire a permanent hatred for these books? The only possible objection I can see to teaching the Bible in every public and private school, and the subject is so important that I am willing to risk the danger, is that the pupils may never read the great book again. Over and over I have asked college students their opinion of certain English classics, and their expression is one of disgust: "Oh, I had to study that at school." There are fortunately noble exceptions; such teachers as the late Mr. George, of Newton, really inspired their pupils.

In order that subjects in the public schools may be taught with vigor and with imagination, it is necessary that the teacher should not be overworked and underpaid. "It is the curse of this world of want and need," said Schopenhauer, "that everything must serve and slave for these." The teachers in our schools, the vast army of faithful, devoted men and women, who wear out their lives in discipline and instruction, ought to be provided for much more liberally than is now the case. How can men and women teach vigorously day after day when their bodies are tired, their nerves overstrained, and their salaries insufficient to support them decently? These persons, more than any others, hold the future destiny of our country in their hands. I wish that those who have never taught and never give a thought to the work of teachers could be put in charge of a room of children in a district school just one hour. Their nerves would be in a frazzle. Yet there are thousands of delicate and refined women who do this hour after hour, day after day, week after week; and then many of them, in the summer vacation, when they ought to be in a sanatorium, go to a summer school, and study strenuously, such is their zeal for learning and self-improvement.

If only the money that is squandered on the building of battle ships and firing off expensive powder into the air could be spent on teachers! If the vast sums wasted on military pensions could be used productively! The teachers in our public schools should not be required to teach too many hours, to manage too many pupils, and their salaries should be substantially raised. It is the best possible investment, for it would help many who are in desperate straits, and it would attract skilled and efficient men and women. And it would be well if every school-teacher, after a certain period of service both in public and in private schools, could have the sabbatical year enjoyed by many college professors. In those rare cases where the salary is high, a large proportion of it could be given; but in most cases, the teacher should have it all. The daily grind of teaching is hard and wearing. If a teacher had every seventh year free from pupils and discipline, and could go to Europe for rest, change, and study, he or she would be so much richer in intelligence and inspiration on the return, so filled with renewed life and energy, that the quality of the instruction would rise enormously. There is nothing quixotic or fantastic about this. It would be a solid, permanent advantage to the country, and it would brighten the lives of those who are devoting themselves to the most important service.

SOURCE: William Lyon Phelps. *Teaching in School and College*. New York: Macmillan. 1912.

D. H. LAWRENCE

"The Schoolmaster": Three Poems
(1913)

See the note on Lawrence's "A Lesson on the Tortoise," above.

I. A Snowy Day in School

All the slow school hours, round the irregular hum of the class,
Have pressed immeasurable spaces of hoarse silence
Muffling my mind, as snow muffles the sounds that pass
Down the soiled street. We have pattered the lessons
    ceaselessly—

But the faces of the boys, in the brooding, yellow light
Have shone for me like a crowded constellation of stars.
Like full-blown flowers dimly shaking at the night,
Like floating froth on an ebbing shore in the moon.

Out of each star, dark, strange beams that disquiet:
In the open depths of each flower, dark restless drops:
Twin bubbles, shadow-full of mystery and challenge in the
    foam's whispering riot:
—How can I answer the challenge of so many eyes!

The thick snow is crumpled on the roof, it plunges down
Awfully. Must I call back those hundred eyes?—A voice
Wakes from the hum, faltering about a noun—
My question! My God, I must break from this hoarse silence

That rustles beyond the stars to me.—There,
I have startled a hundred eyes, and I must look
Them an answer back. It is more than I can bear.

The snow descends as if the dull sky shook
In flakes of shadow down; and through the gap
Between the ruddy schools sweeps one black rook.

The rough snowball in the playground stands huge and still
With fair flakes settling down on it.—Beyond, the town
Is lost in the shadowed silence the skies distil.

And all things are possessed by silence, and they can brood
Wrapped up in the sky's dim space of hoarse silence
Earnestly—and oh for me this class is a bitter rood.

II. The Best of School

The blinds are drawn because of the sun,
And the boys and the room in a colourless gloom
Of underwater float: bright ripples run
Across the walls as the blinds are blown
To let the sunlight in; and I,
As I sit on the beach of the class alone,
Watch the boys in their summer blouses,
As they write, their round heads busily bowed:
And one after another rouses
And lifts his face and looks at me,
And my eyes meet his very quietly,
Then he turns again to his work, with glee.

With glee he turns, with a little glad
Ecstasy of work he turns from me.
An ecstasy surely sweet to be had.
And very sweet while the sunlight waves
In the fresh of the morning, it is to be
A teacher of these young boys, my slaves
Only as swallows are slaves to the eaves
They build upon, as mice are slaves
To the man who threshes and sows the sheaves.

Oh, sweet it is
To feel the lads' looks light on me.
Then back in a swift, bright flutter to work,
As birds who are stealing turn and flee.

Touch after touch I feel on me
As their eyes glance at me for the grain
Of rigour they taste delightedly.

And all the class,
As tendrils reached out yearningly
Slowly rotate till they touch the tree
That they cleave unto, that they leap along
Up to their lives—so they to me.

So do they cleave and cling to me,
So I lead them up, so do they twine
Me up, caress and clothe with free
Fine foliage of lives this life of mine;
The lowest stem of this life of mine,
The old hard stem of my life
That bears aloft towards rarer skies
My top of life, that buds on high
Amid the high wind's enterprise.

They all do clothe my ungrowing life
With a rich, a thrilled young clasp of life;
A clutch of attachment, like parenthood,
Mounts up to my heart, and I find it good.

And I lift my head upon the troubled tangled world, and
    though the pain
Of living my life were doubled, I still have this to comfort
    and sustain,
I have such swarming sense of lives at the base of me, such
    sense of lives
Clustering upon me, reaching up, as each after the other strives
To follow my life aloft to the fine wild air of life and the
    storm of thought,
And though I scarcely see the boys, or know that they are
    there, distraught
As I am with living my life in earnestness, still progressively
    and alone,
Though they cling, forgotten the most part, not companions,
    scarcely known
To me—yet still because of the sense of their closeness
    clinging densely to me.
And slowly fingering up my stem and following all tinily
The way that I have gone and now am leading, they are dear
    to me.

They keep me assured, and when my soul feels lonely,
All mistrustful of thrusting its shoots where only
I alone am living, then it keeps
Me comforted to feel the warmth that creeps
Up dimly from their striving; it heartens my strife:
And when my heart is chill with loneliness,
Then comforts it the creeping tenderness
Of all the strays of life that climb my life.

III. Afternoon in School: The Last Lesson

When will the bell ring, and end this weariness?
How long have they tugged the leash, and strained apart
My pack of unruly hounds: I cannot start
Them again on a quarry of knowledge they hate to hunt,
I can haul them and urge them no more.
No more can I endure to bear the brunt
Of the books that lie out on the desks: a full three score
Of several insults of blotted pages and scrawl
Of slovenly work that they have offered me.
I am sick, and tired more than any thrall
Upon the woodstacks working weariedly.

            And shall I take
The last dear fuel and heap it on my soul
Till I rouse my will like a fire to consume
Their dross of indifference, and burn the scroll
Of their insults in punishment?—I will not!
I will not waste myself to embers for them,
Not all for them shall the fires of my life be hot,
For myself a heap of ashes of weariness, till sleep
Shall have raked the embers clear: I will keep
Some of my strength for myself, for if I should sell
It all for them, I should hate them—
   —I will sit and wait for the bell.

SOURCE: D. H. Lawrence. *Love Poems and Others*. London: Duckworth. 1913.

A. S. NEILL

from *A Dominie's Log*
(1915)

Alexander Sutherland Neill (1883–1973) was the Scottish creator and long-time master of Summerhill School in England. As an ambitious young headmaster and writer he wrote one of the most entertaining diaries of a teacher's thoughts and experiences, A Dominie's Log *("dominie" is a Scottish term for "headmaster" or "schoolmaster"): "I began these log-notes in order to discover my philosophy of education, and I find that I am discovering myself." Below are excerpts from Parts 3, 4, and 6.*

I think that the teaching of history in schools is all wrong. I look through a school-history, and I find that emphasis is laid on incident. Of what earthly use is the information given about Henry VIII's matrimonial vagaries? Does it matter a rap to anyone whether Henry I—or was it Henry II?—ever smiled again or not? By all means let us tell the younger children tales of wicked dukes, but older children ought to be led to think out the meaning of history. The usual school-history is a piece of snobbery; it can't keep away from the topic of kings and queens. They don't matter; history should tell the story of the people and their gradual progress from serfdom to sweating.

I believe that a boy of eleven can grasp cause and effect. With a little effort he can understand the non-sentimental side of the Mary Stewart-Elizabeth story, the result to Scotland of the Franco-Scottish alliance. He can understand why Philip of Spain, a Roman Catholic, preferred that the Protestant Elizabeth should be Queen of England rather than the Catholic Mary Stewart.

The histories never make bairns think. I have not seen one that mentioned that Magna Charta was signed because all classes in the country happened to be united for the moment. I have not seen one that points out that the main feature in Scots history is the lack of a strong central government.

Hume Brown's school *History of Scotland* is undoubtedly a very good book, but I want to see a history that will leave out all the detail that Brown gives. All that stuff about the Ruthven Raid and the Black Dinner of the Douglases might be left out of the books that the upper classes read. My history would tell the story of how the different parts were united to form the present Scotland, without mentioning more than half-a-dozen names of men and dates. Then it would go on to tell of the struggles to form a central government. Possibly Hume Brown does this. I don't know; I am met with so much detail about Perth Articles and murders that I lose the thread of the story.

Again, the school-histories almost always give a wrong impression of men and events. Every Scots schoolboy thinks that Edward I of England was a sort of thief and bully rolled into one, and that the carpet-bagger, Robert Bruce, was a saint from heaven. Edward's greatness as a lawgiver is ignored; at least we ought to give him credit for his statesmanship in making an attempt to unite England, Scotland, and Wales. And Cromwell's Drogheda and Wexford affair is generally mentioned with due emphasis, while Charles I's proverbial reputation as "a bad king but a good father" is seldom omitted.

I expect that the school-histories of the future will talk of the "scrap of paper" aspect of the present war, and they will anathematise the Kaiser. But the real historians will be searching for deeper causes; they will be analysing the national characteristics, the economical needs, the diplomatic methods, of the nations.

The school-histories will say: "The war came about because the Kaiser wanted to be master of Europe, and the German people had no say in the matter at all."

The historians will say well, I'm afraid I don't know; but I think they will relegate the Kaiser to a foot-note.

* * *

The theorist is a lazy man. MacMurray down the road at Markiton School is a hard worker; he never theorises about education. He grinds away at his history and geography, and I don't suppose he likes geography anymore than I do. I expect that he gives a thorough lesson on Canada, its exports and so on. I do not; I am too lazy to read up the subject. My theory says to me: "You are able to think fairly well, and a knowledge of the amount of square miles in Manitoba would not help you to think as brightly as H. G. Wells. So, why learn up stuff that you can get in a dictionary any day?" And I teach on this principle.

At the same time I am aware that facts must precede theories in education. You cannot have a theory on, say, the Marriage Laws, unless you know what these laws are. However, I do try to distinguish between facts and facts. To a child (as to me), the fact that Canada grows wheat is of less importance than the fact that if you walk down the street in Winnipeg in mid winter, you may have your ears frost-bitten.

. . . I find that I am much more interested in humanity than in materials, and I know that the bairns are like me in this.

★ ★ ★

A junior inspector called today. His subject was handwriting, and he had theories on the subject. So have I. We had an interesting talk.

His view is that handwriting is a practical science; hence we must teach a child to write in such a way as to carry off the job he applies for when he is fourteen.

My view is that handwriting is an art, like sketching. My view is the better, for it includes his. I am a superior penman to him, and in a contest I could easily beat him. I really failed to see what he was worrying his head about. What does the style matter. It is the art that one puts into a style that makes writing good. I can teach the average bairn to write well in two hours; it is simply a matter of writing slowly. I like the old schoolmaster hand, the round easy writing with its thick downstrokes and thin upstrokes. I like to see the m's with the joinings in the middle. The *Times* copy-book is the ideal one—to me. But why write down any more.

The topic isn't worth the ink wasted.

★ ★ ★

I picked up a copy of a *Popular Educator* today. Much of the stuff seems to be well written, but I cannot help thinking that the words "low ideals "are written over the whole set of volumes. Its aim is evidently to enable boys and girls to gain success . . . as the world considers success. "Study hard," it blares forth, "and you will become a Whiteley or a Gamage. Study if you want wealth and position." What an ideal!

Let us have our Shorthand Classes, our Cookery Classes, our Typewriting Classes, but for any sake don't let us call them education. Education is thinking; it should deal with great thoughts, with the aesthetic things in life, with life itself. Commerce is the profiteer's god, but it is not mine. I want to teach my bairns how to live; the Popular Educator wants to teach them how to make a living. There is a distinction between the two ideals.

The Scotch Education Department would seem to have some of the Educator's aspirations. It demands Gardening, Woodwork, Cookery; in short, it is aiming at turning out practical men and women.

My objection to men and women is that they are too practical. I used to see a notice in Edinburgh: "John Brown, Practical Chimney Sweep." I often used to wonder what a theoretical chimney sweep might be, and I often wished I could meet one. My view is that a teacher should turn out theoretical sweeps, railwaymen, ploughmen, servants. Heaven knows they will get the practical part knocked into them soon enough.

I have been experimenting with Drawing. I have been a passable black-and-white artist for many years, and the subject fascinates me. I see that drawing is of less importance than taste, and I find that I can get infants who cannot draw a line to make artistic pictures.

I commence with far-away objects—a clump of trees on the horizon. The child takes a BB pencil and blocks in the mass of trees. The result is a better picture than the calendar prints the bairns see at home.

Gradually I take nearer objects, and at length I reach what is called drawing. I ignore all vases and cubes and ellipses; my model is a school-bag or a cloak. The drawing does not matter very much; but I want to see the shadows stand out.

I find that only a few in a class ever improve in sketching; one is born with the gift.

Designing fascinates many bairns. I asked them to design a kirk window on squared paper today. Some of the attempts were good. I got the boys to finish off with red ink, and then I pasted up the designs on the wall.

I seem to recollect an Inspector who told me to give up design a good few years ago. I wouldn't give it up now for anyone. It is a delightful study, and it will bring out an inherent good taste better than any branch of drawing I know. Drawing (or rather, Sketching) to me means an art, not a means to cultivating observation. It belongs solely to Aesthetics. Sketching, Music, and Poetry are surely intended to make a bairn realise the fuller life that must have beauty always with it.

I showed my bairns two sketches of my own today . . . the Tolbooth and the Whitehorse Close in Edinburgh. A few claimed that the Whitehorse Close was the better, because it left more out. "It leaves something to the imagination," said Tom Dixon.

★ ★ ★

When will some original publisher give us a decent school Reader? I have not seen one that is worth using. Some of them give excerpts from Dickens and Fielding and Borrow (that horrid bore) and Hawthorne (another). I cannot find any interest in these excerpts; they have no beginning and no end. Moreover, a bairn does like the dramatic; prosiness deadens its wee soul at once.

I want to see a Reader especially written for bairns. I want to see many complete stories, filled with bright dialogue. Every yarn should commence with dialogue. I always think kindly of the late Guy Boothby, because he usually began with, "Hands up, or I fire!" or a kindred sentence.

I wish I could lay hands on a Century Reader I used as a boy. It was full of the dramatic. The first story was one about the Burning of Moscow, then came the tale of Captain Dodds and the pirate (from Reade's novel, *Hard Cash*, I admit. An excerpt need not be uninteresting), then a long passage from *The Deerslayer* with a picture of Indians throwing tomahawks at the hero. I loved that book.

I think that dramatic reading should precede prosy reading. It is life that a child wants, not prosy descriptions of sunsets and travels; life, and romance.

I have scrapped my Readers; I don't use them even for Spelling. I do not teach Spelling; the teaching of it does not fit into my scheme of education.

Teaching depends on logic. Now Spelling throws logic to the winds. I tell a child that "cough "is "coff," and logic leads him to suppose that rough is "roff "and "through" is "throff." If I tell him that spelling is important because it shows whence a word is derived, I am bound in honesty to tell him that a matinee is not a "morning performance," that manufactured goods are not "made by hand." Hence I leave Spelling alone.

At school I "learned" Spelling, and I could not spell a word until I commenced to read much. Spelling is of the eye mainly. Every boy can spell "truly" and "obliged" when he leaves school, but ten years later he will probably write "truely "and "oblidged." Why? I think that the explanation lies in the fact that he does not read as a growing youth. Anyway, dictionaries are cheap.

★ ★ ★

This morning I had a note from a farmer in the neighbourhood. "Dear Sir,—I send my son Andrew to get education at the school not Radical politics. I am, Yours respectfully, Andrew Smith."

I called Andrew out.

"Andrew," I said, with a smile, "when you go home tonight tell your father that I hate Radicalism possibly more than he does."

The father came down to-night to apologise. "Aw thocht ye was ane o' they wheezin' Radicals," he explained. Then he added, "And what micht yer politics be?"

"I am a Utopian," I said modestly.

He scratched his head for a moment, then he gave it up and asked my opinion of the weather. We discussed turnips for half an hour, at the end of which time I am sure he was wondering how an M.A. could be such an ignoramus. We parted on friendly terms.

I do not think that I have any definite views on the teaching of religion to bairns; indeed, I have the vaguest notion of what religion means. I am just enough of a Nietzschean to protest against teaching children to be meek and lowly. I once shocked a dear old lady by saying that the part of the Bible that appealed to me most was that in which the Pharisee said: "I thank God that I am not as other men." I was young then, I have not the courage to say it now.

I do, however, hold strongly that teaching religion is not my job. The parish minister and the U.F. minister get good stipends for tending their flocks, and I do not see any reason in the world why I should have to look after the lambs. For one thing I am not capable. All I aim at is teaching bairns how to live—possibly that is the true religion; my early training prevents my getting rid of the idea that religion is intended to teach people how to die.

Today I was talking about the probable formation of the earth, how it was a ball of flaming gas like the sun, how it cooled gradually, how life came. A girl looked up and said: "Please, sir, what about the Bible?" I explained that in my opinion the creation story was a story told to children, to a people who were children in understanding. I pointed out a strange feature, discovered to me by the parish minister, that the first chapter of Genesis follows the order of scientific evolution: the earth is without form, life rises from the sea, then come the birds, then the mammals.

But I am forced to give religious instruction. I confine my efforts to the four gospels; the bairns read them aloud. I seldom make any comment on the passages.

In geography lessons I often take occasion to emphasise the fact that Muhammudans and Buddhists are not necessarily stupid folk who know no better. I cannot lead bairns to a religion, but I can prevent their being stupidly narrow.

No, I fear I have no definite opinions on religion.

I set out to enter the church, but I think that I could not have stayed in it. I fancy that one fine Sunday morning I would have stood up in the pulpit and said: "Friends, I am no follower of Christ. I like fine linen and tobacco, books and comfort. I should be in the slums, but I am not Christ-like enough to go there. Goodbye."

I wonder! Why then do I not stand up and say to the School Board: "I do not believe in this system of education at all. I am a hypocrite when I teach subjects that I abominate. Give me my month's screw. Goodbye." I sigh yet I like to fancy that I could not have stayed in the kirk. One thing I am sure of: a big stipend would not have tempted me to stay. I have no wish for money; at least, I wouldn't go out of my way to get it. I wouldn't edit a popular newspaper for ten thousand a year. Of that I am sure. Quite sure. Quite.

Yet I once applied for a job on a Tory daily. I was hungry then. What if I were hungry now? The flesh is weak . . . but I could always go out on tramp. I more than half long for the temptation. Then I should discover whether I am an idealist or a talker. Possibly I am a little of both.

I began to write about religion, and I find myself talking about myself. Can it be that my god is my ego?

* * *

I began these log-notes in order to discover my philosophy of education, and I find that I am discovering myself. This discovery of self must come first. Personality goes far in teaching. May it go too far? Is it possible that I am a danger to these bairns? May I not be influencing them too much? I do not think so. Anything I may say will surely be negatived at home; my word, unfortunately, is not so weighty as father's.

SOURCE: A. S. Neill. *A Dominie's Log*. 5th Edition. London: Herbert Jenkins, Ltd. 1918.

STEPHEN LEACOCK

"The Lot of the Schoolmaster"
(1916)

Leacock (1869–1944) was born in England but grew up in Canada, north of Toronto. While attending the University of Toronto, he taught school, an experience he describes in the essay below. After graduate work at the University of Chicago, he became a professor of political science at McGill University in Montreal. He wrote many books of humor; being thoughtful, honest and serious about teaching, he was also very funny about it: "Now in my opinion (which is a very valuable one) the whole status of the schoolmaster on this continent is wrong. His position is unsatisfactory. His salary is too low and should be raised. It is also too high and ought to be lowered. His place in the community should be dignified and elevated. He also ought to be given three months' notice and dismissed. The work that the schoolmaster is doing is inestimable in its consequences. He is laying the foundation of the careers of the men who are to lead the next generation. He is also knocking all the best stuff out of a great number of them."

"Teachers," said the Minister of Education, swinging round in his chair, "are very cheap just now."

He looked at us fixedly. My colleague and I hung our heads. We realised that we had done a most impertinent thing in asking for a rise in salary. We felt like a couple of dock labourers who had been asking the boss for an extra five cents an hour—only less manly. We didn't exactly shuffle our boots and twirl our rough caps in our hands, while a tear did not, unbidden, course down our grimy cheeks. But we gave whatever symptoms of mute distress correspond to these things in people who have been expensively educated for ten years and have sunk all their available money in it.

We hadn't understood properly about the market for teachers. Somebody ought to have told us about it ten years before.

"Come, come," said the Minister of Education, for he was a kindly man at heart in spite of the rough duties of his office, "we can't give you a hundred and ten dollars a month just now. But what of that? You're young men yet. Keep right on. You're doing good work, both of you. You'll get it in time. Stick at it, my boys, and we'll see that you get your hundred and ten dollars, both of you, before you die."

Very likely we should have. But neither of us remained as school-masters long enough to know.

The incident happened more than twenty years ago and I can write of it now without bitterness; or at any rate with only the chastened regret of one who has spent the best years of his life doing task-work at a salary that began at fifty-eight dollars and thirty-three cents a month and after ten years of toil, expired from exhaustion at a hundred dollars.

That salary is dead and gone now and it is not for me to speak ill of it. I was glad enough to get it at the time. Each month I used to take it from the bank, look at it and then divide it up as fairly as possible, among those who were entitled to receive a share of it.

But I am not here attempting to write a personal biography. I only mention these facts in order to show that on the present subject I am entitled to write with the authority of one who knows.

Nor am I proposing in this essay to write on any such simple theme as that the salaries of schoolmasters ought to be raised. I don't think they should. I think that a great many of them ought to be lowered and that others ought to be taken away altogether. What I propose to show is that the whole position of the schoolmaster is on a wrong basis and should be altered from top to bottom.

Let me explain at the outset that throughout this essay I am talking of what are called technically "secondary" teachers—those who teach in high schools, collegiate institutes and the large private and endowed schools. I am not undertaking any discussion of the status and outlook of the elementary teacher. He is in fact very generally a woman and perhaps deserves to be. At any rate he is not here in question. Still less, am I speaking of University professors. I have dealt with them in an earlier chapter. They form a class by themselves. There is nothing else in the world similar to them. It is the secondary school teacher whom I am calling, for lack of a more exact term, the "schoolmaster."

Now in my opinion (which is a very valuable one) the whole status of the schoolmaster on this continent is wrong. His position is unsatisfactory. His salary is too low and should be raised. It is also too high and ought to be lowered. His place in the community should be dignified and elevated. He also ought to be given three months' notice and dismissed. The work that the schoolmaster is doing is inestimable in its consequences. He is laying the foundation of the careers of the men who are to lead the next generation. He is also knocking all the best stuff out of a great number of them.

All of this is intended as a way of saying that, as at present organised or grown, the whole profession is chaotic. It is made up of young men and old men, good men and bad men, enthusiasts and time workers, martyrs and drones. They are in it, men of all types and ages. Here is a young man fresh out of college with clothes made by a city tailor and with hope still written upon his face; and beside him in the next class room is a poor ancient thing in a linen duster fumbling a piece of chalk in his hand, with the resigned pathos of intellectual failure stamped all over him.

But there is a certain broad and general statement that may be made covering the lot of them. The pay of all the younger ones is far too high. The pay of all the older ones is far too low. Nearly all of them are teachers not because they want to be but because they can't help it. Very few of them—hardly any of them—understand their job or can do it properly. Most of them—in the opinion of those who employ them—could be replaced without loss at a week's notice. None of them retire full of wealth and honour; but when they die, as most of them do, in harness, the school bell jangles out a harsh requiem over the departed teacher and the trustees fill his place at a five-minutes' meeting. Meanwhile the public voice and the public press is filled with the laudation of the captains of industry, of the kings of finance, of boy wizards who steal a fortune before they are twenty-five and of grand old men who carry it away grinning with them after death—to wherever grand old men go. These and such are shining marks from which the public approbation glints as from a heliograph from hill to hill. The poor teacher in his whole life earns no greater publicity than his obituary notice at twenty-five cents for one insertion. And one is enough.

Now why should all this be? Why is it that there are no such things as wizards of the blackboard, boy wonders of the classroom, and alchemists of the chalk stick?

Let us look into the matter. Consider just who the teachers are and why they are teachers.

First of all there is the small, the very small minority, who, with a full choice before them, went into teaching because they wanted to; because they thought it a noble, honourable work at which to spend a life-time—not to be used merely as a stepping-stone to something else; because through their love of the profession they gave no thought to such drawbacks as the low pay, the slighted status of the teacher, the impossibility of marriage with a home equivalent to those of other men of equal industry and endowment—a home such as lawyers and doctors live in, such as kings of finance perpetually find too small for them, or such as those in which the senior clergy, in the pauses of their ghostly duties, take their lettered ease. To all of this the teacher—the enthusiast of whom I speak—has said goodbye at the threshold of his profession. He knew that he could never hope, as a successful schoolmaster, to dress as well as a successful lumberman or dog fancier, or join a club like a banker or play golf and drink whiskey and soda as a broker does. Yet some few men here and there make this deliberate choice. All honour to them for it—or at least all honour that ink and print can give them. They will get no other.

A few such men, and only a few, have I known. "Why did you go into teaching?" I asked long ago of one of my colleagues. "Because I think it a fine thing," he said. At the time I thought him an abandoned liar. Later I realised that he spoke the truth. It took some five years of experience of things as they are to crush the enthusiasm out of him. He left the profession without illusions and without regret. His place was filled by the trustees without a pang: teachers were cheap that year.

The truth is that, as things now are, it is not possible, or hardly possible, for a man to go into teaching for the love of it and at a conscious sacrifice, and to stay in it for the rest of his working life. It can't be done. Human nature is too weak. To make such a thing possible there would have to be no salary at all and the position marked out for the eyes of the multitude as one of conscious martyrdom. If a mathematical master at a collegiate institute were allowed to wear a long brown gown, with sandals and bare feet; if instead of being called Mr. Podge, he were called Father Aloysius or Brother Ambrose; if instead of feeding at a three-dollar boarding-house, he carried a bowl at his girdle into which people of their free will put lentils and peas and sweet herbs—then the job would be all right. Human nature is such that on those terms men would give forth a life of strenuous devotion, asking no higher honour. There would be plenty of applicants for the position of Father Aloysius. Indeed, I might take a shot at it myself. But the unrecognised half-sacrifice of the teacher-enthusiast is not good enough.

Yet after all the enthusiasts of this sort are only a small minority. The same element enters, no doubt, in part into the cases of many other teachers—but only in part and not as the leading motive. The chief cause of most of the schoolmasters being so is because of the peculiar ease of access to the job. It is like a fly-trap, or fish-net: All may walk in; few can get out. What happens is this. There are a great number of youths who begin life with the idea that the way to success lies through a college education. This proposition may or may not be true. It is very likely that the best chance of pecuniary success lies in going into a linoleum factory or a hardware store at fifteen and learning while there is yet time how many cents make a dollar. But at any rate a college education is the recognised and only gateway to the professions of law, medicine and engineering. These appear to offer the best chances of success and the most attractive form of career. They are trees with plenty of branches at the top. The young birds fly straight towards them.

But a college education is a costly thing. To make a college graduate you have to sink in him a thousand dollars in cash, and I know not how much in other things. Funds run low; the young man's savings or his parents' spare money is exhausted. He graduates, as it were, on the brink of bankruptcy. The tall trees look infinitely far and the flight to their branches long and perilous. But standing beside them, close and easy of access, is a stubby tree, a meanly grown thing but carrying all its branches stuck out sideways and very low. This is the teaching profession and into it the crowd of young men, "shoo'd" over the precipice of graduation, are precipitated in a flock.

Not one in twenty—no, not one in a hundred—of these young men means to stay "in teaching." The idea of the average beginner is that he will stay in it long enough to save enough money to get out of it. It is to serve as a stepping stone to law or medicine, or something real.

Let the reader imagine the effect on the profession at the outset of this distorted point of view. Who would wish to be treated by a doctor who was saving up money to become a ship captain? Who would put money in a railroad if it were known that the president and the traffic manager and the rest of them were merely doing their work to get enough money to qualify to be opera singers? Is a judge saving money to be a poet, or a lawyer waiting to run a hotel? Never. But this bad element runs all through the teaching profession like a rotten streak in a board. The thing is used as a mere stepping stone. The young men, those who can and who are not caught, do struggle out of it. Just as they are beginning to know something about the job they leave it and a new set of young men who know nothing about it take their places. Meantime a lot of them—I should say, at a guess, fifty percent of them—get caught in it and can't get out. The net has closed. Perhaps the young man becomes aware that one of the female teachers in the kindergarten department has eyes like a startled fawn and a soul like a running brook. The discovery is too much for him. By the time he recovers it is too late. He is a married teacher in a black lustre coat, saving money to put his eldest boy to college.

Or another fate may overtake the young man. He becomes, to put it very simply, lazy. All men do after the age of about thirty; though the successful ones are able to hide it by a great hustle of mimic activity. For the man on the make there is a whole apparatus of secretaries and subordinates, clubs, rendezvous, appointments, business trips to New York and so forth to cover up the fact that he has ceased to do any real work. Even from himself he hides it. He creates the fiction that he is working with his brain—an inner and mystic process which no one can dispute.

So the teacher, like all other men, gets lazy. It seems harder and harder to take the plunge, to face the loss of his salary, to re-enter a student's boarding-house and open a text book to start the study of law. Something, too, of the mock dignity of his teacher's office has got hold of him and eats into the sillier side of his mind. He has learned to set examinations; he hates to have to pass them. In his class-room he rules; when he says, "Jones, stand up," then up Jones stands. It is hard to give this up and to have a professor say to him, "Mr. Smith, sit down." No, it can't be done. He means to give up teaching. He still talks of law or medicine, or hints that he may go west. But he will go nowhere till he goes underground.

A great part of this trouble springs from the teacher's salary. It is too high. There it is, a hundred dollars a month, let us say, dead certain—no doubt and no delay about it. A lawyer makes (on the average and apart from exceptional cases) a few hundred dollars in his first year: perhaps not that; a young doctor makes on the average, something more than nothing; he walks hospitals, wears a white linen coat and says that his chief interest is in pathology; but what he really wants is a practice and after waiting a few years he gets it. These, and their like, the young engineer, lead a struggling life, subsisting on little, lying much and hoping very greatly. Meantime, the bovine teacher in his stall is as well paid at twenty-three as he will be at forty.

For there it is! The insane idea is abroad that a young teacher, a mere beginner, is as good or practically so as a man of experience. No difference is made; or none that corresponds at all with the vast gulf that lies in every other profession between the tried and successful man and the youth who is only beginning. Compare the salary of a bank junior (you will need a slide rule to measure it) with that of a general manager of a bank. And do the shareholders object to the difference? Not for a moment; the dullest of them will explain you the reason of it in five minutes. And does the bank junior object to the general manager's high pay? Not for a minute; he means to have that job himself later on and he wants it to be as highly paid as possible: in fact that is why he is a bank junior just at present.

Let us reflect for a moment on what qualifications the real schoolmaster ought to have. First, he must possess the knowledge of the things he teaches in the school-room. This is a mere nothing. Any jackass can learn up enough algebra or geometry to teach it to a class of boys: in fact plenty of them do. But apart from the trivial qualification of knowing a few facts, the ideal schoolmaster has got to be the kind of man who can instinctively lead his fellow men (men are only grown-up boys, and boys are only undamaged men); who can inspire them to do what he says, because they want to be like him, who can kindle and keep alight in a boy's heart a determination to make of himself something that counts, to build up in himself every ounce of bodily strength and mental power and moral worth for which he has the capacity. The ideal schoolmaster should be a man filled with the gospel of strenuous purpose.

Theodore Roosevelt (though he would shoot me for saying so) ought to be a schoolmaster. So ought Lord Kitchener and the Grand Duke Nicholas. Indeed, there are any number of unclaimed schoolmasters masquerading in the world to-day as kings and captains merely because the profession is not made such as to call them in. But even strenuousness itself, intensity of purpose, is not all. Strenuousness without the capacity to do things degenerates into mere vague desire of accomplishment, a vapid fullness of intention, which is a sort of mental equivalent for wind on the stomach. Such is the attitude of the man who is perpetually talking of the "full life" and of "developing himself," who goes out into the woods to draw deep breaths and falls asleep after lunch while waiting to begin his life work. Our Schoolmaster must be other than that. He must be the type of man superior not only to the boys he teaches, but superior to the parents who send their sons to him; able to have been, had he so wished it, a better banker than the average bank manager, a better railroad man than the average one, with brains enough to give points to a lawyer and breadth enough to make even a doctor feel thin. This is the kind of man to be a schoolmaster. He is to be found perhaps in the ratio of one in ten thousand ordinary citizens. Things being as they are with the trade, such a man is seldom if ever actually engaged as a school teacher. He is more probably a general, or a bishop, or the head of a great industry or the manager of an international trust or a four-ringed circus, or anything else that knows a good man when it sees him and is prepared to pay a price for him. There lies the point. To get the man you must hand out the pay. And as the pay is not forthcoming all the men of merit either never enter the lists as schoolmasters, or abandon the job before they are twenty-five.

To get and keep the right man it is necessary to pay him an income that will enable him to live with the same comfort and dignity as others of his endowment. There is no need to pay him this at the start. No man with a future before him cares a rush about the initial pay. But the thing must be there as a future, as a possibility, as some-thing to work towards, so that from the first day of his work the man feels that his life is sealed to his chosen profession forever.

I do not mean to argue for a moment that a mere increase of salaries will at once transform the teaching profession. It cannot. You cannot make an incompetent man any better by merely raising his pay. The present situation cannot be remedied by such a simple process as that. Nine out of ten of the present teachers ought not to be schoolmasters at all. They might, at a pinch, get along toler-ably well in the law, or on the bench, or as clergymen, but the idea of entrusting to them the supreme function of training the rising generation is nonsense.

I wish that I had time to organise a school, and that some good fairy would stand the expense of it till it got started. I mean, of course, a real fairy like Carnegie or Rockefeller, not the imitation one of the picture books. I would undertake to show to the world what a real school could be and, more surprising still, what a harvest of profit could be made from it. For the buildings and apparatus I would care not a straw. I wouldn't mind if the gymnasium contained a patent vaulting horse and a pneumatic chest exerciser or whether it just had wooden sides like a horse stable. These things don't matter at all. But I would engage, regardless of cost, the services of a set of men that would make every other school look like—well, look like what it is. I would select the senior masters with the same care and at the same salaries as if I were choosing presidents of railway companies and managers of banks. Let me try to give the reader an idea of what the staff of a first-rate school would look like. The list would read something after this fashion:

RESIDENTIAL SCHOOL FOR BOYS
(Beautifully situated in the Ozark Mountains, or the Adirondacks, or the Laurentians, or any place fifty miles from a moving picture.)

Headmaster . . . . . . Mr. Woodrow Wilson
Treasurer and Bursar . . . . Pierpont Morgan, Esq.
Instructor in French . . . . Mons. Poincare
Russian Teacher . . . . Nich. Romanoff
Military Instructor . . . . T. Roosevelt
English . . . . Sir James Barrie & Mr. R. Kipling
Piano . . . . Ig. Paderewski
Other Music . . . . Al Jolson
Deportment . . . . . . Sir Wilfrid Laurier & Miss Jane Addams
Matron . . . . W. Jennings Bryan
Chaplain . . . . The Rev. W. Sunday

There! That looks pretty complete. I have not filled in the customary office of janitor and messenger. I admit that I might fill that myself.

Readers who are unacquainted with the subject may think that the above list contains an element of exaggeration. If so it is very slight. If the profession were what it ought to be these are the very men who would have been drawn into it. If the list sounds at all odd, it is only because we have reached a stage where it seems quite comic to make out a list of eminent and distinguished men and imagine them schoolmasters. The reader, if he did not appreciate it before, can easily estimate by his attitude towards this list, what he thinks of the status and importance of the school teacher.

But behind this list are facts. All of the instructors above, or people of their class, could be engaged at salaries ranging from thirty to fifty thousand dollars a year. I am not quite sure of the Czar and Al Jolson. But we may let them pass. A school with a staff like this would easily draw a thousand pupils at a yearly fee of two thousand dollars a head. There is not the slightest doubt of it. That would give an income of two million dollars a year. The salaries of the junior teachers would cut but little figure. They would serve, and be glad to, on the same terms as young lawyers or doctors entering on their professional life. With such a staff the simplest of buildings would serve the purpose as well as marble colonnades and Greek porticos. School buildings, as things are, are chiefly used to cover up the schoolmaster. They are like the white waistcoat and three-inch collar of the feeble-minded man.

"But," the reader may exclaim in his ignorance, "where are the parents to be found who will pay two thousand dollars a year in school fees?" Where? Why, my dear sir, you may find them anywhere and everywhere. You may see them in any up-to-date grill room eating asparagus at a dollar a plate; in any of the clubs where they drink whiskey and soda at thirty-five cents; on Pullman cars where they have to ride in a drawing-room to save them from the horrors of an ordinary bed; in steamers where they need a private promenade deck de luxe to keep them untainted by common intercourse. Two thousand a year! It is not worth talking about. You may stretch a string across any fashionable thoroughfare in any prosperous city and in ten minutes catch enough parents of this kind to fill an asylum. True, they don't pay two thousand dollars now. But that is because nobody asks them for it. They have been accustomed to think of a school teacher as a sort of usher, about half-way up in dignity between a ticket clerk and a furnace man. But once let them be able to boast that their little Willie is taught music by a man who costs ten thousand dollars a year, and you will see them on the stampede.

Nor is it only the parents who can afford it who will pay the high fees. There will be also the still larger class of those who can't afford it. There will be no holding them back. In this imperfect world people really appreciate only the things that they can't afford. That is what gives real pleasure. A motor car that is only half paid for, a Victrola that may be removed from the house at any moment, an encyclopedia with payments reaching beyond the grave—these are the true luxuries of life.

There is no doubt whatever as to how parents would act towards a two-thousand-dollar school.

Here I am able to speak with real authority. I learned all about "parents" in my school-teaching days. Every man, according to his profession, is brought into contact with his fellow beings in their different aspects. A car conductor sees men as "fares"; a gas company sees them as "consumers"; actors see them as "orchestra chairs"; barbers regard them as "shaves"; and clergymen view them as "souls." The schoolmaster learns to know people as "parents" and in this aspect, I say it without hesitation, they are all more or less insane.

The parent's absorbing interest in his lop-eared boy (exactly like all other lop-eared boys), his conception of the importance of that slab-sided child and the place he occupies in the solar system, can only spring from an unbalanced mind. It is a useful delusion, I admit. Without it the world couldn't very well go on.

The parent who could see his boy as he really is, would shake his head and say: "Willie is no good; I'll sell him."

But they don't see it and they can't. How often have I sat with parents in my schoolmaster days, listening to their comments and instructions about their boys and nodding with the gravity of a Chinese mandarin while assenting to their suggestions about the boy's training.

My words, or at least my thoughts on such occasions, would have run something as follows: "To be bathed twice and twice only each week: Excellent, very good. A third bath only if an exceptional rise in the temperature seems to permit it: Admirable. I'll rise early and look at the thermometer—Never to be exposed to the morning dew: Ah, no, most certainly not. I shall be careful to brush it off the grass before he wakes. And his brain, a quite exceptional brain,—I was sure it was—on no account to be overstimulated or excited: Oh, assuredly not. And his clothes—true, true, a most important point—and so these are only his second best trousers that I see before me—most interesting—and I am to see that on Sunday morning he puts on his best—precisely, otherwise the impression he makes on the congregation at church might be seriously diminished. And as to discipline—quite so, an important point—a boy that can be led but not driven—precisely—I'll lead him—with a hook!"

Now, do you think that people in that frame of mind care what they spend? Not a particle.

There! I think the theme has been sufficiently developed. There is no need to wear it threadbare. The extension of the argument is plain enough. If the big private schools are remodelled, the others—the government collegiates and so on—follow suit, or follow as far as they can. The tax payer can never, of course, pay enough to make the free high school the equivalent of the two-thousand-dollar academy. But he will (for his own sake, since the tax payer is also a parent) be led on to pay more than he does, or at least to pay it to the men who deserve it. But I repeat I have no wish to wear the argument too thin. No doubt, as many of my friends will assure me, most of the statements above are at best only half truths. But the half truth is to me a kind of mellow moonlight in which I love to dwell. One sees better in it.

SOURCE: Stephen Leacock. *Essays and Literary Studies*. Toronto: S. B. Gundy. 1916.

BERNARD DARWIN

"The Schoolmaster's Profession through a Layman's Eyes"
(1929)

A grandson of the great Charles Darwin, Bernard Darwin (1876–1961) is best known for his writings on golf.

It is rather a singular thing about the schoolmaster's profession that while he himself loves it at least as often as other men love their occupations, few people envy him. Thousands of people in other walks of life wish, wish articulately or inarticulately, that they had chosen otherwise in their youth, before it was too late, but very few of them are heard to wish that they had been schoolmasters. On the other hand, men are frequently heard to thank heaven that they are not schoolmasters, and to assert that perpetually to look after boys would drive them crazy. The inference would seem to be that a man must have a call to be a schoolmaster. No doubt some of the best schoolmasters are born with a talent in that direction and could not have endured to be anything else; but the greater number, among whom are many who turn out equally successful, drift into the profession rather than choose it. They are offered a mastership at a time when they are at a loose end and have not made up their minds. It promises, on the surface, four things: an immediate income, in some cases quite a good one; life in what must be a pleasant place, and, in the case of their own school, perhaps the place they love best in the world; a long reprieve from the sorrow of giving up games and the delightfully long holidays.

It would be difficult to put forward four reasons so likely to appeal to a man who has just taken his degree, on behalf of any other profession. The second and fourth reasons ought to remain good ones forever. The first and third grow less alluring with the passing of the years, for the income, though it does increase, seems to dwindle

171

compared with that of middle-aged contemporaries in other walks of life, and even schoolmasters have to give up football some day. No doubt all four of these reasons seem trivial and superficial ones, to the man who adores his work, but there is a great difference between this passionate adoration, which is rare in any profession, and the ordinary interest which an ordinarily sensible and conscientious man takes in his daily round.

A layman may thank goodness that he is not a schoolmaster; he may be fully conscious of what an extraordinarily bad one he would have made, and yet he may feel envious of one thing in a schoolmaster's life, namely, the never-ceasing opportunity of making friends. Other people may have more friends of their own generation, and may be able to see more of them, but in regard to friends of younger generations, the schoolmaster is likely to be far the richer. Moreover, as long as he is a schoolmaster he will, in this respect, grow with each year richer still, so that if he lives to a hundred he can never feel that all his companions are gone. Moreover, even if he has not, as some have, a genius for keeping friendship warm by letter-writing, he will never lose his friends altogether. They may be scattered to the ends of the earth but, sooner or later, they will come back to their school, and whenever they come their master will be there; there is no need to appoint a meeting place, since one party to the friendship is a fixed point; they cannot miss one another altogether. It is a kind of friendship that, without being sentimental, possesses a quality that can come rather near to tears, and it has an invaluable something which, as a rule, only belongs to friendships between contemporaries, namely, a common background to life. It is, in this case, one seen from different angles, but still it does belong to both parties and it is the feature of friendships that have such a background that they can always be taken up comfortably and easily where they left off. This is not always true of friendships made in grown-up life. If the parties do not meet for a long time, there is often something of an embarrassment in their meeting; each reproaches himself a little for forgetting and wonders if the other is bored.

School friendships, even though they may never have been very warm, seem to be able to stay at the same temperature without any kind of effort, and so can produce at least a calm pleasure free from self-consciousness. And, after all, it is no small bond, between two men or between a hundred, that they have been "at the best house of the best school in England."

SOURCE: Bernard Darwin. *The English Public School*. London: Longman, Green and Co. 1929. [This excerpt appeared in *Unseen Harvests: A Treasury of Teaching*, edited by Claude M. Fuess and Emory S. Basford. New York: Macmillan. 1947.]

BERTRAND RUSSELL

"Education and Discipline"
(1935)

The British philosopher Bertrand Russell (1872–1970), renowned for his rigorous logic, scoffs at Jean-Jacques Rousseau's pedagogical idealism: "The belief that liberty will ensure moral perfection is a relic of Rousseauism, and would not survive a study of animals and babies." Russell, however, rather idealistically suggests that teaching should be necessarily a sideline: "I do not think that education ought to be anyone's whole profession: it should be undertaken for at most two hours a day by people whose remaining hours are spent away from children."

Any serious educational theory must consist of two parts: a conception of the ends of life, and a science of psychological dynamics, i.e. of the laws of mental change. Two men who differ as to the ends of life cannot hope to agree about education. The educational machine, throughout Western civilization, is dominated by two ethical theories: that of Christianity, and that of nationalism. These two, when taken seriously, are incompatible, as is becoming evident in Germany. For my part, I hold that, where they differ, Christianity is preferable, but where they agree, both are mistaken. The conception which I should substitute as the purpose of education is civilization, a term which, as I mean it, has a definition which is partly individual, partly social. It consists, in the individual, of both intellectual and moral qualities: intellectually, a certain minimum of general knowledge, technical skill in one's own profession, and a habit of forming opinions on evidence; morally, of impartiality, kindliness, and a modicum of self-control. I should add a quality which is neither moral nor intellectual, but perhaps physiological: zest and joy of life. In communities, civilization demands respect for law, justice as between man and man, purposes not involving permanent injury to any section of the human race, and intelligent adaptation of means to ends. If these are to be the purpose of education, it is a question for the science of psychology to consider what can be done towards realizing them, and, in particular, what degree of freedom is likely to prove most effective.

On the question of freedom in education there are at present three main schools of thought, deriving partly from differences as to ends and partly from differences in psychological theory. There are those who say that children should be completely free, however bad they may be; there are those who say they should be completely subject to authority, however good they may be; and there are those who say they should be free, but in spite of freedom they should be always good. This last party is larger than it has any logical right to be; children, like adults, will not all be virtuous if they are all free. The belief that liberty will ensure moral perfection is a relic of Rousseauism, and would not survive a study of animals and babies. Those who hold this belief think that education should have no positive purpose, but should merely offer an environment suitable for spontaneous development. I cannot agree with this school, which seems to me too individualistic, and unduly indifferent to the importance of knowledge. We live in communities which require co-operation, and it would be utopian to expect all the necessary co-operation to result from spontaneous impulse. The existence of a large population on a limited area is only possible owing to science and technique; education must, therefore, hand on the necessary minimum of these. The educators who allow most freedom are men whose success depends upon a degree of benevolence, self-control, and trained intelligence which can hardly be generated where every impulse is left unchecked; their merits, therefore, are not likely to be perpetuated if their methods are undiluted. Education, viewed from a social standpoint, must be something more positive than a mere opportunity for growth. It must, of course, provide this, but it must also provide a mental and moral equipment which children cannot acquire entirely for themselves.

The arguments in favour of a great degree of freedom in education are derived not from man's natural goodness, but from the effects of authority, both on those who suffer it and on those who exercise it. Those who are subject to authority become either submissive or rebellious, and each attitude has its drawbacks.

The submissive lose initiative, both in thought and action; moreover, the anger generated by the feeling of being thwarted tends to find an outlet in bullying those who are weaker. That is why tyrannical institutions are self-perpetuating: what a man has suffered from his father he inflicts upon his son, and the humiliations which he remembers having endured at his public school he passes on to "natives" when he becomes an empire-builder. Thus an unduly authoritative education turns the pupils into timid tyrants, incapable of either claiming or tolerating originality in word or deed. The effect upon the educators is even worse: they tend to become sadistic disciplinarians, glad to inspire terror, and content to inspire nothing else. As these men represent knowledge, the pupils acquire a horror of knowledge, which, among the English upper-class, is supposed to be part of human nature, but is really part of the well-grounded hatred of the authoritarian pedagogue.

Rebels, on the other hand, though they may be necessary, can hardly be just to what exists. Moreover, there are many ways of rebelling, and only a small minority of these are wise. Galileo was a rebel and was wise; believers in the flat-earth theory are equally rebels, but are foolish. There is a great danger in the tendency to suppose that opposition to authority is essentially meritorious and that unconventional opinions are bound to be correct: no useful purpose is served by smashing lamp-posts or maintaining Shakespeare to be no poet. Yet this excessive rebelliousness is often the effect that too much authority has on spirited pupils. And when rebels become educators, they sometimes encourage defiance in their pupils, for whom at the same time they are trying to produce a perfect environment, although these two aims are scarcely compatible.

What is wanted is neither submissiveness nor rebellion, but good nature, and general friendliness both to people and to new ideas. These qualities are due in part to physical causes, to which old-fashioned educators paid too little attention; but they are due still more to freedom from the feeling of baffled impotence which arises when vital impulses are thwarted. If the young are to grow into friendly adults, it is necessary, in most cases, that they should feel their environment friendly. This requires that there should be a certain sympathy with the child's important desires, and not merely an attempt to use him for some abstract end such as the glory of God or the greatness of one's country. And, in teaching, every attempt should be made to cause the pupil to feel that it is worth his while to know what is being taught—at least when this is true. When the pupil co-operates willingly, he learns twice as fast and with half the fatigue. All these are valid reasons for a very great degree of freedom.

It is easy, however, to carry the argument too far. It is not desirable that children, in avoiding the vices of the slave, should acquire those of the aristocrat. Consideration for others, not only in great matters, but also in little everyday things, is an essential element in civilization, without which social life would be intolerable. I am not thinking of mere forms of politeness, such as saying "please" and "thank you": formal manners are most fully developed among barbarians, and diminish with every advance in culture. I am thinking rather of willingness to take a fair share of necessary work, to be obliging in small ways that save trouble on the balance. Sanity itself is a form of politeness and it is not desirable to give a child a sense of omnipotence, or a belief that adults exist only to minister to the pleasures of the young. And those who disapprove of the existence of the idle rich are hardly consistent if they bring up their children without any sense that work is necessary, and without the habits that make continuous application possible.

There is another consideration to which some advocates of freedom attach too little importance. In a community of children which is left without adult interference there is a tyranny of the stronger, which is likely to be far more brutal than most adult tyranny. If two children of two or three years old are left to play together, they will, after a few fights, discover which is bound to be the victor, and the other will then become a slave. Where the number of children is larger, one or two acquire complete mastery, and the others have far less liberty than they would have if the adults interfered to protect the weaker and less pugnacious. Consideration for others does not, with most children, arise spontaneously, but has to be taught, and can hardly be taught except by the exercise of authority. This is perhaps the most important argument against the abdication of the adults.

I do not think that educators have yet solved the problem of combining the desirable forms of freedom with the necessary minimum of moral training. The right solution, it must be admitted, is often made impossible by parents before the child is brought to an enlightened school. Just as psychoanalysts, from their clinical experience, conclude that we are all mad, so the authorities in modern schools, from their contact with pupils whose parents have made them unmanageable, are disposed to conclude that all children are "difficult" and all parents utterly foolish. Children who have been driven wild by parental tyranny (which often takes the form of solicitous affection) may require a longer or shorter period of complete liberty before they can view any adult without suspicion. But children who have been sensibly handled at home can bear to be checked in minor ways, so long as they feel that they are being helped in the ways that they themselves regard as important. Adults who like children, and are not reduced to a condition of nervous exhaustion by their company, can achieve a great deal in the way of discipline without ceasing to be regarded with friendly feelings by their pupils.

I think modern educational theorists are inclined to attach too much importance to the negative virtue of not interfering with children, and too little to the positive merit of enjoying their company. If you have the sort of liking for children that many people have for horses or dogs, they will be apt to respond to your suggestions, and to accept prohibitions, perhaps with some good-humoured grumbling, but without resentment. It is no use to have the sort of liking that consists in regarding them as a field for valuable social endeavour, or what amounts to the same thing—as an outlet for power-impulses. No child will be grateful for an interest in him that springs from the thought that he will have a vote to be secured for your party or a body to be sacrificed to king and country. The desirable sort of interest is that which consists in spontaneous pleasure in the presence of children, without any ulterior purpose. Teachers who have this quality will seldom need to interfere with children's freedom, but will be able to do so, when necessary, without causing psychological damage.

Unfortunately, it is utterly impossible for overworked teachers to preserve an instinctive liking for children; they are bound to come to feel towards them as the proverbial confectioner's apprentice does towards macaroons. I do not think that education ought to be anyone's whole profession: it should be undertaken for at most two hours a day by people whose remaining hours are spent away from children. The society of the young is fatiguing, especially when strict discipline is avoided. Fatigue, in the end, produces irritation, which is likely to express itself somehow, whatever theories the harassed teacher may have taught himself or herself to believe. The necessary friendliness cannot be preserved by self-control alone. But where it exists, it should be unnecessary to have rules in advance as to how "naughty" children are to be treated, since impulse is likely to lead to the right decision, and almost any decision will be right if the child feels that you like him. No rules, however wise, are a substitute for affection and tact.

SOURCE: Bertrand Russell. *In Praise of Idleness and Other Essays.* New York: Simon and Schuster. 1935.

IRWIN EDMAN

"Former Students"
(1938)

A philosophy professor at Columbia University in New York, Edman (1896–1954) wrote for popular magazines and spoke about books on radio programs.

Once at a gathering in New York various people were mentioned who in diverse ways had begun to make their young presence felt in the world. One had written a play; another had become a psychoanalyst; still another a distinguished literary critic; one a radical editor; still another a foreign correspondent; and one even "the Iron Man" of big-league baseball. Every once in a while I found myself murmuring with not greatly concealed pride: "He is a former student of mine." Finally, a rather bored young lady looked at me pointedly. "Tell me," she asked, "was Chaliapin a former student of yours?"

I have since tried, not very successfully, to refrain from muttering proudly when the brighter young minds among contemporaries are mentioned: "Former student of mine!" For I cannot pretend to have taught any of them their present accomplishments. They did not learn playwriting, psychiatry, literary criticism, foreign correspondence, or baseball from me. And if I were honest, I should have to claim as former students of mine the hundreds of boring and unpleasant people, the failure and the complacent, successful nonentities, the rakes and the time-servers, whom I had the opportunity once to lecture to and whose quiz papers I once read. There are ten thousand former students of mine, I have calculated, roaming about the world. That does not include half a dozen, including some of the best, I have outlived. It does include hundreds I have forgotten and doubtless hundreds who have forgotten me. I met one of the latter once. It was at a club in New York. He was a little drunk, and he looked at me vaguely. He seemed to recall that he had seen me somewhere. A light dawned.

"I greatly enjoyed that course of yours in—in history."

"Mathematics," I corrected him, gently.

"That's it," he said, "mathematics. You made calculus interesting, I must say."

"No," I said, "it was the theory of functions." I thought I might as well be credited with something even more majestic that I knew nothing about.

I must admit former students generally do better than that, and they greet a former teacher with a touching sense that once long ago they did get something from him. Sometimes it is nothing more than a joke, used to illustrate something they have completely forgotten. But the joke remains, and probably the theory it was meant to illustrate is dated by now, anyway. Sometimes they surprise you by remembering a quite incidental remark. Occasionally it is good enough for you to wish you could be sure you *had* said it and they had not heard it from some other professor—a professor of calculus, for instance. Or they remember some trick of gesture you had, or the way you suddenly, for emphasis, write a single word on the blackboard, or the mordant things you try to say to listeners, cruelties invariably regarded as merely gently whimsical. Or they even remember ideas that, being the first time they had heard them, made a great impression. They are ideas, often, about which by this time you have changed your mind, or lost faith in. One former student told me he had still the notebook he kept in the first year I taught anybody. He promises not to use it for blackmail against me. He insists that I misspelt Malebranche on the blackboard and, as a result, he has misspelt it almost automatically ever since.

Among the students one does remember, there is a tendency to remember them as they were, as, with notebooks before them, they sat as young men of nineteen or twenty in your classroom, or talked with you in your office. I find it hard to realize that time passes, or to realize that though freshmen and sophomores always look the same each year, they don't look the same (though they often are) ten or fifteen years later. Meeting some of them after a lapse of years, one wonders what has happened to them, or whether one could ever have taught them anything, or where they can have learned all they seem to have found out about books and life, or how they could, who had once been so eager and bright, be so stodgy now.

I have had them look at me, too, in obvious wonder that they could ever have believed I could teach them anything and, once or twice, frankly express resentment at what they had learned.

I often wonder what students remember of a "former teacher," and can judge of their memories only by my own. But I wonder, too, what it is that one teaches them; how much difference a teacher can make. The psychoanalysts assure us these days that the great damage we call education is done largely in the first six years of a child's life, and that a teacher can do less and less fundamentally to the mind and character of a pupil after that as he passes from grade school to college. I hope that is so. It appears to relieve many of us of great responsibilities. The freshman comes with a kind of fatal predestination; he is what he is, and a course of a seminar cannot make any very great difference. I realize how momentary a tangent any teaching is upon a student's psyche, or his mental equipment.

Yet is something, and something for which students, doubtless with justice, are not grateful.

"Teaching," Santayana writes in *Character and Opinion in the United States*, "is a delightful paternal art, and especially teaching intelligent and warm-hearted youngsters, as most American collegians are; but it is an art like acting, where the performance, often rehearsed, must be adapted to an audience hearing it only once. The speaker must make concessions to their impatience, their taste, their capacity, their prejudices, their ultimate good; he must neither bore nor perplex nor demoralize them. His thoughts must be such as can flow daily, and be set down in notes; they must come when the bell rings and stop appropriately when the bell rings a second time. The best that is in him, as Mephistopheles says in *Faust*, he dare not tell them; and as the substance of this possession is spiritual, to withhold is often to lose it."

What boredom, perplexity, and demoralization do one's students remember! I once caught a glimpse of what it was. I ran into a former student at a weekend in the country. I had known him fairly well and, even before I knew him, had noticed, as had some colleagues, the sharp, critical eye which he fixed upon one during a lecture. There are always half a dozen students in a class in whose presence one would not willingly be boring or stupid or inaccurate. When one is so unwillingly, one sees the immediate register of disappointment (or is it fulfilled expectation?) in their eyes. S—— had been one of those.

The conversation had been general and desultory. At the end of the evening he came into my room. He sat down on a chair and looked at me sharply. He seemed older than I remembered him, but he had always seemed grown up. He had, I had heard, various reasons for discouragement, both personal and professional, since he had left college. At one point some years ago he had suddenly turned up and asked if I couldn't think of a good reason for his not committing suicide, since he was about to do so. My reasons were not too good, but they seemed good enough. He was here still, not much happier apparently.

"Look here," he said, "I have been wanting to tell you for some years that your former students have a lot to hold against you, especially the good ones, those who got what you gave them."

"What harm did I do?" I asked, weakly. "I am in a worse case than Socrates. At least he could boast at his trial that none of his former students—those whom he was supposed to have corrupted—had appeared to testify against him. But here you come yourself, saying I have done you irreparable damage. Really, a course in the Philosophy of Art can't do that much harm to anyone, not even to those who get an A."

"Yes, it can, and did," he insisted, "and I'm not the only one who was damaged, and you're not the only one who did the damage, though did a good deal. You taught me and a good many others to think that contemplation, detachment, eternal things, that Truth, Goodness, and Beauty, were the proper preoccupations for a young man in this world. Well, that isn't the kind of world we are living in, and you gave us a profound sense of unreality. It's taken me years to get over it and I'm not quite over it yet. But Freud and Marx have helped me, and I wish I had found out about them sooner. I must admit I first heard about them from you, but you didn't sound as if you thought them as important as Plato or Santayana. You made me live beyond my intellectual income; you made me set store by a lot of things that had no more relation to the moving things in the world and to the lives of men than backgammon or Venetian brocades. I admit you woke me up to a few beautiful things and moving ideas, but it was a fool's Paradise. I've reversed the usual order and gone through Purgatory since."

"Well, you've found a new Paradise of your own—the revolution—haven't you?"

"Call it that, but it's one of the forces going on in the world; it isn't the lost causes of sweetness and light."

I tried to say something about the lost causes being the only enduring ones; but S—— suddenly softened a little. "It was a pleasant enough trance while it lasted," he said.

"I'm sorry the coming to was so bad," I said.

★ ★ ★

Former students are not often so bitter, I must admit. They are frequently almost embarrassing in their assertion that you awakened them to think, or to think clearly, or to feel qualities in things and ideas and people they had never perceived before. They can be incredibly kind, even or especially when they think they are being objective and just. For it is difficult to distinguish the persons from the things they communicate, and many a teacher gets a certain glamour in a student's memory because the teacher is associated with that student's first encounter with Plato or Shakespeare, Bach or Phidias. A teacher dealing with great things cannot help sometimes seeming—if only to the undistinguishing young—to be their voice or their oracle; and to a very young mind, if only for a short time, the teacher is confused with the things taught. This may, indeed, be very bad for the teacher, who, in the mirror of his student's generosity, makes something like the same identification, too. His colleagues will correct him, and many of his unbemused students would, too, given the opportunity. For even the luckiest teacher dealing with students avid for ideas will have a good many who look at him as if they dared him to teach them anything. "I never could understand," he said, "why you thought philosophy interesting. And yet you seemed to do so. I was quite struck with that fact. That's the only thing I remember from the entire course."

It should really be a most discouraging fact (I am convinced it is a fact, in any case) that there is nothing much one does for the good student, and nothing very much that one can do for the poor one. In the case of the brilliant successes among former students of mine, I am convinced they were in essence as sophomores what they are now. If they are now learned men, they were already on the road to learning in their sophomore year. One of my former pupils can lay claim now to an erudition that I shall never have. But he was an erudite sophomore, and a little disturbing to an instructor in his first year of teaching. Another, though he is wiser about the world now, was wiser then than I shall ever be about it, and wrote almost as clearly and well then as he does now. The campus politicians are now real politicians, some of them, and not only in the field of politics.

Sometimes there are apparent changes: the aesthetes become hard-boiled or disillusioned; the sentimentalists, cynics. But even in those cases the change is not always a real one.

Now that I have been teaching more than twenty years and have thus seen five generations—a college generation being four years—of college students, former students seem to return. I do not mean that they come back in the flesh as one did recently with his ten-year-old child to the campus; I mean one recognizes in the sopho-more or junior there in the first row a replica of some predeces-sor not so very different of classes long ago. If I had known fewer students I should have been readier to predict what will become of them. It is easy enough with the run of the mill, though even with them, so rapidly is our world changing, it is not so easy as it used to be. There are not so many fathers' businesses to go into; the typical pre-lawyer may not find an office to be a lawyer in; the young snob and richling may find the world in which he can be both of those things vanishing under his feet. It is not easy even with the "origi-nals," who also, for a teacher long in harness, fall into types. How was I to guess—how would anyone have guessed—that the editor of the best college humorous magazine in ten years, neatly ironic, merrily skeptical, and amusedly disillusioned, would turn into an uncom-promising revolutionary, the Washington correspondent of the *Daily Worker*? How was one to suspect that the playboy whose life was bounded by fraternities and dances and drinking would be sobered by something or other into becoming a diligent professional classical scholar—a pedantic one at that? How could I have dreamed (though I might have done so) that the withering cynic of his class, whose god was Swift, should have become a mystical and fanatical rabbi?

I suspect that in each of these cases, had I been wiser or known my student better, I should not have had much occasion for sur-prise. There is much one does not find out about students, since it is natural that a teacher does rather more of the talking. And there is a lot one would never find out from the way in which students talk to a teacher.

There is only one thing by which I continue, with a foolish and persistent naivete, to be surprised. I expect, somehow, that a student ten years after college will still have the brightness and enthusiasm, the disinterested love of ideas, and the impersonal passion for them that some develop during their undergraduate days. Time and again I have run into them, and wondered what the world has done to them that that passionate detachment should have gone. I know some of the things, brutal or familiar enough to the point almost of banality: a family, the struggle for a living, a disillusion with the status of contemplation in the nightmare of a violent world. But it is not revolution or disillusion that surprises me; both are intelligible. It is the death-in-life that assails the spirits of young men who had been alive when I knew them in college. A fierce hate, a transcendent revolutionary contempt for ideas, especially traditional ones, a revolt against the academy; all these things are not dismaying. They are symptoms that life is not dead and that spirit lives on in some form, however tortured or fantastic or unprecedented. It is when spirit is utterly dead, when the one-time eager youth becomes precociously middle-aged, that one feels above all that education is a failure. One awakened something for a short time. But did one? Perhaps I have, like a good many teachers, flattered myself. It was not we who awakened them; it was the season of their lives, and the things and ideas which, despite us, for a moment—if only for a moment—stirred them. There are times when, if one thought about former students too much, one could not go on teaching. For the teacher meeting his former students is reminded of the fact that Plato long ago pointed out in *The Republic*. It is not what the teacher but what the world teaches them that will in the long run count, and what they can learn from the latter comes from habits fixed soon after birth and temperaments fixed long before it.

There are just a few things a teacher can do, and that only for the sensitive and the spirited. He can initiate enthusiasms, clear paths, and inculcate discipline. He can communicate a passion and a method; no more. His most serious triumph as a teacher is the paradoxical one of having his students, while he is teaching them and perhaps afterwards, forget him in the absorption of the tradition or the inquiry of which he is the transient voice. Lucky for him if later his students feel his voice was just. As in the playing of music, it is the music, not the musician, that is ultimate. And in the art of teaching, it is what is taught that counts, not the teacher. It is a great tribute to an artist to say that he plays Beethoven or Bach, and puts nothing between them and his audience. But in so doing he becomes one with both the composer and the listener. In the listener's memory he anonymously shares the composer's immortality. The teacher, too, is best remembered who is thus forgotten. He lives in what has happened to the minds of his students, and in what they remember of things infinitely greater than themselves or than himself. They will remember, perhaps, that once in a way, in the midst of the routine of the classroom, it was something not himself that spoke, something not themselves that listened. The teacher may well be content to be otherwise forgotten, or to live in something grown to ripeness in his students that he, however minutely, helped bring to birth.

There are many students thus come to fruition whom I should be proud to have say: "He was my teacher." There is no other immortality a teacher can have.

SOURCE: Irwin Edman. *Philosopher's Holiday*. New York: Viking Press. 1938.

MARY ELLEN CHASE

"The Teaching of English"
(1939)

Chase (1887–1973) was a novelist from Maine who taught English at Smith College. As she reflects on the various goals she has had and methods she has used, she observes: "Of all the excellent teachers of college English whom I have known I have never discovered one who knew precisely what he was doing. Therein have lain their power and their charm. I have come, indeed, to think that a firm hold upon definite objectives and methods by the teacher of English is likely to mark him as mediocre or even as poor at his job."

1.

My grandmother, who died at eighty-seven, was as she grew older more and more perplexed over the meaning and significance of my profession in life. Whenever I returned home for summer vacations, she always cornered me and asked exactly what the teaching of English meant. Since no such pedagogical term was used in her day and generation, she added to her bewilderment a kind of uneasy suspicion lest this strange subject to which I gave my time and strength was in some way inferior to those more obvious subjects such as Latin or mathematics. Upon each return we used to have disturbing colloquies of this nature:

"Just what do you do when you teach English? Do you mean that you teach your students to read?"

"Yes, and a great many more things."

"What things?"

"Well, I try to teach them to write as well as to read."

"What do you mean—to write?"

"To say what they think in good English."

"Do you mean *grammar*?"

"Yes, partly. But there is a lot more to it than grammar."

187

"What, exactly?"

"Well, I try to teach them to write good sentences that mean something."

"Do you mean you teach them to be writers?"

"No. I can't teach them to be writers. But I try to teach them to say what they think."

"Do people nowadays have to be taught to say what they think?"

"Yes, and they have to be taught to think straight."

"To think straight about what?"

"Well, about the things they do think about, and the things they read."

"What things do they read?"

"Oh, poetry and essays and novels."

"Can't they read those things by themselves?"

"Well, I try to show them what poetry and prose mean, not just what they say in so many words."

"You mean you read things like Shakespeare and Dickens in your classes?"

"Yes, and many other things, too."

"It can't be so hard just to read things and talk about them as to teach, say, Latin or arithmetic, is it?"

"Yes, I think it's a great deal harder."

"Well, maybe. But it doesn't seem so to me. . . . Do you like teaching English?"

"Yes, I like it better than anything else in the world."

After such a conversation as this with my grandmother I always felt a kind of odd insecurity assailing me. I wondered if the teaching of English was as vague an exercise and occupation as my own answers to her questions. I felt, in fact, sure only about two of my answers: first, that the teaching of English is at once the hardest teaching in the world to do and, second, that it is more fun to do than anything else in the world.

2.

After twenty-two years spent in the teaching of college English I still believe true the first of my contentions to my puzzled grandmother: that English is the most difficult of all subjects to teach. Unlike others more tidy because more clearly defined, English has no *terminus ab quo*, no *terminus ad quem*. More closely related to life than any other study, even than the sciences, it embraces literally everything within its invisible and illimitable boundaries. And yet, on the other hand, in itself it baffles definition. It is a language, yet, because of the very necessity of its use, it lacks in most imaginations the dignity and the charm of an ancient or even a modern foreign tongue. It is an art, yet again the familiar and the necessary, the daily and the commonplace, dim its aesthetic qualities and possibilities. It seems the handmaiden to other subjects rather than the mistress of them all, simply because no other subject can be understood without it. Thus the teacher of English is hampered at the start by misconceptions so natural and inevitable that they are doubly hard to put to rout.

Of all the excellent teachers of college English whom I have known I have never discovered one who knew precisely what he was doing. Therein have lain their power and their charm. I have come, indeed, to think that a firm hold upon definite objectives and methods by the teacher of English is likely to mark him as mediocre or even as poor at his job. Our objectives are as nebulous and intangible as are our methods, for the simple reason that we are dependent for the efficacy of both upon the multifarious imaginations of our students. The success of our teaching like the nature of it is forevermore conditioned by the capacities of the minds with which we work, by the wealth or poverty of perception, by the presence or absence of humor, by the possession or lack of understanding and vision. The meaning and value of any piece of literature are rarely the same to any two persons; the arrangement of words in a sentence may mean everything, something, or nothing both to those who read them and to those who labor to write them. *Man proposes, but God disposes* is a truth to be learned as quickly as possible by all teachers of English! And it is through the extreme flexibility of his mind, through the recognition that he is but a variable means to a most variable end, that the teacher of English reaps his variable reward.

Once at Hillside I was endeavoring to teach a stupid and somewhat sullen boy of thirteen the fundamentals of English grammar. We were dealing one morning with adverbs of manner, those sprightly parts of speech which add life and action to their verbs. Seeing the necessity for extreme simplicity in my explanations, I made the insecure announcement that most adverbs of manner end in *ly*. I wrote various of these on the blackboard: quick*ly*, slow*ly*, gent*ly*, noisi*ly*, smooth*ly*, stern*ly*, silent*ly*. Then I turned to the boy and said:

"I want you to think quietly for a few minutes and then give me some adverbs of manner of your own."

"I don't need to think," he said instantly. "*July.*"

Since that day I have had many such doors so summarily slammed upon my objectives that I have learned to look upon them merely as my own loosely defined and pleasant possessions, which may never become, indeed, often *can* never become, the property of those whom I teach. I have learned that for one student who sees reality and excitement in an adverb, there are many who will never see a part of speech other than as a part of speech. I have learned that for one student who comes to college with a sense of the dignity and the delicacy of words, there are many, even from the best schools, to whom the writing of English is stupid and useless and the careful and thoughtful reading of it only a bit less so. I have learned that my methods must be as different and varied as the different and varied personalities of my students, who from the start are governed by forces over which I have small control. I have learned that to know precisely what I am doing in any given class at any given moment is a state of mind as intolerably dull for my students as for myself and as arid as the proverbial Valley of Baca.

It is, then, this very necessity for elasticity of mind on the part of the teacher, for quick and intelligent changes in approach, which makes the teaching of English such a difficult job. We deal with the most personal and most fortified of possessions, with thoughts and feelings, suggestions and impressions, notions, fancies, predilections, ideas. We learn, if we are any good at our work, to welcome opposition, opinions different from our own, heresies, heterodoxies, iconoclasms. Our delight lies in the activity of awakened minds to any end at all. For we deal not with ends but with means. If Karl Marx dictates the criticism of certain of our students, we keep our heads; if James Joyce rather than Wordsworth proves the bread of life to others, we rejoice in this form of nourishment, strange though it may be to us; if Pater's style stirs someone to rebellion, we turn to Hemingway until the rebellion is quelled, if it ever is. We learn that we can be firm toward our own loyalties and yet not immovable toward others. Our one aim is to intensify the powers of thinking and of feeling in those whom we teach; and the only method we have of doing this is to open, through countless ways, every possible avenue to thought, emotion and expression and to keep ourselves alive as we are doing so.

3.

I feel sure that all honest teachers of English admit from the start that their job, difficult as it may be, is, first of all, a self-indulgence. For I still believe true the second of my contentions to my grandmother that the teaching of English is more fun to do than anything else in the world. The best of us have come into the profession because we have been unable to keep out of it. In one way or another we fell in love with books early in life, with their words and phrases, their music and rhythm, their people and their events, their meaning and their thought; and to attempt to convey to others our own passion has been the simplest means open to us of continuing therein ourselves.

Most college professors of English like, as they reach what is known as the "top," to stick to their own fields of study and enthusiasm. This becomes their own particular form of self-indulgence. If they are mad about Chaucer or Shakespeare or the Seventeenth Century, they like to teach within their own boundaries. They are not eager to meet the incoming hordes of college freshmen, who, for better or for worse, write themes which must be read, and read badly the books assigned to them. They prefer to deal with students who have gone through the mill of Freshman English and who have, presumably, come out refined and ready for more delicate and costly nourishment. But, unlike the majority, I am one who, even after twenty-two years of trying to teach English to freshmen, still find its ways ways of pleasantness if not always paths of peace.

Source: Mary Ellen Chase. *A Goodly Fellowship*. New York: Macmillan. 1939. [An excerpt appeared as "The Teaching of English" in *Unseen Harvests: A Treasury of Teaching*. Edited by Claude M. Fuess and Emory S. Basford. New York: Macmillan. 1947.]

L. S. SIMCKES

"Want to See My Bottom?"
(1970)

Lazarre Seymour Simckes is a psychotherapist, playwright, translator, and novelist who has taught at several universities, including Yale. In his essay, he demonstrates the kind of writing and thinking he encourages in students.

Two basic contexts, the world inside or close to the student and the world distant and perhaps alien. Two centers of attention, the family and the stranger. I take it as my initial task to push each student to see, on the one hand, the particular drama of his own family and, on the other, the possible dramas in the lives, only partially shown to him, of strangers. At the outset, therefore, I give my students the following two assignments. I ask them to write (not mail) a letter of accusation to a member of their family, preferably the mother or father, in which they bring up all the details of resentment, disappointment, blame, they can remember and analyze—Kafka's long, nearly novella-size, unmailed letter to his father, published as "Dearest Father," is a document I encourage them to read in this connection. The simple importance of such a letter is that the student is addressing somebody, for the trouble often with the early stories students write is that they lack the poignancy of an immediate necessity. Why is the story being told, the reader wonders, and to whom? The student may be hampered from creating an imaginative natural voice because an audience is missing. The letter is a bridge to fiction. The complex importance, however, of such a letter is not just that the student is talking about what he knows and feels, but also that in exposing the genealogy, as it were, of his being he is breaking a taboo of shyness. He is telling me, a stranger, secrets. The business of art, though, is giving away secrets.

As a second assignment, I ask them to prepare at least five pages of eavesdropping upon strangers. I expect them to pay murderous attention to the conversation and action of people of varied ages at restaurants, bars, on streets, until something about these strangers is revealed to them, until something hits them. To make out some manner say of Dostoyevsky who had a passion for following strangers like a detective and making shrewd guesses about them. Of course, the student may take wrong or weird suggestions from his few observed facts, from his collection of gestures, voices, clothes; a hand always jumping to an eye may hint that the person before him is playing at being sick, or it may evoke, for all I know, the image of a train crossing a bridge. The point is that the revelation is double. Something about the stranger may be revealed, but something also about the student. And the object of a writing class is to enable a student to find out what interests him, what excites his imagination, and what is exciting about his own imagination. Sometimes, too, the imagination, following its own interests, discovers curious truths. During an office hour, a student once told me about her angers against her mother, angers stuck from the days of childhood when her mother would insult her in front of others. I suggested that she write a story in which, perhaps, an intense precocious child, in order to get back at her mother, drops pieces of paper around the house and the yard, for anybody to pick up, notes condemning her mother. The girl stared at me and said, "That's what I did. I dropped them everywhere."

Both assignments meet much resistance. As for the letter, one student at Harvard said it was "metaphysically bad, morally bad, and bad all around," because the parent would have no chance to reply. Do you fantasize? I asked. He did. Do you have fantasies in which you carry on arguments against your parents? He did. Do you give them a chance to reply? He didn't. Subsequently he submitted two brilliant letters, five pages to each parent, ten to a friend, and his later fiction inherited much of the energy and freedom present in his letters. A girl at Vassar insisted that she was interested not in the *givens* of her life but in her own private *choices*: her family was something given to her, her loves were something she herself chose. As for eavesdropping, one Harvard student, as soon as he heard the assignment at our first meeting, got up, shouted, "It's a sin!" retrieved his sample manuscripts, and left for good.

So far I have been speaking of *initial* shoves, initiatory pushes into certain directions. The ultimate burden of discovery lies in the domain of the student's luck and ambition. My intention is not to bully or enslave. Right off I announce that I always keep in an important pocket my agreement with Sir Joshua Reynolds that "Few are taught to any purpose who are not their own teachers." I claim, they must teach me as much as I teach them, teach me *before* I teach them. I say, they have the right to insist upon their own ways despite the advice of any teacher just as I have the right to insist on my ways despite them. In any case, I try to throw away the whip of grades. I try not to be the dog obeyed in office. My first two years of teaching, it is true, I gave out a total of two D's. but the third and fourth years, no lower than a C. And the fifth, B was my floor. Next year I expect to give all A's, and as soon as possible thereafter no grades whatsoever. On the one hand, my progress as a teacher has been toward a willingness to impose a personal or eccentric scheme upon my class, and, on the other, to have that scheme upset by anything improvised by the students which is exciting. Each class must help invent the pattern of its own schooling. One day at Vassar, I ended a class with the joke that we would meet next time under the table. And, the next time we met, there they were, under the big table, where I joined them. To be sure, this was somewhat silly, but the ladder toward creation is long and it takes, sometimes, a few foolish steps. Once, just once, I brought in three toy figures, a Norwegian yokel and a Japanese boy and girl with springy heads. And we sort of played dolls. Objects can be handled; language lacks a certain tangibility. By playing with these toy people, suggestions emerged concretely and immediately. Place the yokel in between the Japanese couple, you have perhaps the man who brought them together or the man who may break them apart. Knock the yokel to the ground, other possibilities suddenly exist—betrayal, death, dreaming. *Where* a person is helps to establish *what* a person is. My aim was to free their attitudes toward their own material. Let them deal with what they are extremely familiar but let them also take advantage of their freedom to translate, transpose, invent, in accordance with other commitments and compulsions, alien perhaps to preliminary givens. Let them also write about a country they've never been to, except in some fantasy.

At Stanford, in its less cosmopolitan or experimental days (1960–61), I began my teaching. I was a Teaching Fellow for Freshman English. *Oi vai!* The trouble was, we were encouraged to teach in some (though not absolute) accordance with a text book. I understood that the more we relied on it, the more we were blessed. But using it was always a trick and an embarrassment, and after the rhetoric book came the casebook. From description, boys and girls, to argument, to research! Instead of twisting my days into such a shape, I should have rebelled completely. For instance, to me it makes more sense to start a year of Freshman English by allowing the students, individually or collectively, to select some writer that interests them. Thereafter the agreement would be, as they read the man's works and life, they follow as many other interesting or unfamiliar references or leads as possible. They'd go from link to link, jump from item to item, they way you would if you were looking up a word in a dictionary and came across another unfamiliar word— you'd look up that word too. Learning takes place best when you need to learn, when something arrives to explain something else, when one thing actually leans on another. What should always be avoided is that paper fan, that schematic spread which encourages a concern for patching up holes in one's knowledge, as an act of protection against insult or social stigma or, worse, college failure. So, a student beginning with a modern figure would obviously be led to some art of an earlier period, and not necessarily literary art. Keats might point to the medieval ballad or Greek art. There would certainly be an explosion of references, a chaos of sorts, the center might not hold. But, after all, until there is sufficient chaos there is no need to talk of order. Chaos is a sign of chaos, but also a sign of coming order. Introducing order too soon is as bad as introducing it too late. Perhaps the greatest benefit of this kind of approach is not just that each student has his own course but that the teacher himself is taking his own course. In this context, information becomes excitement, becomes insight, and the dictum of Sir Joshua is heeded all around.

When I was a student, my teacher told me: "Give the reader time to know your characters. Introduce them one at a time. Slow down." As if he were some speech therapist and I the poor fellow whom others would understand if only I learned to speak more slowly. The advice is kind and good, but like any rule in art, when followed too closely, it threatens to pinch the neck of discovery. A story can get the reader to read it in almost any way it wants; at least it can try. If a student's most interesting work emerges from a deep sense of fantasy where motivation is ruthlessly or comically inadequate, there is no place any more for the conventional though useful demand for motivation. Order enters the writing class as it enters a story, experimentally, tentatively. It is ultimately the last thing created although being created all the time.

For myself, I want something more intense, more chaotic, than the usual informality and relaxation of a writing class. I want the crater of art to be hot. Rules tend to go cold, but perhaps not personal ones. At Vassar, after my having stressed the priority of "bad" experiences, i.e., confusion, pain, failure, embarrassment, these must be exposed and handled first, i.e., without acknowledgement of despair and fantasy the language of hope and reality is dishonest, a student complained that if she tried to write a "sad" story it would come out all wrong, she had nothing tragic to tell, she was a very happy person. The story she had already handed in was the tale of her witty, energetic grandmother. It turned out, however, that her grandmother was in fact not merely senile but grotesquely immobile. And as for herself, before school started she had jumped out of a moving car, luckily only breaking a leg. I should add that her speaking voice had one peculiarity, it always sounded as though she was crying. For a vision to have depth and truth, it must deal with pain. But pain, it must be remembered, is the source of comedy as well as tragedy, *contra* Aristotle. That laughter and grief are both necessary is an important discovery. Cruelty is not the only outcome of an honest encounter with one's own experience. A writer's vision is as brutal as it is tender. This girl ultimately wrote a poignant monologue of comic self-abasement, called "The Hawker," in which the speaker pleads to give everything she has away: "Hey, anybody need a favor? Just ask. . . .Want to use a phone? Use mine. I'll leave the room. . . . Here, take my chair. Go on. I'll be sitting on the floor anyway so you might as well prop your feet upon my shoulders." Her last piece of prose was a letter to me in which she declares herself mad. Also in the letter was the title for a story which she unfortunately never managed to write: "What would it look like if I were a stranger?" In short, a student of mine is encouraged to imagine the extreme; I agree with Durrenmatt, a story is not complete until it has taken its worst possible turn.

A further priority—the priority of oral language, the spoken word. Children are able to use their imaginations when speaking but less so when writing. Because the rhythms of the imagination are too often subject to punishment under the school rules of decorum and diction. A second-grader talking about the kick of a gun said to me: "It pulls back, like when you're walking and the guy pulls you back." This precise little image is liable to be erased in a classroom. Standards of expected or correct usage simply rob children of their own ways of saying things, and their own ways are usually inventive, ambitious, exciting. No wonder many students enter college empty-handed. Rhetoric, it should be pointed out everywhere, has colloquial as well as academic sources. We say, "Tomorrow I'll see you, I'll see you tomorrow," and that's an example of, heaven help us, *epanalepsis*. I asked a four-year-old girl how big her brother was; she answered: "He's up that high." I asked her why she had a band-aid on her finger; she answered: "My meat is opened." One child at a nursery for "disadvantaged" children came up to me all of a sudden and screamed: "What's a buddy stuck in your ear?" "What do you mean?" I said. He said: "It means you're upside down and a little beer in your mouth and you're crying so hard." Fantasy, babbling, disturbed nonsense, are important places of energy for language to appear—and in an uninhibited though maybe difficult fashion. But art is difficult communication. One day I had my Vassar class talk, or rather babble, facing the wall, one by one. That is, I wanted to break down for a moment their reliance upon a realistic situation as the occasion for language, I wanted to astonish them with their own complicated resources, with the possibility in their own mouths for rich strange language. It was difficult, and I didn't pursue it enough. Some students, misunderstanding me, sounded like Shakespeare's Pyramus with his "O wall!" My mistake was, I didn't try it again.

Why not try the following? (I intend to.) Ask a student to make up a story in class and then have the others heckle, or argue against him. If he says, So-and-so was a short old man, you yourself shout out, That's a lie, he was tall and young. The hard job of convincing an audience, of adding details, metaphors, images, will slap the storyteller in the face. Let everybody argue back and forth, boast back and forth, tall-tale fashion, kid-stuff fashion. For what purpose? Under these circumstances, (playfully) insulting circumstances, the storyteller may be forced in class to invent more convincingly. In any case, the problem of convincing an audience, of finding the appropriate and necessary details for a story, is dramatically there.

What releases another's language and imagination is something of a mystery—in my case, one certain key is the approach to madness, so it is natural for me to throw my students somewhat in that direction. In my fiction, God is a bum. Once I asked my students to shut their eyes and then write down whatever they saw. In this private world behind our own eyes, the pace of metamorphosis is amazing.

But sometimes you can wait an hour before the visions come, like waiting strike time for a Long Island train. It might have been better had each student told his visions to another student who would act, for the time being, as amanuensis to the prophet. Anyway, despite the near illegibility of their blind script, it was a good idea to let their minds wander, let them daydream in class to their own benefits. A very familiar thing became strange to them. I was interested in showing them they could write about anything. Again, to show my students that the narrative imagination takes hints from all places, to encourage them to include anything in their stories, I read a small passage from Wittgenstein's *Blue Book*:

> Suppose I pointed to a piece of paper and said to someone: "This color I call 'red.'" Afterwards I give him the order: "Now paint me a red patch." I then ask him: "Why, in carrying out my order, did you paint just this color?"

Then I myself ask: Is there anything dramatic here, anything that suggests some particular relationship? After a while, somebody catches what I am after, the tyranny in the voice of the speaker. To tell a person to do something and then ask him why he has done it, that is a form of interrogation which might issue from the realm of espionage. Or it might signal a babyish or senile approach to another human being, or the magician's way with his prepared hoaxes. Wittgenstein's "philosophical investigation" of the justifications we have for any act amounts to a kind of torture. A classroom itself, with its constant questions, could inspire terror, with its dialectics, one will breaking another, one will embarrassing another. Isn't Wittgenstein's passage a parody of a reign of terror? Given such authority and such vulnerability, anybody can turn you around, make it impossible for you to act or think about your actions, drive you crazy.

You may feel that the only decent and direct way to get students to write is to let them alone altogether until they come up with something, until they find their stories and the language adequate for these stories. Why antics and pranks? In part I agree with you. But I am talking about beginners, who need shaking. At Vassar, after the letter assignment, the best work adopted the form of a message or a plea, to somebody expected or gone or dead. The assignment worked. I have had students whose early work was silly and whose final work was so good the class confused it with the work of the class master.

Certainly what shook these "late bloomers" most was being exposed to the style and performance and conversation of other students, but also what helped was stepping on the crazy ground of the course itself. With one hand I push my students away, so they'll be on their own, with the other I force them to need me.

In his 1887 *Myth, Ritual, and Religion*, Andrew Lang tells of an American who, living among Amazons in order to take down their myths, was unable to get the Indians to tell him a single story, not by coaxing, not by offers of money. Once, however, he overheard a steersman telling his oarsmen a story to keep them awake. Thereafter, when the American told this story to other Indians, they responded by relating a story to him. The simplest way, perhaps, to get students to tell you stories is by first telling them your own. In this respect I have been a tiny bit delinquent. I've assigned my fiction or encouraged students to read it, but not yet read it in class.

All the teacher is trying to do is make the student accessible to himself, make him as bold as possible. That, though, is an enterprise bound, in many cases, to encourage resistance. A resistance of a strange sort. Once I asked a class to compose a list of their own shames, not to be handed in, and a student wouldn't begin until I assured him again that the material was not required to be submitted. But when he was through, this student handed in his list. In truth, the more I have helped my students be accessible to themselves and the more I have used my imagination to release theirs, I have found myself fearing that I myself may become less accessible to myself, have less imagination for my own purposes. And with fear comes anger. Such nightmares, however, are inevitable, like fearing you'll turn academic if you teach one course. Certainly this fantasy of robbing myself to pay my students is not the whole story. The rabbis say that when God smashed the first Temple he said he had bad students, and when he smashed the second he admitted he was a bad teacher. I haven't smashed any temples yet.

To conclude, an important agreement between student and teacher is that the student not be shy and the teacher not be angry. Most of the time anyway. A few years ago, while I was visiting a certain rabbi, his five-year-old daughter suddenly asked me, "Want to see my bottom?" Her father and mother present, I said: "Yes, certainly!" So she turned round, lifted her dress, and—since she was wearing no underwear—there at once was her bottom. "Oh," I said, "what a lovely bottom!" So she let the hem of her dress go, turned back round to face me, and raising now the front hem to her mouth said: "I'm sort of shy." Of course, there at once was her shy, or actually sly, side. The lesson? A shy side may be bolder than a bold side.

SOURCE: *Writers as Teachers: Teachers as Writers.* Edited by Jonathan Baumbach. New York: Holt, Rinehart and Winston. 1970. Used here by the kind permission of Dr. Simckes.

RON PADGETT

"The Care and Feeding of a Child's Imagination"
(1976)

Padgett, born in Tulsa, Oklahoma, in 1942, attended Columbia University in New York City. He became one of the writers known as the "New York Poets" and for several years ran the publications program at Teachers and Writers Collaborative, a nonprofit educational group. In an anthology of his writings on poetry, he comments on his venture into teaching: "As a hand-to-mouth poet who had never taught, I thought the job sounded challenging but would give me time to write poetry and live my private life. However, as I worked with many different children, I became impressed with the beneficial effects poetry writing was having on their private and social selves. I felt I was being given a rare opportunity for a poet in the twentieth century—to be directly useful to society without compromising myself."

I still find it hard to recognize myself when the teacher introduces me formally to the class as "Mr. Padgett, the poet who is visiting us today. . . ." I feel dazed as I walk to the blackboard, draw an oval shape on it, and say, to a group of seventh-graders, "This is you." They giggle. "I mean, this is a blob. . . ." More giggles. "Let this blob represent the you that is your imagination, your personality, your mind, your Self, whatever there would be left if your body disappeared." I write the number 24 above it to represent one day and draw a line through the blob to mark off 8 hours for sleep. Pointing to the 16-hour part, I say, "This represents your mental self in the awake state, the you that is here right now. Most people think this part is the whole story. But when you lie down and go to sleep at night, your mind keeps on working, just differently, and sometimes very odd things happen in it." (By now the kids see me zeroing in on the dream-mind.) "This other part of the mind interests me a lot. When I was little I hated to go to sleep, but now I love it, because I'm curious to see what's happening over in that mysterious part of my mind. Last night, for instance, I dreamed . . ." and I go on

201

to recount last night's sleep extravaganza. By the time I'm finished, hands are up, kids anxious to tell me about their favorite dreams or nightmares, dreams that are repeated or continued the next night, funny dreams, romantic dreams, or how you can be in a dream and outside it at the same time. Then I ask, "Were you ever in a car, or a room, or outdoors, and suddenly you have this creepy feeling, that this has all happened exactly the same, sometime before?" Some gasp. Fifteen minutes ago we were total strangers. Now they are really excited about their own personal mysterious imaginative experiences.

I ask everyone to write down either a dream or a déjà vu experience, being as specific as they can in their descriptions. Not "a monster chased me," but "a green man with fiery pink hair all over his body walked toward me." No, they needn't sign their papers, and, no, don't worry about spelling or grammar. This is not a test. A few kids complain, "I never remember my dreams." Often they will go on to write about an actual dream they were hesitant to acknowledge. Others respond to "Remember a scary dream you had when you were little."

I read their dream writings aloud, including my own and the regular teacher's. Suddenly the room is filled with a sampling of the classroom unconscious. The anonymity adds to the fascination.

Dream Poem

I dreamed I was in a gigantic room. Everything was made of tiles, the walls, floors, everything. The only piece of furniture was a gold throne. I thought to myself, "What am I doing here? Oh well, I'll sit down." Then all of a sudden the left and right corners of the room opened. I could see beams of light coming in the corners. Very strong light and I could hear cheering. I stood up and a big dinosaur ran through the corner of light. I screamed and ran out the opposite beam of light and fell on a cloud that had sand particles on it. Then I dreamed I fell asleep. I've had this dream 4 times.

—Christine Riblett

I suggest they keep a diary of their dream lives that they can use as a basis for short stories, fantasy tales, or science fiction. (I've found it helps to replay details from my dreams before I open my eyes in the morning and then write them down immediately.)

Because my basic interest is in creative writing, I encourage kids to say whatever they want, no matter how wacky, weird, or unconventional, and to forgo, if they wish, rules of spelling, grammar, rhyme, and meter. They also have the freedom to write anonymously (until they feel confident enough to sign their work). Kids who have a terrible time spelling simple words naturally dislike writing but are often good storytellers. I take dictation from them, either individually or as a group. I don't want poetry writing to be confused with "schoolwork."

I am not, however, an "anything goes" type. I discourage personal viciousness and constant use of obscenity in writing. Doubtless therapeutic for some, they disconnect most children from their larger, more interesting selves.

I also discourage the kind of competitiveness that makes most kids feel anxious, unloved, and defeated, or vainly victorious: I do not single out the "best" works. Creativity should not be turned into a contest. I let kids talk while they work, move around the room, share ideas, copy from each other (if they feel they must), in short, behave in any way that isn't damaging to the group or to themselves. I encourage them to pay attention to their ideas, to take themselves seriously, even if what they're writing is funny, so that they know that the content of their fantasies is not only acceptable, it is welcome.

A crucial moment for emphasizing this comes when I read the poems aloud. I pause to comment on things I like, as much with my tone of voice as with outright remarks. In fact I praise the poems like mad. Praise makes the kids feel good about what they've done; they've gone out on a limb in their writing, and by damn it worked, somebody liked it! Gradually they gain the self-confidence to write as well as they always could have, with greater ease, pleasure, and satisfaction. They come to appreciate their imaginations, and from there the imaginative lives of others.

By "imaginative lives" I don't mean just the world of the unconscious. One poetry idea called variously Here and Now, Right Now, or Poem of the Senses has the kids focus their attention on the immediate present. In order to present the Right Now idea I secretly study the walls, ceiling, desks, view outside, details of clothes, and gestures that stand out a little, while the teacher introduces me. "This room is very interesting," I begin. "Look at that crack on the wall: it looks like a bolt of lightning. The reflection on the clock face forms a bent shiny rectangle. A yellow pencil is lying on the floor pointing to a red tennis shoe that goes up and down. Do you hear that humming? I feel a little cool breeze on my face as I walk back and forth, and I feel my heart beating in my chest. Do you feel yours? I feel my throat vibrating as I talk. I don't smell anything." Laughter.

"Right now this room is the way it never was before and never will be again because tiny details are constantly shifting." I hold up a piece of chalk and let it drop onto the floor, where it leaves a small bite of chalk. "That chalk falling is now three seconds into the past. . . . What I'd like you all to do is to blot out the past and future. Make yourself one big receiver of impressions: notice what you see, hear, feel (touch), smell, and sense right now. This can be outside your body and mind, like the light powder on the chalkboard; or inside, such as feeling your lungs fill with air or sensing an idea happening in your mind. Make a list—in sentences—of things you never noticed before or things you think no one else will notice. Not boring stuff like 'I see a wall,' but clear details, such as 'There are thousands of little holes in the green cinder blocks, each casting a shadow.' Or say what it reminds you of: 'The Vietnamese landscape is pitted with shell holes.'"

To make things easier I write on the board:

I see	I feel	I believe
I hear	I think	I imagine
I taste	I sense	I wonder
I smell	I know	etc.

The kids start craning their necks. Consciously focusing on details in the room is peculiar for them but exhilarating.

I see the dark mouth of a cave.
I hear the shouts of millions.
I feel high.
I think I am getting drunk off this class.
I smell a blue sea.
I imagine I am flying.
I know I am mad.

—Todd Robeson

This type of poem also shows how repetition is a good substitute for rhyme and meter in teaching poetry to children because it creates a poetic structure without inhibiting their freedom of expression.

Actual events become dreamlike when they sink into the past. "Wouldn't it be great if you could get in a time machine and go back into the past?" I ask one class. "To see George Washington remove his false teeth or Christ right up there on the Cross, a prehistoric man learning how to make fire, the real live Cleopatra, the Titanic sinking. . . . Or into the future. What would we look like? Would we live in plastic bubbles? Hmm. As far as I know, we can't get into the future, but we can travel back into the past by using our own personal time machines, our memories."

I talk about how odd it is to have something on the tip of one's tongue, how wonderful it is to remember something beautiful and valuable that happened to you, how dim and dreamy to remember back to the age of three, or two. . . . If only we could remember how it was before we were born! Finally I say that today I want everyone to get into their own time machines and travel back to something they remember from long ago. It doesn't have to be an earthshaking story, but it should be as specific as possible, recalling colors and details. I tell them to start each story with "I remember . . ."

> I remember when my sister was two, it was her birthday and we went shopping to get a cake at Pathmark. We had to wait on line for about 2 hours and when we got home my mother found out that my sister was sitting on the cake the whole time.

> —Carl Johnson

> I remember when I was 3 or 4 my father was very made at a '59 Ford and so mad he threw the keys at it and busted the ring and the keys went flying in the air and he came inside and mowed over everything and anything including me and he blamed me for it. It took us 3 hours to find 20 keys and we still didn't find one key, the key to the car.

> —Tom P.

Dream Poems, Here and Now Poems, I Remember—these depend directly on the personal experiences of the writers. There are other poetry ideas that are more mechanical but no less fun, such as acrostics.

I ask the kids to volunteer a word or a name, the first one that comes to mind. One kid calls out "Jackass."

"Okay, I'm going to write this word in the traditional Chinese fashion, up and down."

J
a
c
k
a
s
s

"Someone give me a word, any word, that starts with J."

"Jackknife," one kid says.

"Yes, that's good. Any others?"

"Jupiter."

"Japan!"

"Jellybean!"

"Those are all terrific. Let's take jellybean." Which I do. "Okay, now what word begins with A?"

"Ambulance?"

"Great! Now let's put jellybean and ambulance together by adding some things before and after jellybean."

By now the kids are cracking up or staring in amazement at this peculiar teacher or racing ahead in their minds. In any case they are learning how to do an acrostic.

We finish the example at the board and I read it aloud:

The Jellybean drove an
    Ambulance to South
    Carolina because he was a
    Kook who
    Always
    Started
    Speeding wildly

Everyone's laughing.

"Pick a word of your own," I tell them—"and do an acrostic, just as we did at the board, putting in anything that pops into your mind, no matter how silly."

Onions

July smells like
Onions when it is
Hot and
Niagara Falls
Runs dry because
Onions clog the
Immense
Merging of the
Entire
Roto Rooter Company

—John Roimer

Another writing method kids enjoy is collaborating as a class, dictating lines to someone at the board. This is also a good way to start with a class that hates writing, like one fourth grade group I taught. Here is their class collaboration:

God and His White Underwear

Angels are workers of God
Angels are the shoeshiners of God
Does God wear shoes?
No, he's a spirit
He might wear spiritual shoes
He puts on his underwear
It's pink and white
He goes to New Jersey
There he visits his family
In his family are George Washington, Babe Ruth, Mister
    McGoo and Mister Boogie
They dance
Then God takes an elevator
Like Jack and the beanstalk
And he's a rocket
Going to the moon, to the sky, to outer space.

In a more advanced fourth-grade class the kids chose partners and wrote alternating lines. These fourth-graders had a lot of experience writing poetry, which can be seen in this sample that still makes me dizzy with envy:

What's Inside the Moon?

What's inside the moon?
　　　There's hot water inside
What's the sky made of?
　　　It was made out of white snow.
If you cut the sun open what would you see?
　　　Terrible looking enemies.
When you write you look at your words have you thought
of
　　　cutting open a letter to see what's inside?
　　　No. But if a person was crazy the answer would be
yes.
What's inside colors?
　　　There's pink stars.
Where is the end of the universe?
　　　In back of the swimming pool.
How old is adventure?
　　　It is 60,000 years old.
Which color is older, black or white?
　　　Black because you can outline me.

　—Vivien Tuft and Fontessa Moore, P.S. 61, New York City

Sometimes with younger kids I sit down at the class typewriter and wait for them to come over and start dictating to me. One second-grade class didn't need much encouragement. They rushed over to dictate:

Sneezes of Hair

In the middle of the night
A hand comes out and says, "Hiya, honey,"
And kisses her in the lips
And she makes him baldheaded and he says, "I'm bald!
　I'm bald!"
And he puts pepper on his head
And it sneezes up.

It became so exciting, one kid climbed up on top of my head, searching for sneezes of hair, I guess.

At first, kindergartners were hard to teach because of their inability to write words or to concentrate very long, but I found them so much fun to be with that I usually let them look in my pockets, pull my beard, put toys on my shoes, etc. Then one day I enlisted the aid of five sixth-graders, good poets who had been writing for several years. I gave them some ideas for poems the kindergartners might like: "You know how your mother or father always says the same things. What do they say at your house? If your dog or cat or fish could talk English, what would they say? If a tree or a leaf or a mountain could talk, what would they say? A table? Imagine a talking table! A talking shoe? The moon talking! A glass of milk!" We broke into flying wedges, each sixth-grader in charge of three or four little kids. They worked much better with the sixth-graders than they had with me. Here are two poems dictated that day:

Poem

When a leaf drops it goes
tic, thoup, roasp,
wee wee weeee ahhhhh

My Daddy Says

My Daddy says walk the dog
My Daddy says clean the cat
My Daddy says keep the tiger in the cage
My Daddy says brush your teeth
My Daddy says meow
My Daddy says wa wa wa Indian
My Daddy says eat the dog and leave the cat
My Daddy says ruf, ruf, ruf
My Daddy says feed the monkeys bananas
My Daddy says I drive him bananas
My Daddy says don't get dirty
My Daddy says play it cool

I encourage kids to use my ideas in any way they like, even to the point of replacing them with their own ideas. One boy, San

Lum Wong, newly arrived from China and just beginning to learn English, wrote the following poem when I asked his class to write Love Poems:

The Funny World

The world is funny. The earth is funny. The people is funny.
Somebody in funny life. Somebody given a life change the
funny. The magic is funny. The funny is magic. Oh, boy a
funny funny money happy.

I defy you to write something in Chinese half as beautiful about love after three months of studying that language.

Sometimes a student will hand me a manuscript, something written at home in private. Such a poem was that of Liz Wolf, a seventh-grader:

I Kiss No Ass

I follow no footsteps because the ones I start to make I end
And I don't need your sun
'Cause I am my own sun, I can make light for myself, so I
can
   see the light
I don't need your gentle fingertips because I have my own
   two hands
And I have no room for hassles
No time, I don't have any need for it and it doesn't have any
   need for me
You can use your army and shield to knock me down
But my feet are planted to the ground
You tell me to "kiss ass"
I want to say, "Don't they know I have a mind too,
I'm not stupid!"
But what I say is "I kiss *no* ass."

Once kids come to appreciate their own writing, they have an improved, in fact a corrected, opinion of themselves, because one's language is as integral a part of one's self as an arm or leg. By getting in touch with their creative imaginations—which is sometimes a scary business, not a cutesy-pie world of daffodils and little hills—

they see more clearly into themselves, and this clarity gives them a sense of personal value. Creativity is not something to be tacked on to the curriculum; it's essential to growing and learning.

Educational administrators and classroom teachers are beginning to see that imaginative writing is not just a "cultural enrichment" to which they "expose" their kids. By having kids indulge themselves in the wild and wacky world of the imagination, presto: schoolwork improves, school becomes a bit more fun, and the printed word loses some of its tyranny. When kids can look at books and articles and say, confidently, "I write too," they are much less likely to acquiesce to the printed word without question, less likely to become mindless victims of mindless power.

SOURCE: Ron Padgett. *The Straight Line: Writings on Poetry and Poets*. University of Michigan Press. 2000. "The Care and Feeding of a Child's Imagination" first appeared in *Ms.* magazine in May 1976; it is republished here by the generous permission of the author.

JOHN RIDLAND

"Grading"
(1984)

The poet and translator John Ridland, born in 1933, taught English and writing at University of California, Santa Barbara, from 1961 through 2005.

> *"An experienced teacher can grade anything."*
>
> —An experienced teacher

He grades the cat on being cat
(straight A), the grapefruit on juiciness
(B+) and sweetness (B), his wife
on sleeping soundly (last night, D
minus); he grades the morning (C
+, *Be more definite*), the dog
for coming quickly when she's called
(A−, *good dog, good dog*), for
fetching the paper (*Fetch it!*—F).
In broad daylight he grades the moon
last night at midnight, *Well defined,*
clear and complete (pure A, pure A);
his breakfast lunch and dinner (Pass);
his shoes (Unsatisfactory);
of course he grades the morning paper
(*low C for content, C for form*);
the window (B, maybe B−,
Try to be more imaginative).

He grades the way he drives to school
(B+ *woops*, D), the radio—
rather, its choice of music (A
+, for Segovia's guitar

212

followed by Goodman's clarinet),
the fat opossum in the road
(plain D for *Dead*), the old man trudging
in red sweatsuit and jogging shoes
(Not Pass), the parking lot (OK),
colleagues for cordiality
(A, B, C, D, none of the above)
and courage in the line of duty
(*Withheld: cf. the Privacy Act*).

He's graded God (*You should do better
than this, with Your Advantages.
Try to improve by putting more
of Yourself into it: C–*);
and *homo sapiens* (*Barely passing,
YOU ARE IN TROUBLE!*); and himself
(Delivery, B; Coherence, C;
Organization, D; Good will,
A! A!), and grades his grading (C,
Inflated, whimsical), his life
(B+ *as far as it goes, keep going*);
Tomorrow and tomorrow and
tomorrow (*Where's your outline?* C,
No, Incomplete. *Please see me soon.*)

SOURCE: *Writing Poems*. Edited by Robert Wallace. 2nd edition.
Glenview, Illinois: Scott, Foresman and Co. 1987. Reprinted here
by the kind permission of the author. Copyright © 1984 by John
Ridland.

MARVIN MUDRICK

"'Week One': A Class in Eighteenth-Century English Prose"
(1989)

Marvin Mudrick (1921–1986) was a writer, critic, and English professor as well as the founder and provost of the College of Creative Studies at University of California, Santa Barbara. The College of Creative Studies was an experimental program that as its fundamental basis allowed for undergraduates to work creatively and independently in the arts and sciences. After Mudrick's death, a former student, Lance Kaplan, published a book of transcripts of Mudrick's classes and talks. In the excerpts below, from September 25, 1984, the first meeting of the class that fall quarter (which I attended), I have focused on his statements and thoughts on reading, reading assignments and his favorite book of nonfiction, Boswell's Life of Johnson. *A bracketed ellipsis [. . .] indicates not a pause but an excision by me.*

I think talk without the reading is bubbles, is of no importance, and reading without talk is pedantry. And so I try to set up the class in such a way that you will be really drowned in reading. For instance, I expect you to read the entire *Life of Johnson* by Boswell by next Tuesday. That's about fourteen hundred pages in the edition that you have. Of course if you are really serious English majors you would have read it a long time ago anyway. You certainly would be familiar with a lot of the material.

I'm inclined to think myself that it's—you'll check me on this, because some of you have heard me say The Greatest This and The Greatest That, and you probably know that it's the latest superficial enthusiasm that I have—but I do think that it's the greatest work of nonfiction ever written. And I also am inclined to think that it's one of the two greatest books ever written. The only book that for me comes anywhere near it, and is greater than, for certain reasons, is Chaucer's *Troilus and Criseyde*. But I don't have any doubt that it's the greatest book of nonfiction ever written. It's fascinating. And

214

certainly the greatest nonfictional character in literature—I mean the character of Johnson. . .

[. . .]

I don't think there is any alternative to reading. That is, reading gives you certain things that you cannot get in any other way. Johnson himself is as good an illustration of that as anybody who ever lived. Johnson's wit is unimaginable without the range and depth of his reading (and his extraordinary memory too). And I know that most of you are very young and of course you live in the age of television, and so probably most of you don't even know what the excitement of reading is, since you have this alternative from practically infancy.

I have to repeat my little song and dance about reading. I don't know any alternative to very hard reading in order to know what reading is. The kind of reading that you do for most of your classes is absolutely ridiculous. I mean it's trivial, it's minimal, it's conducted under false auspices—that is, you're *not* reading scripture. Literature is not religion. The study of literature is not the study of religion. The significance of reading—I mean the *reason* you read is to be entertained. And there is a sense in which you always have to have excess before you can have sufficiency. So in order to know what reading is like, you in effect have to read to excess, you have read overmuch, you have to be *driven*.

And once again, I can only depend on my own experience. Unlike most of you—all of you, I guess—I grew up in the age before television (and even radio was just beginning), and so for me a great time was to go to the library after school, and I went at least two or three times a week. And for me the most exciting thing in the world was a thick book with small print, because that meant I had something that would *last* me (instead of these wretched little books—that's another thing I hate about children's lit, I mean these wretched non-books which are put out, with large illustrations and no type in them—and of course they're drivel, besides, in addition to everything else). I loved books with small type—preferably without illustrations, because illustration took the place of the print that I would rather have. And I read it, and I read *any*thing, anything at all, it didn't matter. Because reading was great fun, it was extremely entertaining. It's true that *nobody loved me* [*laughter*] . . . *I was all alone* . . . I was very unsocial, and so I read.

I'm sure by the way that that was true for Johnson too. Johnson was of course a very strange-looking person with all kinds of tics from childhood. So what he did was essentially to lock himself up in a room (his father was also a bookseller—his father conducted a bookstore). So he read everything. And there's no alternative to it. And even at your age, if you have any serious interest in literary studies, you have no alternative to sitting down and piling in. And you read as hard as you can . . .

The worst thing that's done in these classes that you take is that the pretense is that you're going to understand everything you read. If you understood everything you read, you don't belong in school, you belong in heaven. I can tell you that your *teachers* don't understand everything they read, and they've read very little, and it's all fake—practically all of it is fake. You read for pleasure, and when you see something that you don't understand you simply pass it by. And if you discover that you're not reading as fast as you would like because you want to get to the end of something, turn over a lot of pages and get somewhere else. Fake it—*for yourself*. I mean, knowing that you're faking. Eventually you'll want to read it all, or most of what you're reading.

If you say to me, Do you seriously expect all of us to read the *Life of Johnson* by next Tuesday? Of course I don't. Most of you are phonies anyway as far as literature is concerned. You've never even read a Shakespeare *play* which has been assigned to you in one week, and that you should be able to read in an hour and a half. *I* know all that, and if you think that I'm going to act as a kind of policeman over you, you really *are* out of your mind. *I* don't care whether you read it or not, except if I catch you. I'm certainly not going to get headaches about whether or not you do the assignments. You're damn fools if you take a class like this and *don't* do the assignments, because you won't make sense out of any of it. And if you've reached the point where you are accumulating numbers and that's *all* you're doing, then you're beyond hope anyway.

You take a class like this because you get a chance to plunge into some of the juiciest material in the world in books. The eighteenth century, I have come to be more and more convinced, is the most important century in human history. Everything comes to an end there, and everything has a beginning. I recently have finally figured out what the word *watershed* means, and the eighteenth century is the great watershed of human history. Everything that came before comes to an end in the eighteenth century, and everything that produces what we call modern occurs in the eighteenth century. I mean you think of things like the French Revolution, and that's of course extremely important. The so-called Enlightenment. . . . Johnson is one of the great figures of the Enlightenment, and paradoxically he's particularly important in the Enlightenment because he consciously opposes it. Johnson is the great resistant force of the eighteenth century. That is, what he would like is for things to be as he fondly imagines they might have been at certain times in the Middle Ages (he never says that). But of course Johnson would have been burned at the stake within thirty seconds if he had lived in the Middle Ages, because he supports all the positions, but he supports them with such a sense of his own personal liberty—his right not to be bothered, his right to say what he pleases—that he is inconceivable earlier than the eighteenth century, he is just inconceivable. Nobody would have been able to get away with things the way Johnson did before the eighteenth century. So he is, almost against his will, one of the very greatest figures of the Enlightenment.

Certainly the two major literary figures of the European Enlightenment (for me anyway) are Voltaire and Johnson. And if you wonder (those of you who know anything about the eighteenth century) why I exclude Rousseau. I think Rousseau himself is a kind of counterrevolutionary, and is not really . . . he is neither an enlightened man nor, except by historical accident, a figure of the Enlightenment. He's essentially a moral reactionary, an intellectual reactionary.

Okay, you see already (those of you who are paying attention) that the fact that you haven't even read encyclopedia articles is something of a disadvantage when people are talking. Because some of you have no idea who Rousseau is, except that he's a name; Voltaire is just a name; Johnson is just a name—all of these people are just names. And the function of a course like this, if it has any function at all, is to compel you to read so hard and so much that these names begin to have substantiality for you; they'll begin to exist in space and time. And if you have no interest in that kind of experience, then you really shouldn't take this course.

I remember—once again I'll give you a personal experience—I remember (this was in the late '50s—no middle '50s) I had a number of enthusiastic students. It was just after [the literary journal] Spectrum had started, as a matter of fact, and some of the earliest people associated with *Spectrum* were very anxious to take extra courses. And we really worked rather hard in those days in the English Department—I mean I taught four courses, including two freshman courses—and they wanted me to teach extra courses in authors like Dostoevsky and Tolstoy because such courses weren't available. So I remember, for instance, teaching one semester a course in Tolstoy, another semester a course in Dostoevsky. And because I have a lousy memory and have to read what I'm teaching, shortly before I teach, and take detailed notes, I would prepare for the Dostoevsky course by starting to read the novel as soon as I came home from school, about three o'clock in the afternoon on the day before (because that was the only time—the classes met at my home one evening a week). And I read. And I read, and I read, and I broke for dinnertime, and then I read, and I read all night. And I usually was able to finish the novel by about six or seven a.m.—I was in better shape in those days, so I could then get up and start my day.

I didn't feel it was any imposition, it was absolutely fascinating to me. *You* people would stay up all night getting drunk or fucking some attractive member of the opposite sex, so why you should think that reading can be any less attractive necessarily, I don't see why. *Chacun a son goux,* as we say. [*Laughs.*] I can tell you that until you develop some such attraction for reading you aren't going to be anything like a serious student of literature. Unless reading begins to take you over in some such sense, then you might as well forget about literary studies. And you *really* ought to forget about teaching, because it will be the most miserable—I mean, some of the unhappiest people I ever knew are professors of English who hate to read, hate books, hate intellectual activity . . . they really are virtually out of their minds with self-hatred. It's a waste of time.

So I don't think I'm putting you through anything loathsome, disgusting. As I say, I don't expect you to be able to do this really . . . *very* well, anyway. But I expect you to make an effort, and I start you with—I love the fact for instance that Boswell, using a relatively new word, said (while he was writing the book on Johnson—in fact even before he started) he said: This will be the most entertaining book in the world. And that, as far as I know, is the first really modern use of the word *entertain* in a good sense. And he was right. I think it's probably fair to say that it is the most entertaining book ever written. And Boswell knew it, and by the way his friends thought he was absolutely crazy, out of his mind. DO YOU MEAN TO SAY THAT

YOU HAVE THE NERVE TO COMPARE THE BOOK THAT
YOU'RE GOING TO WRITE ON DR. JOHNSON WITH
MASON'S *LIFE OF GRAY*? (And all of you are very familiar with
Mason's *Life of Gray*, aren't you? It's on every reading list . . . I mean,
even the people in this English Department wouldn't dare put that
on a reading list. In fact I think most of them have never heard of
it.) [*Laughs.*]

That's the sort of thing that Boswell had to face up to, because
he was doing something absolutely unique. Not only unique—it's
never been done again. In fact the only thing that I know like it,
the only thing that's remotely like it in literature since—that is, the
combination of circumstances and personalities that made it possible—are the books brought out by Craft and Stravinsky, that is,
which record Stravinsky's conversation. Those are the only books I
know of which are at all like Boswell's biography of Johnson. This is
one of the greatest men who ever lived being recorded—accurately,
frequently, also being provoked into doing even more talking than
he would have done otherwise—by this *nut*, whose purpose is to get
Johnson to talk as much as possible, and who will ask him all kinds of
questions like: What would you do if you were locked up in a castle
with a newborn baby? [*Laughter.*]

[. . .]

[*Mudrick is led to an important passage in* Life of Johnson *and after
reading from page 615 (Oxford edition, 1980) and making observations
upon it, asks:*]

Do you get a little vibration of what feeling you might have reading a passage like that, if you knew who Gibbon was, how important
he was, who Johnson was, how important he was, who Boswell was,
how important he was? You see how exciting it would be to imagine these extraordinary men in the same room together at the same
time—who could scarcely abide each other, some of them. And
there they are, I mean before our eyes, speaking as they would speak
at the time. And by the way, Boswell was the only person that I can
think of who ever lived who consistently presented people behaving
domestically in this way. Imagine, you wouldn't have that anecdote
about Gibbon and Johnson if it weren't for Boswell. And you would
know that from time to time they were together, but what did they
say? How did they feel? Were they *really* afraid of each other? How
much did they dislike each other? In what *way* did they dislike each
other? And so on. And Boswell gives it to you.

What books give you is history. And there is no substitute for history, in the feeling you have that you have about the human race. You can be smart as all get-out, but your smartness will be . . . Whenever I hear about noble savages—and I am impressed when people are telling me how smart, say, Indians are, or savages (I'm using *savage* not in the pejorative sense)—I always think that their intelligence often has an extraordinary *breadth*—that is, they can know about everything on the face of the earth, if you take *earth* to mean dirt, and *sky* to mean sky—but they know nothing whatever in depth, because depth is history. If you don't know history, you have lost the third dimension—if you don't have a sense of what people were like in the past, and who lived in the past, and what they did. And you don't get that except by plunging into books. Nothing will give you that but books.

Where does Johnson get by with, for instance, understanding that lectures are a fake? Johnson understands in the 1760s . . . They had started giving lectures at Oxford, and Johnson disapproved of them. He said: What can you learn from a lecture that you can't learn from the books that the lectures have been taken from? Which is, of course, exactly what you have to say about lectures. [. . .]

What is the use of a lecture, will you tell me that? And the ludicrousness of a university *paying* these people to read from their notes, which were obsolete before they were written. What would you rather do: find out about the Roman Empire from the lectures of some tenth-rater, who if he had a few brains would steal from Gibbon, but probably hasn't even read Gibbon, at least since graduate school—or Gibbon? I mean, one of the most extraordinary minds that ever lived, giving you a sense of another period too, an entirely different period. This just baffles me. But Johnson knew that instantly, he knew it instantly. He looked at it and he said that's ridiculous, why should they have things like that?

STUDENT: Maybe the use for lectures is that the instructor has to give tests, so he's telling you beforehand what's going to be on the test—but it's intentional.

MUDRICK: That may be. You don't regard that as a serious justification for lectures, though, do you?

STUDENT: Well, if he didn't lecture he wouldn't be able to give a test, because it would be so broad.

MUDRICK: And if he didn't give a test, he wouldn't be able to lecture. [*Laughter.*] Yes! there's a real problem there, that's true! Yes?

STUDENT: What do you mean by a lecturer? Do you mean someone who's reading from something, or somebody who's talking—

MUDRICK: *I mean somebody who is presenting you with canned material,* who knows what he's going to say before he says it. Anybody who knows what he's going to say before he says it is either a lecturer or an actor. Actors sometimes at least deal with interesting material. I mean they're reading interesting material. Yes?

STUDENT: The implication of that is, that maybe in twenty years we can all stay at home and watch lectures instead of going to the university.

MUDRICK: It's true of course—that's the implication of university education, that is, the teacher really is obsolete. Johnson makes the point—and I assume I must have stolen it from Johnson years and years ago because I had no idea that lectures are invalidated by the existence of books. As soon as you have books you don't need lectures. If you're growing up in the Middle Ages, let's say, and you're going to Professor Abelard's class and you happen to be Heloise, the teacher has all the books. So the teacher is both the professor and the library. You have no alternative. And obviously if he has more than two or three students he can't lend out the books. When Chaucer, for instance, talking about his young scholar, the Clerk, says that he has "twenty bookes at his beddes heed," and you say twenty books— why, my God, you have twenty books on the *floor!* [*Laughter.*] Twenty books in those days meant virtually the entire *range* of what was written. For one thing the books were collections. A book in the medieval sense was a kind of anthology, it had enormous variety of material. But even so, that was all there was.

There is a very interesting modern example of this that I love, because it shows exactly what conditions must have been like in the Middle Ages. There was a teacher here, a young German who grew up in Vienna, and the first university he went to was the University of Vienna just after World War II. And of course Vienna had been bombed to the ground, there was nothing left. (For those of you who imagine by the way that European cities, with the possible exception of Paris, exist as they did in the pristine past—that is, they tried to reconstruct. Prague for instance was bombed to the ground, and then was rebuilt according to architectural specifications. . . . But anyway—) So the University of Vienna had been destroyed, the library had been destroyed, the books had been destroyed and so on, and so the students went to lectures. And they had no alternative—

there were no books, you couldn't get any books. And he took a class in Kafka, and the class in Kafka consisted in the teacher *reading synopses of Kafka's stories to the class*—detailed synopses of Kafka's stories—because there were no copies of Kafka's stories available.

And that was what going to class with Abelard might very well have been like. I mean you can assume that Abelard was a brilliant teacher, and also he was showing off for Heloise and so on, so he probably made a few smart cracks from time to time. But still, he had all the books, and the students had to take the word from him. But *you* have the books. *You* can use them, you can read them. And if I serve any purpose in my humble way, I serve the purpose that Johnson, say, serves to Boswell when Boswell says: *Well, what do you think about this passage in this book, Sir?* Or: *No, I disagree with you, and I think this.* And Johnson will go off, Boswell will go off, and so on. That's the only purpose. What in the world *business* do I have telling you what you're supposed to think about something which you haven't even read? I mean, does that make any sense at all? It doesn't to *me*. So unless you read, we have nothing to talk about, we really have nothing to talk about.

We can talk about the birds and the bees. One of the reasons I talk about sex so much is that that's about the only interest we share. [*Laughter.*] I don't know of any other interest that you and I share. And we share very little information. So I have to talk about sex. (It's a lie, but it's a good story.) So read! Why would you be taking an advanced English class unless you liked to read? If you don't like to read the *Life of Johnson*, forget it, really forget it. If you don't find this book interesting, you just should take up another line of work, that's all there is to it. Because Boswell was right—it's the most entertaining book ever written.

Now I don't mean you don't have to make some effort to get into a book which after all was written almost exactly two hundred years ago. So that it's a different time, and especially at the beginning, when Boswell is trying to establish the sense of this character—he's writing, after all, for people who understood that Johnson was the greatest Englishman of the eighteenth century, and that he's just a misty literary figure of the past. Well, you have to make that effort at the beginning. You have to give Boswell the chance to introduce him.

Another thing about reading is the notion that some of you have been given (and this, too, really is quite the reverse of what it's intended to be). That is, your teachers will tell you: Never read anything without making every effort to understand every word of it. THAT IS THE *DEATH* TO READING! If you allow yourself to get into that frame of mind, you will never get through a single book—never get through a single *interesting* book. You read because you expect to come to something that's going to entertain you. And you keep reading as hard as you can to try to get to interesting parts, and you turn the pages as fast as you can. And I'm not talking about speed-reading, which I know nothing whatever about, so I'm not qualified to speak of it. I don't read that way myself. I can't read that way (I mean I suppose I wish I could), I don't know anything about it. And I am *not* a fast reader.

But what I'm expecting you to do, and I really wish you would try to talk about this a little because I'm sure—I don't want to lose those of you who had the courage to come back for the second half of the class, I wouldn't like to lose anybody. And I *am* serious. I'm not going to punish you in any way—I will be grateful if you have done as conscientious a job as you can. And once again the notion of conscientiousness as trying to understand every word—*that* I don't go for. You are conscientious because you try to read in such a way as reading should be done, which is to get as much fun out of it as possible, and if you don't understand something the first time around, keep going, just keep going. Try to cover as much of it as you can. One thing you try to bring into play as much as possible is the completion compulsion.

This notion—that all obsessions are bad—is crazy. Many obsessions are very good, in fact we couldn't live without a lot of obsessions. I have an obsession about completing chapters for instance. I have to complete a chapter before I stop reading anything. So it doesn't matter what the time is or what's going on.

STUDENT: There aren't any [in the *Life of Johnson*].

MUDRICK: No, I know, but there are years, and it's divided by years.

Any way that you can develop a habit which compels you to do something which in the short run might not appear to be particularly attractive to you but in the long run does appear attractive to you—develop it like crazy. It will serve you in very good stead, and the astonishing thing is that eventually you may even develop a liking for what you have forced yourself to do—that's the most astonishing thing about it. Because it really is quite as easy to develop good habits as bad ones, good addictions as bad addictions. And I should think that the function of our lives, especially when we're young, is to develop as many good habits (the trouble is, when you say "good habit" everybody says, "Yeah, I know what that is"), good *addictions*, good *obsessions*. Things that don't really make any sense if you consider them rationally—I mean, why am I forcing myself to do this?—but there is some hope of future gain.

I don't know of any obsession that you would be better off to develop than the obsession for reading. It is really, of all obsessions and addictions, the one that will serve you best throughout your entire life. Every once in a while, I revise my notion of what pleasures sustain themselves best as you get older (because every year I get older—so, you see, then something diminishes). At the moment my feeling is that the only two habits that pay off completely, continuously, without diminution, and indeed I think with intensification if you practice them properly, are reading and eating. I don't mean stuffing your mouth three times a day with anything that's there, or overeating because you have suffered some kind of emotional setback; I mean really discriminating. If you really eat, you know the difference between shit and Shinola or chalk and cheese. And if you really read, you know the difference between this and that. And that of course is part of the enormous pleasure that you get from it.

[. . .]

For those of you who think that books will be outmoded, and for the things that you read about, it's not true. There is no substitute for books. (And certainly I'm all for all modern improvements.) The invention of language was certainly the most extraordinary invention in human history (it's much more significant than the wheel, for instance), and more particularly the invention of written language. There is a cohesiveness . . . there is a correspondence between a book and the mind such as exists between no other external object and the mind. There is a sense in which a book is the objectification of a human being. And there is nothing else like that at all. A computer isn't like that, a TV image isn't like that, a floppy disk isn't like that. And I think part of the reason is that the use of the eye in reading is special. The use of the eye in looking at images is much less . . . comprehensive than the use of the eye in reading words. The effort that the eye has to make in conjunction with the mind while looking at words brings into action functions which are brought into action by no other human activity. There is nothing which so animates human beings.

And I know that I'm struggling for words here, *animates* is not quite right, and you can think of all sorts of things. . . . For instance, I happen to be mad about music, and I am really fonder of music than I am of literature, it's more exciting to me. Nevertheless I would stick by what I just said, that there is always a sense in which language involves more of me, or books involve more of me, than music does. Music involves a part of me more intensely than any book does, but books involve more of me than any music does. And this I think is of some significance, I mean even for your own examination, your own interest. Because it is true that music is more exciting to me, much more exciting, than books. Maybe that's one of the things wrong with it, that it is so exciting to me that there is a sense in which it takes me out of myself. Books keep me inside myself, most of the time. I am where I am. I am within my limits. There is a sense in which music for me is sanctioned sentimentality, though music is not sentimental. Music makes me believe that I am bigger than I am. And for a moment maybe I am, but it's unsustainable. Books very seldom do that to me. Yes?

STUDENT: That sounds like the difference between love and friendship.

MUDRICK: Yeah, to some extent. Maybe another way to put it is to say that music for me is like passionate love at the beginning, and books for me are like love after many years if it sustains itself. [. . .]

SOURCE: *Mudrick Transcribed: Classes and Talks by Marvin Mudrick.* Edited by Lance Kaplan. Santa Barbara. 1989. Reprinted here by the kind permission of the Mudrick family and Lance Kaplan.

BOB BLAISDELL

"It's Greek to Me"
(1994)

Bob Blaisdell (born in 1959) is the editor of this book. He teaches English at the City University of New York's Kingsborough Community College in Brooklyn. Since 1995 he has taught writing workshops at a soup kitchen in Manhattan. This essay is based on his experiences learning Greek as a graduate student and working at a residential school in California for children with learning disabilities.

"Bob, how about you then? I think it's your turn, isn't it?"

"It is? Okay, here goes." I read the Greek aloud, in a pronunciation that I continually realize differs from the one Professor M gives it, or from the ways the other half-dozen students read it. I try to at least hit the accent right, and put myself into something like the frame of mind I have or had when I read French or Spanish aloud. I fail to elide two vowels into a diphthong, and Professor M corrects me: "*You-geneis.*"

So I say, "Huh?" (though immediately I repeat his correction), and I repeat it again after his reiteration: "*You-geneis.*"

When I finish the sentence, he says: "Okay, that's enough of the Greek aloud. Now some translation." He does not want us to write down our translations of passages anywhere, and he does not like us putting the English word in pencil above a tough vocabulary word. "Otherwise you're not translating, you're just reading a translation—it's your own, sure, but it's not going to help you any. Read it enough times to yourself so that you know what it means, but don't write down a translation. Okay, now go ahead."

It is a tricky passage, but I have read it a dozen times at least, aloud to myself, silently, silently and slowly looking up word by word, checking the notes from two different reader's editions of the *Anabasis*, as well as having read (Professor M would not approve) the translation by Rouse. I know this translation cold, or so I think, and

226

I confidently (cockily) begin my translation: "There was a spring there, and near the road of Midas—"

"The *road* of Midas?"

"The Midian road?—Wait. Okay, 'The spring being of Midas—'" I have panicked: I'm not reading the passage but *remembering* the meaning, as if the words weren't to be read, but to be a kind of visual prompt for telling the story.

Professor M gets a pained look on his face, and I start to stammer, because I like and respect him and feel grateful that he has passed me along to second-year Greek. He has seemed favorably disposed towards me even though I am probably the seventh best student of Greek in a seven-student class. "What's your subject?" he asks in his weary voice.

I have regained some composure—anyhow, I know the answer: "Road!—I mean, spring!"

"Right. So go on."

"There was, near the road, a spring—"

"'The' probably."

"There was near the road, a spring—the! spring . . ." But again, instead of reading slowly, figuring out phrase by phrase the relationship between words, I see those familiar lines of Greek prose, they look like a picture, not language, and I tell about them or explain them the way you might describe a painting, but knowing or fearing that I am about to be corrected for errors. It matters that the participle, the meaning of which I am drawing a blank on, is in the middle voice, and when I confess, in agony, "I forget 'kaloomeneh'," he tells the answer (though he habitually does not):

"'So-called.' That's not an easy one. But it comes, of course, from '*kal-e-oh*.'"

I *am* reminded, and I push on, slowly, and stumblingly, being corrected or "adjusted" a half-a-dozen times in about four lines. I'm exhausted, disappointed in my flub of a tricky but familiar, extremely familiar, passage. I sigh when the bearded Religious Studies graduate student from last year's class gives me a quick look of sympathy and a shrug, as if to say, "Yeah, that *was* tough." But *he* rarely messes up. He probably has as much anxiety as I do about Greek, at least he expresses it plenty, but he is very good, and the class knows it and Professor M knows it. Anyhow, I shrug back at him as if to say, "I apologize for wasting everyone's time." Because it is agonizing even if it's not on your account when Professor M asks those leading questions.

When the class is over I get up to go; I'm usually the first one out of the room. Professor M (his colleagues call him, out of affection I'm pretty sure, "Papa Joe") says to my apologetic look on my way to the door, past him at the blackboard where he is erasing everything (as a courtesy to the next teacher), "Hey Bob, you're doing all right. Really, I think you're coming around." I can't bring myself to thank him or deny it, so I shrug, smiling (but again apologetically) and leave. I start on my way back towards the English department, where I'm a graduate student, already planning for my next reading of Xenophon: tonight, two hours. I do want to do well, I'm not optimistic that I will, but I am determined (at least momentarily) to keep at it steadily.

★ ★ ★

Before I started graduate school I worked in Southern California for three years at a residential school for children with learning disabilities. I'll call it Our Lady of Hope. The children lived and went to school on the grounds. As part of the school's residential staff I would teach the kids among other things table manners and domestic skills. The kids I liked best and worked with the most were in a coed group, and they were usually the youngest or scrawniest or most backward kids in the school. Michou was about ten, maybe eleven, when we got to be friends. She was skinny and Polynesian-looking, with big front teeth, and cute. All the other kids in the group looked up to her; she was the queen. She spoke as well as most ten- or eleven-year-old girls, could articulate anything, and to look at her you couldn't figure out how she could be retarded. She did not look slow or act slow. She was responsible, dressed with a degree of taste, and was well-liked by staff and kids. It sounds bad to say, but she was so wonderfully "normal."

It was not until after maybe my first year that I realized for myself the extent of her limitations, which I had heard about: she could not tell time, she could not read. She could copy words well enough, but read them, no. Some of the least social, most severely developmentally disabled kids could tell time (even without having a concept of what time was—which Michou certainly did; the hands and numbers just did not translate themselves into "time" for her). She could not work with numbers or written words. Something didn't click, but she was so bright otherwise and attractive, that I could not resist feeling that something would or had to click sometime, and that she would *become* the all-around normal kid she seemed (her parents shared this hope). Meanwhile, some of the kids with Down syndrome could read off simple sentences and could tell the correct time to the quarter hour.

"What time's it, Miche?" I would ask, showing her the toy clock, its hands indicating 4:30.

"My my, Bob, you forgot to shave today, didn't you?" She put her finger on my cheek.

"Miche."

"Hm?"

"What time's it?"

"Do we have to?"

"Yeah."

"It's um . . ." She touched the clock hands. "What time do you want it to be?"

"Where's the little hand?"

"This one?—Um. Near the four.—It's four o'clock. Can I get my snack now?"

"No, no. Look, you're right, the little hand's on the four. Where's the big hand?" (Understand, reader, that she had probably been run through a time class at least a hundred times over the past two years.)

"Six. It's six o'clock."

In spite of not being able to read, she would sometimes sit on her bed, or at the play table with an open book or coloring book, reading aloud to one of her group-mates (who could have read for themselves, though with little or no comprehension, with a teacher prompting them).

"Now, Dorrie," she would say in a teacherly tone, "sit down. No, put your purse down."

"Down?"

"Yes, down.—Yes. And I'll read this to you." If I got too close or seemed to be observing her, Michou would clam up, embarrassed, as if she knew she wasn't fooling me. But if I kept myself busy with another kid or other kids I could overhear her.

"Dorothy, look. 'And Bugs decided to have a picnic with all his carrots.'" The sentence under the coloring-book picture read: "Bugs enjoys a carrot picnic." And she would continue, happily, except to rebuke Dorothy occasionally for her inattention.

Sometimes at night after all the kids were put to bed and I was cleaning up the residence, or doing homework, or filling in charts at the same play table where Michou would "read" her books in the afternoon and evening, she would wander out of her dormitory and, in an appropriately quiet voice, pipe, "Hi. Whatcha doing?"

"Oh, Miche, you should be in bed."

"But I can't sleep."

I would frown, and then continue my work, which she took to mean (and of course correctly) I would let her sit up with me for a while if she were quiet. "What are you reading?" she would ask.

"Poems."

"Poems?"

"You know, 'Roses are red, violets are blue, come smell my feet—'"

"—Pew, pew, pew!"

"Right."

"It's for school?"

"Yeah."

"I'll be right back. I've got homework too."

And she was off, though I was whispering after her, "Miche, no, don't go in there rustling stuff around. You'll wake up Dorrie." She ignored me, and rustled in the dark dormitory, and then I heard her in the hallway, and then she came in and sat at the opposite side of the table. "I think I'll color first." She opened a Dukes of Hazzard coloring book.

"Isn't that Leonard's?"

"He said I could use it."

"Oh."

"Let's see, where was I?" And she opened the book up. She put her finger on the caption under a picture of a fat sheriff shaking his fist, and she then pretended, glancing up at me self-consciously, but trying to play it cool, to read the words (they were in large-type capitals and easy for me to read upside down): "THOSE DUKE BOYS, I'LL GET THEM YET!"

She said instead, her finger slipping along that caption, "The Duke boys sure make me mad!" And she laughed, delighted with the sheriff's vexation. She knew that coloring book very well, and knew the adventures to come, and could have summarized the entire plot in fifteen seconds. But she was not reading, she just knew how it all went. She knew all the letters and could sound out easy words, but she rarely could force herself to keep her attention on the words. She would guess the word, or the sense, and keep moving. The agony of learning was particularly acute for her; it seemed to shame her.

"Miche."

"Hm?"

"Let's color." I closed my Norton Anthology.

"Okay. I'll go get my big box of crayons."

"No, no, you'll—" And she was off into the dark dormitory again. When she came back I had moved her chair to my side and had opened the coloring book to another page.

"Oh, this one," she said. It was a picture of an out-of-control sheriff's car about to dive into a pond. She put her finger on the first word. "'It'—'The,' I mean."

I nodded, trying not frighten her with encouragement. "And this word . . . hmm.—'The car takes a bath,'" she said quickly. She flipped the page so I wouldn't stop her and point out word by word the correct reading: "The sheriff and his car take a plunge."

"Let's color something else," she suggested. She found a picture of a young woman in a work-shirt, smiling. There was one word under the picture, and she knew what it was: "DAISY."

"All right," I said. "We'll color Daisy. Then you gotta go to bed.— How about blue hair?" I liked to tease the kids by suggesting incongruous colors.

"Blue!?" she said, wrinkling her nose, and then, catching on, smiling. "Okay! Then how about a green face?"

"Green!?"

"Well, maybe she's got a stomach ache."

SOURCE: First published, in a slightly different form, in *Hudson River* (Number 50), edited by Robert Lapides. New York. March 1994.

STEPHEN VINCENT

"In Class"
(1994)

Born in 1940, Stephen Vincent is a poet and publisher who lives in San Francisco.

Azuonye sits in front. He's tall.
He loves to raise his long arms
to discuss literature. Yeats. Achebe.
Wordsworth. Okigbo. Shakespeare.
An ear for two worlds, and more. I
change the subject. We speak
about how the children
are named. That in his village,
six weeks after birth, it is
the grandmother who visits.
If there is a dimple in one place
and not another, the grandmother
says it is this uncle or great uncle
or cousin and not another. He demonstrates.
He points to his neck. He wears
an open-collared shirt.
There is a large birthmark, purple,
almost black, under the jugular.
Its wide diamond shape
cuts a sharp angle
down to his chest. "I am named
after a distant uncle," he says.
"The man was assassinated
with a machete
in an act of revenge."
The class—many of the students
are from the village—

suddenly ricochets into laughter.
Even Azuonye, as if already
divided by fate, breaks into
an odd smile. Only gradually
can I turn the class back
to a poem by Yeats.

SOURCE: *Educating the Imagination: Essays and Ideas for Teachers and Writers*. Vol. 2. Edited by Christopher Edgar and Ron Padgett. New York: Teachers and Writers Collaborative. 1994. Reprinted here by the kind permission of Stephen Vincent.

KENNETH KOCH

"The Butterfly and the Rhinoceros"
(1995)

Kenneth Koch (1925–2002) was an American poet and professor whose books about teaching poetry writing to children, among them Wishes, Lies and Dreams *and* Rose, Where Did You Get That Red?*, inspired teachers and poets the world over: "You do whatever you can to make literature something that belongs to students rather than something that is distant, remote. One way to make it belong to them is to have them write it and not to treat it with so much respect that it's unapproachable." In the selection that follows, Judy Kravis, an English poet and teacher, interviewed him for her book* Teaching Literature: Writers and Teachers Talking. *In "The Butterfly and the Rhinoceros" he tells his history of teaching poetry.*

The first time I taught a poetry writing workshop was at the New School for Social Research. It was long before I taught at Columbia and the students who came to this workshop were adults, which meant they were anywhere from eighteen to seventy. To some extent when I started to teach I was teaching people to write from the point of view of a style that John Ashbery and Frank O'Hara and I wrote in. It wasn't exactly a common style, but we had something in common. I wanted to bring into the workshop the experiences I'd had outside of school which had helped me to be a better poet, such as reading other poets and being influenced by them, trying new forms, using ways of writing that brought unconscious experiences in, such as my dreams, and so on.

Then I got a job at Columbia and within three or four years I was teaching a writing course there. I used the same kind of techniques I'd used with the adults at the New School. It was after I'd been doing that for a number of years that I taught in the schools. I used very few texts outside of those that the children wrote. I would tell the children to write a Wish Poem and I'd get them excited about their wishes and then I would use the Wish Poems of the fourth-graders to interest the second-graders, the Wish Poems by

234

the second-graders to interest the third-graders and so on. Later I found a way to bring already written great poetry by adults into the classroom. I taught Blake's "The Tyger." I read the poem aloud. I explained everything in it that the children didn't understand. I dramatized it a little bit so that they would understand it more. I got to where Blake says: "What immortal hand or eye / Could frame thy fearful symmetry?" and nobody in the sixth grade knew what symmetry was. I started making up a drawing on the board: symmetry is when something is exactly the same on this side as it is on the other, and then I got a bright idea. I said, "I have good news for you. You're all symmetrical, try it out." I don't think anybody's been so excited about symmetry since Blake. So the very things the children didn't understand were exciting to them.

After we'd gone through the whole poem, including the penultimate stanza which I never completely understood—I don't think it's fair not to teach things one doesn't completely understand, if, after all, one has gotten a lot out of them oneself: "When the stars threw down their spears, / And water'd heaven with their tears." I'm not sure I know what Blake's talking about there. I presume he's talking about the end of the war in heaven. But the kids in the sixth grade had a pretty good idea and they said, "Well, it sounds like, after God made the world, it rained so that things would grow, and the spears are like lightning."

Then I told the children to write a poem, like Blake's, in which they imagined they were talking to a mysterious beautiful creature, even a dangerous sort if they liked. For a magic moment they could communicate with it, they could ask it anything they wanted. They asked if there could be more than one animal and if the animal could answer back—one of the points of Blake's poem is that the animal doesn't answer—but I said yes, because that would make it more enjoyable and seem more real. I think that there are three or four poems inspired by Blake's "The Tyger" which show that the children had a better reading experience of Blake than most people do in college classes, mostly because they paid so much attention to the details of the poem, and to feeling like it and writing like it. Some of the poems they wrote are really good.

Children learn more from participating and acting than from merely listening. There's a lot they didn't understand about Blake, but there's a lot that they did. You know when you're about ten years old you're closer to believing you can talk to a dog. Children are much closer to Blake in one way than adults are. After I taught this poem, I looked in a textbook, a ninth-grade textbook which had Blake's poem in it, and above it in bold black letters much larger than the type of the poem it said: "The tiger is a symbol of God's wrath. Now read this poem." That's really something to take the experience away from the children.

I had a very touching experience when I was teaching children. There was a little black girl named Fontessa Moore in third grade and Fontessa was obviously a lively, spirited little girl and she was eight years old and she wouldn't write a poem. All the other children were writing and I tried to cajole her into writing too. So in the second or third class the subject was colors. I had told the students to write a poem about the colors of things that don't really have colors. I said, "Close your eyes," and I'd whistle and say, "What color is that sound?" And they'd say, "Red." "Green." "Blue." Fontessa wrote a technically perfect poem about how black and white people might be different outside, but they're really the same inside and they should love each other. I thought she'd probably copied it out of a book or magazine. But it would be silly to accuse her, an eight-year-old, of plagiarism. I said, "Fontessa, this is a perfectly made poem, but this has been said so many times, don't you think it's sort of corny, it doesn't seem very interesting, it seems kind of boring and I think you're very funny, why don't you write poems that are more like you?" So she said, "You mean I can write a funny one?" And I said, "Yes." So then Fontessa began to write in other classes and a lot of words were spelt wrong and obviously she hadn't been willing to write because she was very bad at spelling.

David Frost used to have a weekly show and he found out about my work and invited me and four or five of my star students on to his show. Fontessa was there and he admired her very much and actually invited her back on the show a second time. When she was in sixth grade, in emulation of my book *Wishes, Lies and Dreams*, she made up her own book of poems, which she made copies of and a dedication page, on which she thanked people, and she said, "I want to thank my parents, I want to thank Mr. Ron Padgett but most of all I want to thank Mr. Kenneth Koch. I used to think I never would amount to anything, but he taught me that spelling didn't matter and I love him for that." It makes me very sad when I think of it, you know, the harm it's done to children in school, putting spelling before expression. So somehow you have to avoid that trap. I tell the children, "Don't pay any attention to spelling or anything like that when you're writing. At the end of the term I want you to turn in a notebook of your poems; by that time you can find out how words are spelt." Another thing I do is if I collect the poems, the children know in advance I'm not going to make any marks on them. It's hard for teachers to resist marking misspelt words. Also, you don't want to write comments on all their poems because even if you write "This is wonderful," the kids will know you're lying. Sometimes they're not wonderful and you don't want to write "This is stupid," so I try to get it all done in class. The kids read their poems, we respond to them, and it's all over.

Someone wrote to Wallace Stevens one summer when he was in his fifties or sixties and said "What have you been reading?" and he wrote back and said, "Well, I haven't done much reading but I've been doing a lot of writing, which seems to me a very intense form of reading." At Columbia I teach a course in modern poetry in which students do imitations of four or five of the writers we study every term and they all think it's the best part of the course. You know one can talk for a long time about inscape and sprung rhythm and so on, but when you have to turn into Gerard Manley Hopkins and crowd all those words into a line, you really know what it feels like. You feel the excitement and you read him better; you get the music.

Another course I teach at Columbia is called Form in Poetry. I start with ballads and then go on to sonnets by Wyatt, Sidney, Spenser and Shakespeare. Then I do Shakespeare's songs, Campion's songs, Jonson's songs, John Donne, and I go through the Romantics on my way to modern poetry and the subject is the form of poetry. So we talk a little bit about pentameters, rhyme schemes, stanzas, but the interesting thing about the course is that instead of writing papers the students do a lot of poetry writing. They write extensively in the style and in the form of every poet that we study and it seems a wonderful way to learn literature.

I do have them write an essay at the end of the term because it helps make them organized, but I have them pick one of the imitations that they've done or write a new one and write a piece of bogus scholarship in which they claim they've discovered this manuscript and demonstrate whether or not it's genuine—that is, genuinely by Keats, Shakespeare or whomever. I let them have one page to be silly and then they have to write five or ten pages in which they're serious.

You do whatever you can to make literature something that belongs to students rather than something that is distant, remote. One way to make it belong to them is to have them write it and not to treat it with so much respect that it's unapproachable.

Of course, there are limits to students'—or anyone's—ability to write like the poets I was teaching, but these limits are instructive, too. In my Form in Poetry class I was having the students write sonnets in the style of Shakespeare. First I had them practice writing the first lines of sonnets—you know the first lines of Shakespeare's sonnets are like trumpet calls—"Let me not to the marriage of true minds" or "When to the sessions of sweet silent thought"; they're very grand. Then I taught them how to write the couplets, the sort of soft thoughtful conclusion and how to construct the whole thing, and one young woman said after having tried, "There's something that I'm finding it very hard to get and that's that he seemed so confident, with the world so much in his control. The world doesn't seem to me that way." I thought that was brilliant. It led to some very interesting perceptions of Shakespeare's poems.

If I taught an introduction to poetry, I would start off with a few poems that I like and I would let everybody have a copy of the poem and I would read the poem and say, "What do you think?" Poetry is written in a different way from the way almost all other things are written. Poetry is deliberately suggestive rather than definitive. You don't read poetry to find out how to get to the door or how to open a can or how to play tennis. You read poetry for some other reason. Therefore the language may seem vague and may make you excited, happy or unhappy, or thoughtful without your knowing why. The first response to a good poem is certainly not to understand it intellectually. The best way to understand one poem by Yeats is to read ten poems by Yeats. The same thing with a new friend who starts talking to you and you don't know if he's serious, if he's joking or what. You find out after you've talked to the person for a while. So, I'd say to the students, "I'd just like you to listen to this poem. I'll read it twice—it's almost impossible to understand a poem the first time you hear it or read it. Then you just tell me something you like about it because the first step in understanding a work of art is to like it, to get pleasure from it, because art is constructed so as to give pleasure, that's the nature of its construction. A good analogy is music. If you listen to a piece of Mozart or Stravinsky and you don't feel pleasure, either Mozart or Stravinsky is not any good or you're not understanding what's going on, you're not hearing the harmonies or dissonances that are supposed to make something happen to you. Sometimes I can read a poem and understand it immediately and even imitate it. But it takes a long time to be able to do that and there are still poems by Wallace Stevens and even Yeats that I don't understand."

We were reading a very difficult early poem by Yeats, "The Rose of the World," in my class at Columbia once: "Who dreamed that beauty passes like a dream? / For these red lips, with all their mournful pride, / Mournful that no new wonder may betide. . . ." To me, and later to my students, the poem is close to incomprehensible. Poetry is so seductive, it's so pretty on the surface, that it's very hard to understand what it says, there's this dazzle, it's like trying to see what the sun is made of. We read the poem and I said, "You may not understand it, it may be incomprehensible at first, but is there anything you like about it?" Finally somebody raised his hand and said, "I like the way this guy talks as though what he's saying is very important." That seemed to me a wonderful perception about Yeats's style and tone and a good way to start talking about his poem.

When I read the beginning of *Paradise Lost* to my fifth- and sixth-graders I said, "What do you think of that: 'Of man's first disobedience, and the fruit / Of that forbidden tree'?" Some little girl in the back row raised her hand, a very skinny little girl, and she said, "It sounds like the preacher." I thought this simply stated version of a recognition of the ceremonious nature of Milton's language was awfully good.

But to change education is really tough. I thought I was making a big difference with my work in teaching children to write poetry and it's made some difference, but sometimes I felt it was like being a butterfly trying to influence a rhinoceros. It's tough. I had a friend who worked in the Southampton Library—Southampton is a pretty sophisticated community—but she said that my book *Wishes, Lies and Dreams* had come up for purchase by the library but they decided against it because in it I said that spelling shouldn't matter for children when they wrote poetry.

In my modern poetry class at Columbia I used to give one long paper at the end of the term. But there were so many flaws in these papers—it's hard to write about poetry. The first and most natural response to reading a good poem is not to write a critical essay about it. The most natural response is to write a poem or call up a friend and read the poem, or read more poems or be excited but certainly not to write a critical essay, although it's wonderful to write clearly. But it's not easy. So I changed my assignments because I was getting papers at the end of the term in which the writers didn't know how to give evidence and didn't know what they were supposed to say about a poem. What I'm doing currently is having the students write three or four short papers. In the first they take a poem that we haven't discussed in class and do a prose paraphrase of it, and then write a two-page essay saying in detail which version is better, the prose paraphrase or the poem, and why. The students learn a great deal about what you can't get into a paraphrase. Of course what the essay turns out to be about is what the way in which meaning is communicated by line, meter, repetition, transitions, strange juxtapositions and so on.

I teach some poets in translation. I resisted this for years. People say you don't get anything from poetry in translation; poetry is lost in translation. Nonetheless I don't know ancient Greek and I can still get something out of Homer and anyway twentieth-century poetry is international. I mean, if you don't know Rilke and Lorca and Pasternak, you don't know what's going on. A number of my students know a foreign language, so one assignment I give them—which is voluntary—is to translate a poem of which there are two other translations. They give me the three translations, theirs and the other two and the essay of five to ten pages is on why their translation is the best of the three. One question I always have on the modern poetry exam is this: I print a poem ("Leda and the Swan," say) and ask the students to imagine that three other poets have also written poems on this subject. Describe their poems, quote from them as much as you can and justify your opinion. So I give the students a chance to be creative in exams. I have to make the exams interesting, otherwise it's very tedious to grade them.

Another question that I like a lot is I take for example a poem by Yeats, "Among School Children," and I write a rhyming couplet version which makes the main idea extremely clear. The question I ask is: which version of Yeats's poem do you prefer and why? I try to develop the students' taste. I am always asking them how they like a particular poem. I tell them some things that could conceivably be wrong with it: isn't Lawrence in bad taste, a bit vulgar, corny? Isn't

Hopkins a little over-excited? Because I want them to participate in the whole thing.

When I teach poetry writing, I never give people grades on the works that they write, I just write comments and in my academic classes where the students write poems as sort of a sideline, I don't give A, B, C, and I don't lower a student's grade because he or she doesn't write good poetry. Spelling and punctuation wouldn't have any effect on my grading of the writing of poetry or stories but it probably would have an effect if I were teaching a course like teaching people to write simple prose. One has to train people to go out into society and be effective; they have to learn to spell and punctuate, though a course in modern literature is hardly an appropriate place to do that. It makes it hard to enjoy literature.

SOURCE: Judy Kravis. *Teaching Literature: Writers and Teachers Talking.* Cork, Ireland: Cork University Press. 1995. Reprinted by the kind permission of Judy Kravis.

BILLY COLLINS

"Introduction to Poetry"
(1996)

The poet Billy Collins (born in New York City in 1941) was a professor of English at Lehman College in the Bronx. In 2001 he was named the Poet Laureate of the United States.

I ask them to take a poem
and hold it up to the light
like a color slide

or press an ear against its hive.

I say drop a mouse into a poem
and watch him probe his way out,

or walk inside the poem's room
and feel the walls for a light switch.

I want them to waterski
across the surface of a poem
waving at the author's name on the shore.

But all they want to do
is tie the poem to a chair with rope
and torture a confession out of it.

They begin beating it with a hose
to find out what it really means.

SOURCE: Billy Collins. *The Apple that Astonished Paris*. Fayetteville, Arkansas: University of Arkansas Press. 1996.

GERRY ALBARELLI

"Questions"
(2000)

Albarelli teaches writing at Sarah Lawrence College. His memoir about his five years teaching in a yeshiva in Brooklyn, Teacha! Stories from a Yeshiva, *is full of marvelous, often humorous scenes depicting the difficulties and surprises of teaching. "Questions" is one of the fourteen stories.*

The morning rabbi is in a hurry to leave. He sees me at the door of the classroom we share. He's getting into his coat, fixing his big black hat like a black plate on his head. Boys are all around him, they try to detain him but he knows how to shake them off. He nods hello at me (this is a new thing, he used to just push past me). I want to ask him something but he says, "Must to go!" pointing a finger in the direction of his hat. "I'm late to catch a bus."

At the door, he looks back over his shoulder. "Any problems, leave me a note."

The problems begin right away.

I'm standing in front of the old faded and broken blackboard covered with Hebrew characters from the morning's Torah lesson. "Who wants to erase the blackboard?" I hand the eraser to the nearest volunteer. Joel Bierman is under the impression that he is my assistant. I didn't hand him the eraser and so he immediately takes offense. He always does whatever needs to be done, hands out tests, collects homework, washes the blackboard. He even has his own "assistant's" desk, pulled up like a wing attachment to my own. As long as I am lavishing attention on him, he's all right. The minute he is circulated back into the general population he becomes no end of trouble. Now he picks up a piece of chalk and starts to play tick-tack-toe on the blackboard right there where it was just cleaned. Another boy joins him.

"Joel Bierman, stop it."

He looks at me and draws a circle; the boy next to him draws an X.

243

"Give me the chalk."

"No!"

This goes on for ten minutes. I tell him he's not sitting in the assistant's chair today. I move him to a new seat, nearby, where I can keep an eye on him. He scribbles all over his neighbor's notebook. I change his seat again. This time he's sitting next to a fat boy. He shoves the fat boy off the bench. The boy is on the floor, crying. Joel Bierman is looking at the boy and then at me and shrugging as if it were the boy's own fault for being so fat.

"Maybe you want a new teacher." He shrugs. "Keep this up and you're going to a new teacher."

"Good!" he says.

"You want a new teacher?"

"Yes!"

"All right!" Then we are walking down the hall together toward the principal's office. This is the day I finally solve the problem, the ongoing problem of Joel Bierman. I deliver him to Rabbi Steiner. "He'll be better off somewhere else," I say, leaving him there.

He's back for his coat when the final bell rings. He runs in, enjoying his new celebrity as he relates his experiences in the new class to other boys. He waits in the doorway till I look over at him, and he shouts, "The new teacher is better than you!"

"Goodbye, Joel Bierman," I say.

He glares at me and leaves.

Two days later I'm teaching and the door to the classroom opens. A man stands there—probably my own age but with his tall hat and his long peyahs and his beard he looks much older to me. He is clutching what looks like a brocaded pillow. "Teacher," one of the boys says, "it's Joel Bierman's father."

The boys when they see him become quiet, sheepish almost, as though he were everyone's father.

The man bobs his head politely. "I can see you outside?"

Then we're out in the hall, standing under the broken clock. "The boy feels bad. He wants to come back to class. He's very sorry."

"Oh no, I don't see how he can come back," I say. "He needs too much attention."

"I know, I know. I'm having the same thing at home."

"But I have thirty-three students," I say.

"I have thirteen children," he says.

I say nothing. He smiles. "I know what the teacher is saying."

The door opens, a boy looks out at us.

"What is it?" I ask the boy who is peering out into the hall. He doesn't answer, goes back inside.

"I appreciate what you are saying," Mr. Bierman says. "But he was crying. I felt bad. I said I would talk to you." He shrugs and smiles.

"I would like to but—"

The door opens again. This time it's another boy.

"How about I make you a proposal?" Mr. Bierman says. "Teach him at the house."

"Oh, I don't think so."

"I'll pay you. What do you usually get?"

"I don't usually do it."

Then he's offering me a certain sum, two, three times a week. "It's a lot of money," he says.

"Really, it isn't—"

Then he offers a higher sum. "It's a lot of money," he says, though it isn't a lot of money. "But I must to. Why I do this, teacher? I want they should know the language of our country."

Rabbi Katz and Rabbi Steiner in their black caftans come around the corner in quiet conversation.

"Think it over," says Mr. Bierman.

"I'll think it over."

The two rabbis are watching us. Mr. Bierman says, "Oh, one thing: don't tell it for anyone. Not even for the rabbi."

A few days later, I'm in a cab headed to a housing project near the Brooklyn Navy Yard. The school day is over and it's already dark outside. Joel Bierman is waiting for me outside the entrance to one of the tall apartment buildings. He's standing with a few other boys, packing up snow into snowballs and throwing them at the passing cars. Three snowballs splatter against the side window of the cab just before I open the door.

Joel Bierman comes away from the other boys, takes my hand, slipping his fingers through mine, and leads me to the front door. He's smiling as if to say, Father has fixed everything. The teacher is coming to my house.

We stand in the lobby, waiting for the elevator. The door opens and we get on with about five Hasidim. They look at us curiously. Joel Bierman stands in front of me, looking over his shoulder every once in a while.

Then I follow him down the hall. A door opens. Mrs. Bierman
stands there in the doorway with a girl next to her and many children
in the living room behind her. She wears a scarf around her head.
"Good evening, Teacher Albarelli," she says, stepping aside. I follow
her in. She closes and locks the door behind me.

I follow her to a bedroom lined with bunk beds, a small table in
the center.

"It's okay?" she asks, motioning to my new classroom.

"It's fine."

The next night another boy joins the private class, Joseph, a third-
grader. I sit down the two boys at the table. They pull out brand new
composition notebooks.

Mrs. Bierman starts to close the door. "No fighting," she says.

The next week two more boys join the class.

Toward the end of the week there are six small boys sitting around
the table.

An older boy, thin, tall, pale, maybe fifteen years old, shows up
about half an hour into the lesson. He's wearing a tall black hat
and a gabardine. He stands and watches for a while. I don't realize
at first that he's there for the class till he sits down and takes out a
notebook.

"What's your name?" I say.

"Call me Mendy," he says.

"What would you like to learn, Mendy?" I ask.

"I want to know how things work. Bring me a book."

This is the unexpected solution to the problem of Joel Bierman.
Back at school, he has become less of a problem.

He is not supposed to tell anyone about the private classes, but I do
see him whispering to his friend Meyer Teitelbaum. I know what it
is he's saying from the way Meyer Teitelbaum's eyes fixed on me are
opening wide in surprise and from the way he, Joel Bierman, laughs
when I ask him what it's about.

At home, Joel Bierman is always breaking out into fits of laughter.
He laughs at everything. He laughs at his own mistakes. He laughs at
mine when I try to say something in Yiddish. "My arm have rind,"
he says. "Your arm has what?" "Rind! Rind!" pinching the skin
on his arm. "No, a lemon has rind, an orange has rind." He flings
himself back in his chair and laughs; he pitches forward, puts his
laughing head down on the table. He gets up and falls down on one
of the lower bunk beds, he's kicking his legs and laughing helplessly.

His older sister Sarah comes in to see what all the noise is about. "What?" she says.

He tries to tell her but he can't get the words out.

"You're miserable," she says, smiling a little.

Mrs. Bierman comes in, watches him for a while and says, "Isn't this one a character? Sometimes I wish he would cry, you know what I'm saying?" Soon I'm a regular fixture there: three nights a week, occasional Sunday afternoons.

I'm sitting in the bedroom with the four boys reading them a story from a book of Yiddish folks tales. The story of an evil Gentile who plots to kill all the Jews and dies himself in a snowstorm, devoured by wolves.

At the end of the story, the small boys clap.

"You like it?" says Mrs. Bierman, sticking her head inside.

"Sure, sure!" they say, wagging their fingers.

I'm there all through the winter, all through the renovation of the kitchen.

"Teacher, the kitchen is finished," Joel Bierman whispers to me at school one day.

"They want me to see the new kitchen," I say to Mrs. Bierman, motioning to the boys next to me when I walk in on her in the kitchen. Usually I go straight to the bedroom. The new kitchen, completed only yesterday, has a wrap-around bench like an ice-cream parlor, good for so many children.

"It's very nice," I say.

"You like it?" She shrugs. "Practical."

The little girl Leah is at the kitchen table, drawing. She gets up and shows her mother the picture.

The mother just nods.

I admire the drawing.

"She's taking art lessons," Mrs. Bierman says.

"Really? Where?"

She waves her hand dismissively, in Leah's direction and then, as if Leah weren't right there, she says: "It's nothing. As long as *she* thinks it's something."

My landlady, my Brooklyn landlady, is always asking me questions: "How come they wear those big hats? Why don't the men shave? How come they live in the projects? I thought they all had money."

Now that I'm here all the time, in his Hasidic bedroom with the books with Hebrew characters on the shelf in this room where the small boy Naftali comes in to have a look at me, touches my beardless face and laughs; where another boy pushes open the door and sets a plate of steaming cabbage down on the table, saying, "Mein mother says eat it," in this house where Hungarian and Yiddish and Russian (but no English) are spoken, I have a few questions of my own. Not like the landlady's questions. More basic:

What is the yeshiva? The school on a street of warehouses. This brick building with the snow swirling in front of it. Who are the rabbis on the steps? What is this European history doing in Brooklyn? What about the parents? What do they want? How about the older boy at home?

As soon as the lesson is over, Mendy stands up and puts on his coat. Even if he just took it off. Sometimes he's at shul and has to miss the class. He puts his coat on as soon as he sees I'm ready to leave. "Walking the teacher to the subway?" his mother always asks.

"You really don't have to," I always say. He doesn't answer, he just goes ahead and waits for me by the elevator.

I don't ever see Mr. Bierman at the house. He leaves me an envelope with cash once a week. I do run into him once, many months later, on the street. He's on his way down the steps from the elevated's. I'm just about to go up.

"Teacher," he says, smiling, recognizing me before I recognize him.

"How are you?" I say.

"How's things?"

"I'm just coming from your house."

"How's it going? How's the behavior?"

Then he asks about the older boy. "And Mendy?"

"Oh, Mendy's very smart, a very smart boy."

"Yes, I know. I worry for him," he says, adding, "I want he should have a good future."

Then there are the questions that Mendy asks, walking me to the subway, week after week. He asks these questions as though everything depended on the answers.

"How they know the weather?"

"What means geology?"

"Who was Con Edison?"

"Thomas," I say. "Thomas Edison."

"No," he insists, politely embarrassed by my ignorance. "Con. Con Edison."

We're standing across from the elevated train.

"Teacher," he says, one day, "why is it we know from the Torah that the earth is five thousand years old but the museum have bones that are a million years?"

"Oh. That's a good question," I say. "You should think about that question for a long time."

We stand there on Broadway, where the neighborhood changes (all the signs here are in Spanish: BOTANICA, LLAMADAS LARGAS DISTANCIAS, POLLO ASADO); where the Dominican barber is sweeping hair out into the street; where the trains keep coming in at regular intervals and pigeons burst out of the elevated supports at the approach of the oncoming train, like dark rags flung up against the gray afternoon sky.

SOURCE: Gerry Albarelli. *Teacha! Stories from a Yeshiva*. Thetford, Vermont: Glad Day Books. 2000. Reprinted here by the generous permission of the author.

JERVEY TERVALON

"A Novel Education"
(2000)

For five years, the novelist Jervey Tervalon (born in 1958 in Los Angeles) taught high school English in his old neighborhood; he recreated the lives of his students and some of his experiences as a teacher in his prize-winning novel Understand This. *He earned his master's degree at the University of California, Irvine. Tervalon now teaches at various southern California colleges.*

My days teaching at Locke High School are exhausting to remember. I wasn't cut out for the grind and humiliation. After five years I took the easy way out, retired my chalk and eraser and returned to college to pursue a master's in fine arts. Yet there are moments I recollect fondly, including the time a student named Shauntell slumped on the steps of a bungalow classroom, clutching a copy of a fat 19th-century novel and weeping.

"Tervalon," she said, "I don't know why you gave me that book to read. It just made me cry."

"That's good. That's what a tragedy is supposed to do."

"You're a sick man, Tervalon. Getting your kicks making your students cry."

I hadn't anticipated tears when I casually suggested to this shy, intelligent underachiever that she read Leo Tolstoy's *Anna Karenina*. I had said it was one of my favorite novels and that she might like it. But I often tossed off such comments. Shauntell was the rare student who took such a suggestion to heart. Now she had reached the book's conclusion—Anna's death under the wheels of a locomotive. Tolstoy had transported Shauntell from Los Angeles' cruel streets to the cruel salons and parlors of aristocratic Russia. An enormous journey in many ways; in others, not a long trip at all. Like Shauntell, I had a passion for reading (friends wouldn't loan me books because I read in the shower and returned the volumes waterlogged). Like Shauntell, I'm a product of California public education.

I attended Los Angeles' Foshay Junior High School in the early '70s. Franz Kafka's *The Penal Colony* will give you a sense of what it was like to be an 11-year-old boy in that harsh, incomprehensible world. Foshay's lawmen were gym teachers packing walkie-talkies and squash paddles for corporal punishment. They were soon outmatched by the new gangs sprouting in the surrounding neighborhoods. One summer they just appeared, wearing sporty bomber jackets with thick fur collars, shiny, starched Levi's and a black or red handkerchief. They sprang from the concrete, the lawns, the backyards and the schools. Some big head pootbutt with bad teeth and breath would get the "look"—slit-eyed, barely even a nod, trying damn hard to exude menace—and kids started converting, so many on that sullen, silly trip. You'd hear, "What, fool? This is Crip here," and the shooting would start.

Reading clued me to look at gang life differently than most kids did. In Bram Stoker's *Dracula*, I confronted the nature of evil. Not the simplistic evil of comic books but something seductive that had to be resisted. I saw the various gang sets as fascist wannabes, ruling the streets like sadistic police officers, willing to shoot or beat down anybody silly enough to oppose them. I couldn't drive a stake through the heart of gang violence, but it became clear that I needed courage to live the life I wanted.

Our schools, like our city blocks, were small, self-contained towns that gangs battled for as if they had natural resources or religious significance. Self-defense, preemptive strikes, the need to never be caught slipping became a way of life. Because adults were fighting different wars at home and abroad, teens owned the hallways and streets. Junior high felt like *Lord of the Flies* with sawed-off shotguns. I risked being robbed or chased on my way to the Baldwin Theater or my girlfriend's house. It seemed inevitable that sooner or later we all were going to meet some stupid, embarrassing fate like the disabled protagonist in *Johnny Got His Gun*, who dreams that he is fed upon by rats.

In my mind, the consolation prize for having suffered through this was the opportunity to attend the University of California system. I had a decent SAT score and grades, but most important, I had college-level reading comprehension. That prepared me for higher education, if not for being the rare person of color among the 700 students in my cultural anthropology class. The day my father drove me to U.C. Santa Barbara, fog hung over Storke Tower. The campus was as idyllic and mysterious as Middle Earth in *Lord of the Rings*. The students I met there were different than those back home. The guys seemed obsessed with keggers and bongs, and the girls' worries focused on weight and eating disorders.

One quarter, I took a class from the notorious scholar Marvin Mudrick. He had us read three of Shakespeare's plays each week. "Read them on the toilet, on the bus, read them like the sports page," he said. My boyhood passion found a focus.

SOURCE: *Los Angeles Times*. January 23, 2000. Copyright © Jervey Tervalon. Used by the kind permission of the author.

JEAN TROUNSTINE

from *Shakespeare behind Bars*: "Rose"
(2001)

Trounstine (born in 1946) teaches English at Middlesex Community College in Massachusetts. Her account of teaching drama at Framingham Women's Prison shows that through reading and acting, the women, like all students, are able to awaken their consciousness of their past and present. Trounstine describes below a class session that draws out an estranged student.

We're in the middle of watching Sir Laurence Olivier's film version of *The Merchant of Venice* when Rhonda taps me on the shoulder. "You always get the best for us," she whispers.

"Thanks," I whisper back.

"Even if we do have to watch this in two parts without popcorn," Kit adds.

I scoot my chair into the row behind Rose, who's sitting at a desk. Everyone else is in metal chairs. I note that Mamie is absent. Cody has sent word that she has a visit, which probably means she won't show up at all.

It's just after Valentine's Day, and Rose is making a card in the classroom while she watches the film. A pink heart filled with glue dollops sits on the desktop in front of her. She pastes the heart onto a black square that she's cut out of construction paper, and then, pulling a glitter pen out of her pocket, she carefully draws silver swirls all over it. She does this with her left hand but manages to use the crippled right one to help her hold the paper in place.

On the screen Olivier is decked out in an elegant suit and tie, meeting his adversaries for dinner to discuss Antonio's plight. He is agreeing to loan money and does it with a bow and a tip of his hat. Kit says, "I like this movie better than that lame first one. That Shylock seemed like a rotten person with a lot of money who would stop at nothing when crossed. This one's got class."

"*Shhh*," Bertie says. "Save it." She's moved her chair in between Dolly and Kit, and sits as close as she can to the screen.

Dolly leans across Bertie to tell Kit that she disagrees. She likes David Suchet's interpretation in the other *Merchant*. "He's a pushy guy with heart, simply headed in the wrong direction. My type of man. This one's too polite."

"You're wrong," Kit says.

"*Shhh!*" Bertie repeats. "I can't hear the Shakespeare." She pinches Dolly playfully on the cheek.

"Oww," Dolly says. "You're dangerous."

Rose looks up from her card and says, "Maybe Shylock can be interpreted in different ways." Gloria makes a sort of deprecating snort, as if she thinks Rose is full of herself.

"Good point," I say. "But Bertie's right. Let's talk about it later."

It's been difficult integrating Rose into the class, since she doesn't make jokes or take things lightly. I don't want to praise her too much or draw attention to her status as a newcomer. Unlike the others who've taken writing, literature, and play-reading classes, Rose has not gone through the college program, and although she's quite bright, she is still not comfortable with the group. In the semidarkness I watch her put the glitter pen back in her pocket and blow on her card. Silver scatters across the paper heart.

Everyone's quiet for a while, watching the film, and then, in the trial scene, after a broken Shylock has been told he must give up his wealth and convert to Christianity, Olivier exits the courtroom. At this moment it seems to all of us that Shylock might not be able to bear his fate. His daughter has abandoned him to a Christian; he's all alone in a Christian world. Then comes Olivier's famous scream, making us imagine he has thrown himself down the stairs or in some way taken his own life. Some of the women are pushed to tears. Bertie covers her ears at the piercing sound.

"I like old movies," Kit says as I turn on the lights. I suggest we just sit and talk for a while.

Bertie curls up next to Dolly. She puts her head on Dolly's shoulder and says she feels sympathy for Olivier's Shylock. "He's the outsider."

Rhonda's the first to head to the window to have a cigarette. She says, "Shylock's driven to revenge, obviously, because his daughter betrayed him." She takes a deep drag on her Newport. "That's why he has to get his pound of flesh. He's been disgraced."

"Maybe," says Dolly, "but he sure as hell doesn't have to try to kill someone for it, does he?"

"Right, Ma," Bertie says softly.

"I'm not sure he doesn't want to die," Dolly continues.

I ask the women to tell me why some of them teared up when Shylock seemed so broken in the last scene.

Dolly says, "It's simple. We believe that everyone deserves a second chance, even Shylock."

"Yeah," Rhonda says to Dolly, "but second chances aside, do you really think most cons in here would care about a Shylock? I mean, really." She takes another weary drag from her cigarette.

"He deserves justice too." Bertie echoes Dolly.

"Maybe, maybe not," Rose says. "But I know his pain."

Dolly crosses to the window and, with a friendly nudge, shoves Rhonda aside to light up. Dolly's been trying to quit ever since Recreation held a week-long smoke-out a few months ago, but she's been on her Camels tonight. "Remember last week," she says to Rose, "when we came to class late after the Code 99? No one knew what was up. Jean freaked—a buncha guards in yellow jumpsuits marching down the hallway with guns and helmets. We all thought someone had tried to kill herself in Max. I thought it was you, Rose."

"Nahh, she's too stubborn," says Kit. She winks at Rose, who doesn't respond. "But, hey, I don't know," Kit continues. "Coulda been any of us."

"Speak for yourself," Rhonda says, heading across the room. She sprawls out in her chair.

"I wasn't in Max," Rose tells Dolly. "I knew the girl, though. She was in my support group. They say she hung herself."

I look at Rose. I'm imagining belts, clothes tied together, guards on break paying little mind to the possibility of death.

Rose is looking at the floor, her face contorted. It bothers her that someone would think she tried to kill herself. "I've never been in Max or on any sort of Iso, for that matter," she says, and then she twists her hands together, looking around skittishly, "except for, you know, my own." The women are silent except for Kit, who coughs uncomfortably.

Suddenly Rose pulls out a script from under her seat and sits up, waving it at me. "Do you think Rhonda's right? Will anyone in here care about Shylock when we do this play?"

"I think they will," I say.

"But these two-bit bitches ain't gonna see no Laurence Olivier up on that stage," says Gloria. Mamie chuckles.

"Let's try something," I say, brushing Gloria's comments aside. "Ladies, are you game?" I am up, out of my seat.

"You are one wacko," Kit groans. "Nobody in here would expect anything of us after watching that movie."

"Rhonda, you and Gloria are on your way somewhere."

"To a party," Gloria says.

I point at her as though she's won a prize. "Okay, to a party."

Kit perks up a bit at the word "party" and sits up in her seat. I begin pushing the TV into the corner, making more space for an improv. "Bertie, you and Kit will make an entrance, chatting." Kit makes a face, all growl. I ignore her. "You all knew each other and aren't interested in people from other neighborhoods coming into your scene. I'll tell you when to enter."

Gloria shoves her chair into another corner and heads to the cleared space. Rhonda pulls Bertie to her feet. Dolly pesters Kit until she's up. By now the energy in the room has shifted.

I direct Rose to the doorway. "Rose, you make an entrance, and as the new kid in town, try to get to know people."

Rhonda and Gloria immediately begin horsing around, cutting up folks they know and others they create on the spot. They hold make-believe glasses of something in their hands, calling out to an imaginary bartender whom they place in the audience. It's clear that on their way to the party they've stopped at a bar.

Rose enters and crosses to where Rhonda and Gloria are toasting. She tells them she's heard that there's a late-night party after the bars close, and she asks where it is. Gloria and Rhonda are acting like they're getting a little tipsy, repeating phrases and slurring their words. They snub Rose. Rose tries again, but as she moves toward them, the two friends make their way around her to another side of the bar.

When I give them the cue, Bertie and Kit come through the door with a "Wazzup?" to Gloria and Rhonda, and the four of them make a mini-circle, shutting Rose out. Kit asks the imaginary bartender for refills. From the audience Dolly passes them drink after drink, having decided she's the bartender.

When Rose again asks about the party, they brush her off and drink up. Rose keeps trying to break in, moving behind one or another of the women, even using the tried and true "You dropped your wallet on the ground" routine.

Finally Rose throws up her hands and turns to the rest of us. "I can't do this. I can't. They won't even talk to me." She slumps into a chair by the table, still "onstage." I can feel her sinking. I know I am taking a risk, but I hand her a script and show her where to start reading. She looks at me, her eyes trying to find some reason to trust my direction. I motion the other women who've been in the improvisation to take seats in the audience.

"Go ahead," I say. "Give it a shot."

Rose begins to read, haltingly, "Hath not a Jew eyes? Hath not a Jew hands?" and she pauses. It is Shylock's famous monologue, in which he expresses his sense of being wronged by the Christian merchant and betrayed by his daughter.

Rose is so full of emotion that at first she seems afraid to throw herself into the scene. I ask her to look at her hands, and she does— first one, then the other—and finally, without my asking, she repeats the line, this time with feeling, "Hath not a Jew hands?" She says it louder, letting the word "hands" resonate inside her, letting her sense of injustice build as she goes on, "Organs, dimensions, senses, affections, passions?"

"I get it," she says, turning to me. "Shylock is really talking about how hurt he is, even though he sounds mad. I get it." Tears are in her eyes, but she's unflinching, almost excited. I ask her to finish the monologue.

She pours herself into Shakespeare's words—"fed with the same food, hurt with the same weapons, subject to the same diseases"— and she pauses—"healed by the same means, warmed and cooled by the same winter and summer as a Christian is?"

She stands, clutching her script, walking to the center of the cleared space, and gestures with her free hand, the crippled one, cutting through air. She's forceful now, crying out as though she is accusing us all. "If you prick us, do we not bleed? If you tickle us, do we not laugh? If you poison us, do we not die? And if you wrong us, shall we not revenge?" She walks over to her seat, lowering herself into it, and says softly, "The villainy you teach me I will execute, and it shall go hard but I will better the instruction."

Everyone is dumbstruck. Rose places the script on her lap and looks at me. Her eyes are watery, and the struggle gone from her voice. "Does it really hurt like this, for actors, onstage?"

"Some actors pretend," I answer, "but they're not good enough to play Shylock."

Rose nods, somewhat for my sake but more perhaps for her own, drinking in the idea that she can communicate something about herself through this character. She looks at me. "You know, Jean, I want a beard, a long one, white, like those pictures of God. And a scroll. Shylock has to have something to wave around."

SOURCE: *Shakespeare Behind Bars: The Power of Drama in a Women's Prison*. Ann Arbor: University of Michigan Press. 2004. (Originally published: New York: St. Martin's Press. 2001.)

TAYLOR MALI

from *What Learning Leaves*: Four Poems
(2002)

America's best political and social advocate for teachers is the intense and often funny slam-poet Taylor Mali (born in 1965): "What am I, really, but a propagandist who mollifies teachers into accepting the status quo? I sometimes feel that way when I am worn from the fight. But I always come back to the fact that being a teacher is one of the greatest jobs in the world, and sometimes the people who have chosen to walk that noble path simply need to be reminded that there is a vast army of educated and grateful citizens who have their backs. Someone needs to remind teachers that they are dearly loved. I'm that guy," he writes in his 2012 memoir, What Teachers Make: In Praise of the Greatest Job in the World. *A former teacher, his "What Teachers Make" (see the third selection below) is the most famous poem in English about teaching.*

What Learning Leaves

My children have all gone home
leaving me with nothing to do
but grade, plan, record, worry,
and call their parents.

Jenny's mother ends the conversation by telling me
that I seem like the only teacher who understands
that learning is fun,
that it should leave you feeling refreshed.

I look around my room and think,
in the parlance of the sixth grade, *no way!*
Learning is tiring, frustrating, often boring,
and as for feeling refreshed, their blood sugar levels
are so low by three o'clock that the only thing

259

my students have the energy to do
is beat each other up and scream.

Refreshed is not on the list of what learning leaves.
What is you ask?

Overturned desks and tipped over chairs
as if learning does damage before finally coming to rest.
Staples and mangled paper clips, no longer able
to hold anything together.
Pencils dulled by sleep or splintered by imagination,
some too short to sharpen, but still too long to throw away.

Pens! Hundreds of pens.
Most of them almost empty, chewed at the ends,
barely capable of writing.

Used Kleenex. Learning leaves wads of it
all around my classroom. Because learning produces snot.
It's what lubricates the educated mind.
Learning is messy and disgusting.

And let's not forget the paper.
Handouts and class notes from mine and other classes.
Unused sheets of lined paper,
gum wrappers and Pokemon cards,
hundreds of little three-hole punches,
the disgruntled homework in the trash can,
always the bad grades, the crumpled quiz that
failed by please, please, please . . .
just five, four, three . . . two points.
Learning grows as a tree, from a rustling pile of loose leaves.

This is the wake of my teaching:
this mess tells me I'm doing something right.
I can't get to sleep on Sunday night.
I'm wasted like the unused piece of paper in the trash can,
like the pen with chewed ends, almost incapable of writing.
And inside my mind there are overturned desks
and partly erased blackboards.

★ ★ ★

Please See Me

If all the year were playing holidays,
To sport would be as tedious as to work;
But when they seldom come, they wish'd for come,
And nothing pleaseth but rare accident.

—*Henry IV, Part 1*

And speaking of rare accidents, come in,
shuck off your book bag, please, pull up a chair.
Let me tell you why I didn't grade your paper.
See, you're either average or lazy, and you better know which
  one you are because I'm sick of hearing, "I didn't understand!
I don't know why," when the truth is, "I don't care, and I
  didn't even try."

I know you all.

You'd rather be suspected of being stupid,
because you know you're not,
than be accused of being lazy, because you know you are.
I don't think you're stupid,
but if you expected me to fall for that,
then maybe I am wrong.

Which is to say, this is not your best work.
I'm not asking you to write the paper over again
unless you deleted the file after printing it in which case,
I'm asking you to write the paper over again.

Look at the next lines:
When this loose behavior I throw off
And pay the debt I never promised,
By how much better than my word I am,
By so much shall I falsify men's hopes.

That's what you're doing, isn't it?
You're getting by at four so that when you turn up the volume
you can go all the way to eight and I'll be impressed.

But life goes to eleven, baby,
And then it keeps on going.
So tell me I ain't seen nothing yet.

Tell me you can do much better than this.
Falsify my hopes and shine.
Otherwise you'll always be what you are now:
dismissed.

What Teachers Make, or You Can Always Go to Law School If Things Don't Work Out

For every teacher who has ever made a difference

He says the problem with teachers is,
*What's a kid going to learn
from someone who decided his best option in life
was to become a teacher?*
He reminds the other dinner guests that it's true
what they say about teachers:
Those who can, do; those who can't, teach.

I decide to bite my tongue instead of his
and resist the temptation to remind the other dinner guests
that it's also true what they say about lawyers.

Because we're eating, after all, and this is polite company.

*I mean, you're a teacher, Taylor.
Be honest. What do you make?*

And I wish he hadn't done that
(asked me to be honest)
because, you see, I have a policy
about honesty and ass-kicking:
if you ask for it, I have to let you have it.

You want to know what I make?

I make kids work harder than they ever thought they could.
I can make a C+ feel like a Congressional medal of honor
and an A- feel like a slap in the face.
*How dare you waste my time with anything less
than your very best.*

I make kids sit through 40 minutes of study hall
in absolute silence. *No, you may not work in groups.
No, you may not ask a question.*

Why won't I let you get a drink of water?
Because you're not thirsty, you're bored, that's why.

I make parents tremble in fear when I call home:
Hi. This is Mr. Mali. I hope I haven't called at a bad time,
I just wanted to talk to you about something Billy said today.
Billy said, "Leave the kid alone. I still cry sometimes, don't you?"
And it was the noblest act of courage I have ever seen.

I make parents see their children for who they are
and what they can be.

You want to know what I make?

I make kids wonder,
I make them question.
I make them criticize.
I make them apologize and mean it.
I make them write, write, write.
And then I make them read.
I make them spell *definitely beautiful, definitely beautiful,*
definitely beautiful
over and over and over again until they will never misspell
either one of those words again.
I make them show all their work in math.
And hide it on their final drafts in English.
I make them understand that if you got *this* (brains)
then you follow *this* (heart) and if someone ever tries to
    judge you
by what you make, you give them *this* (the finger).

Let me break it down for you, so you know what I say is true:
I make a goddamn difference! What about you?

★ ★ ★

Undivided Attention

A grand piano wrapped in quilted pads by movers,
tied up with canvas straps—like classical music's
birthday gift to the insane—
is gently nudged without its legs
out an eighth-floor window on 62nd street.

It dangles in April air from the neck of the movers' crane,
Chopin-shiny black lacquer squares
and dirty white crisscross patterns hanging like the second-
    to-last
note of a concerto played on the edge of the seat,
the edge of tears, the edge of eight stories up going over, and
I'm trying to teach math in the building across the street.

Who can teach when there are such lessons to be learned?
All the greatest common factors are delivered by
long-necked cranes and flatbed trucks
or come through everything, even air.
Like snow.

See, snow falls for the first time every year, and every year
my students rush to the window
as if snow were more interesting than math,
which, of course, it is.

So please.
Let me teach like a Steinway,
spinning slowly in April air,
so almost-falling, so hinderingly
dangling from the neck of the movers' crane.
So on the edge of losing everything.

Let me teach like the first snow, falling.

SOURCE: Taylor Mali. *What Learning Leaves*, Newtown, Connecticut:
Hanover Press, Ltd. 2002.

ELIZABETH GOLD

from *Brief Intervals of Horrible Sanity*:
"Every Child Has a Voice"
(2003)

Elizabeth Gold is a poet and writer who successfully taught for many years in New York City colleges. When she took a job as a high school English teacher, she encountered many difficulties and frustrations with the students and administration; she analyzed her new situation with wit and humor in the liveliest, funniest book on teaching, Brief Intervals of Horrible Sanity: One Season in a Progressive School: *"They are marvelous, the voices of Cindy Fernandez. They rise and fall, they tremble with ardor and outrage, there is one soft as a baby's. She reminds me of my Communist labor organizer grandmother, long dead now, dead even when I knew her—the cause dead, done in by history, and only her voice, her gorgeous orator's voice, trembling not with the power of the events that were coming, that they, the workers of the world, would make come, but with the events that had passed. Yes, I see in Cindy that kind of power. That raw, that unfeminine, that . . . eloquent. The only difference is, my grandmother spoke up for justice, for the new world coming. And Cindy Fernandez, well. She speaks for Cindy Fernandez."*

Every child has a voice. That's what Leon [the principal] likes to say. Sometimes, as I walk through the halls, head pounding, it seems that every child has two voices, *four* voices. Burbling up in the classrooms. By the lockers. In the gym, especially the gym. The stairwells. In the principal's office. Outside the school, where Vincent stands, sophisticated in army jacket and blue eye shadow, smoking a cigarette.

There's the *I know the answer* voice. The *I don't care* voice. The *Fuck you* voice. The *Listen, could you help me?* voice. The *Could I trust you, could I tell you a secret?* voice. The *Please don't call my parents* voice. The *Fuck you, I don't care, call my parents* voice.

The *I'm going to beat the fucking shit out of you* voice.

265

The *Watch me lie to the principal* voice.

Every child has a voice.

But of course it's not true. It's no more true here than anywhere. Some students choose—or are chosen by—silence. They sit at their desks, as some tempest plays itself out, quietly drawing monsters or unicorns, or reading mysteries or wrestling magazines under the table. Or they do nothing. They sit and they sit, and there is not even a window to look out of. Where they retreat I do not know. Or if there is a voice inside them, whispering, *Wait, this will pass, wait, soon you'll be eighteen, and then twenty-one, and then . . . and then . . .*

I hope they are listening to a voice like that.

I suspect a lot of them are not.

No, not every child has a voice.

But Cindy Fernandez has twelve of them.

★ ★ ★

They are marvelous, the voices of Cindy Fernandez. They rise and fall, they tremble with ardor and outrage, there is one soft as a baby's. She reminds me of my Communist labor organizer grandmother, long dead now, dead even when I knew her—the cause dead, done in by history, and only her voice, her gorgeous orator's voice, trembling not with the power of the events that were coming, that they, the workers of the world, would make come, but with the events that had passed. Yes, I see in Cindy that kind of power. That raw, that unfeminine, that . . . *eloquent.* The only difference is, my grandmother spoke up for justice, for the new world coming. And Cindy Fernandez, well. She speaks for Cindy Fernandez.

She sits in the back of 9B, a big fat girl crammed into the tiny teen fashions of the day. A mass of nymphet ringlets tumble down her back, but with her plucked brows and matronly bosom, she is nothing like Lolita. She looks years older than the skinny little boys of ninth grade, some of them still staging duels to the death with plastic dinosaurs they smuggle into school. And of course, she *is* older. She is seventeen years old, a seventeen-year-old ninth grader. Not a stupid girl. Actually, rather a smart one. Yet her peers are almost graduating, and here she sits. And sits and sits and sits. Failing again. Extravagantly failing. Failing with verve and bravado. A mystery to me, because let's face it: ninth grade isn't that interesting the first time around. By the third it must be deadly. So why not try to leave? Tenth grade makes a bit of a change.

Cindy Fernandez. Maria Callas without the soprano. Emma Goldman without the politics. Mae West without the one-liners. A diva without a stage.

Until one day she finds it.

★ ★ ★

Three weeks into March, I have to give grades.

How can I give grades? Even as a kid I didn't care about grades. There was a little bit of the Adam Patel in me. It was *meaning* I cared about, even if I wasn't sure what meaning meant. I was the kind of kid who didn't cheat because to cheat would be to admit that one strove not for enlightenment but for arbitrary approval, and a pat on the head.

Okay, I was a dope. Too high-minded to live. And as is often the case with us high-minded ones, we get ourselves into scrapes that the more sordidly practical avoid.

But still. How can I give grades? I've been here a total of three weeks, which is not very long, but long enough, one would think, to do *something*, but for the life of me, what have we learned except that Britney Spears may—or may not—have acquired breast implants?

She did.

She didn't.

She did.

She didn't.

Oh come on! Nobody grows three sizes overnight!

She's just getting fat, that's all!

What do you think, Elizabeth?

What do I think?

Grades.

So, okay, I have to give them, but even Leon has realized the absurdity of the situation: one marking period, three teachers, one, at least, with a nervous breakdown. How can I accurately dole out grades?

"Just give the ones who are doing the work an S," he says. "Give the ones who are not, a U. Leave room for comments, then you're done. Can't do much more."

All right, this I can do. *Peter Garcia, S. Sarah Patel, S. Erica Reynolds, S. Alfonso, the brilliant, eccentric Alfonso . . . well, what do you expect?* U.

It unnerves me, writing down the grades. I try, a little bit, to give people points not simply for *doing* it, but for attempting to think, but it's not easy. The push to give reward merely for showing up is strong. If I don't, I've got an 80 percent failure rate on my hands, maybe more. But what do I do with those crumpled scraps handed to me? What are they evidence of? Learning disabilities? If they are—and how do I really know?—how am I supposed to evaluate them? And if not learning disabilities, what's the problem? Emotional disabilities? Grand Ennui? Or is it too much self-esteem, the idea that any old thing you do is wonderful, because so are you?

Are they simply missing Sharon, or April? The instability of the universe getting them down? That's Leon's theory.

Man, I don't know.

Go through the motions, I think. They don't care. Haven't I heard Alan and David and Randolph and Sammy cry out when I finally resorted to the dullest teacher trick in the book, the threat of failure, haven't I heard them say, *I don't care, I'll just go to summer school*?

Didn't seem like much of a solution to me, who wants to be in school in the middle of July? I don't, and I would get paid for it. But I guess if a kid is poor, if there is no camp to go to and he's too young to get a job, or if he simply suffers from lack of imagination, summer school relieves the mind from trying to figure out what happens next, it provides institutional comfort and torpor.

Robert, S. Ahmed, S. Ken, S. Silvia, U. Adam, S. David, Randolph, Sammy, Ricardo, Jose, Lucille, Cindy, U, U, U, U, U, U, U.

Do they really expect anything different?

★ ★ ★

In a few days, it will be Parent Teacher Night—a night I dread. The grades will be handed out then. But surprisingly, one morning, the kind of quiet that falls upon a classroom right before the grades are given out, a kind of exhausted anticipation, suddenly overcomes 9B.

"You know," announces Cindy, "no one in the ninth grade is going to get credit for English class."

She announces it so authoritatively that immediately almost everyone accepts it as true. Hell, *I* accept it as true.

And that means summer school, she says. *Everyone* is going to summer school.

At that second, she's done it. She's shaken the champagne bottle. She's worried out the cork, and now those voices the students have are spraying around the room. Everything they have hated about the School of the New Millennium, everything that, with all their complaints, they kept inside, it's out now. All the teachers coming and going, the chaos of things beginning, the promises made and not delivered, it's all out now, and there's so much fury in the class-room, that teachers start getting accused of crimes that are hardly crimes—Vivian, for instance, who had the temerity to get . . . preg-nant, yes, pregnant, how dare she, didn't she know she was going to need three months of emergency bed rest, shouldn't the school have made plans? Shouldn't they have known? Why should the students suffer for all the fumblings of adults, why should *they* all have to go to summer school?

Never have I seen the students so galvanized, candy and Walkmans and Britney Spears forgotten.

"We need to talk to the classes," says Cindy. "*I'll* talk to them. We've got to demand our rights. We'll make sure no one goes to summer school! No one!"

"Uh, Cindy," I start to say, "some people will go to summer school, no matter what . . ."

But Cindy pays no attention. "After all," she announces, "I'm seventeen, older than any of you, I've been here longer than any of you, I *know* what this place is like."

And now I'm thinking how ridiculous it is, that she should be sev-enteen and here. Raging against summer school when she shouldn't even be going to summer school at all. This girl has a brain, and no fat girl shyness, she is more than willing to shine. So why has she squandered her power?

I don't know. But I know people that do. I know that sometimes the only power you think you've got is the power to throw it away.

I don't care, I don't care, I don't care.

So, the students are busy organizing. I don't know exactly what they're doing, but now I am the one who doesn't care. Let them or-ganize. Get their complaints and confusions out of their systems. Let us begin again with mutual acceptance, and good will. Meanwhile, I'm puzzling over the riddle of Cindy Fernandez. All those years of failure.

Suddenly I make a decision: *I will save her.*

You see, she and I have something in common. Not only a certain self-destructive streak, a talent for resentment, but something else: Cindy is a poet. She belongs to the spoken-word-here-are-my-feelings-they've-never-been-felt-before teenage school of poetry.

Of course I have heard it before, but it doesn't matter. She's got some talent, and some feeling, she's got *something*, does Cindy Fernandez.

What would happen if I recognized that something?

Now I'm the one who's high on power: I will show her the world, I will remake her, I will save Cindy Fernandez.

Independent study, I think. She's old enough to be removed from the classroom, and surely it must be humiliating to be sitting here, the oldest student in the room. So we'll study poetry together. We'll read Dickinson, and Neruda, and Ahkmatova. Classics. Why not? She's got the brain for it, I know it. She'll write her own poems, of course she will, and attend a poetry reading, and give a poetry reading—a dramatic girl like her would blow any audience away—and together, on my own time, we will fight for Cindy Fernandez. I will give her the recognition I craved, but never got for myself.

That'll give her something more challenging than summer school to think about.

And then it is the end of class, and the students rise to their feet, and as Cindy Fernandez is leaving the room, I stop her, and tell her my plan.

"What do you think?" I say. "You could really do it. It would be a challenge, but you could really do it. You would like it. You could really *learn* something, you know? You really could."

Are there tears in her eyes? And is she crying because of my offer, or because of the exhaustion of being Cindy Fernandez?

"Okay," she says. Acting like she's doing *me* a favor.

But I've been seventeen. I know how difficult gratitude can be.

I massage the School of Millennium knot in the back of my neck. "Good. We'll talk about it tomorrow."

She smiles weakly and leaves the room.

But I am not alone. Peter Garcia is standing in a corner, watching me.

He has not participated in any of the uproar, though Peter Garcia does have a voice—two voices as a matter of fact. His *I love skateboarding* voice and the other voice he uses to get around his world and to define it. They are both voices I like, though the first I hear only while eavesdropping—it is the voice reserved for the other boys who love skateboarding, too. The second is the one he uses with me. That voice is honest and direct and clear. Peter Garcia never wheedles or rails. He doesn't know how. He doesn't want to. What he does is tell it like he sees it, and he sees a lot, does Peter Garcia.

"Hey," I say. "What's up?"

"I wrote something for you," he says. "I just want you to read it."

Some people are hypocrites, he has written. *They demand their rights, but they never want anybody else to have any.*

I feel hot, weak, embarrassed. I know who he's talking about. Have I made a miscalculation?

"Oh, *Peter,*" I say. "Maybe if she speaks she'll get it out of her system."

He shakes his head and sighs.

Oh, the stupidity of adults. The well-meaningness of their mistakes. What else can Peter Garcia do but practice patient forbearance?

For he knows a lot. I don't know how he picked it up or if it's just an innate something in him, but he knows. And in a little while, if I'm smart enough and pay enough attention, I might know a little bit, too.

SOURCE: Elizabeth Gold. *Brief Intervals of Horrible Sanity: One Season in a Progressive School.* New York: Jeremy P. Tarcher/Penguin. 2003.

JENNIFER NAUSS

The Long Answer
(2003)

Jennifer Nauss (born in 1968) earned her master's degree from Stanford University. She was teaching at Thurgood Marshall Academic High School in San Francisco when she wrote this poem. She teaches now in Washington, D.C.

Saturday night—
New faces from various places
mingle
The person to my right asks
        the commonplace question
        of the over-25 generation,
        "What do you do?"

I am an actress
        My critics tell me when I'm bad
        and I don't mean as in good
I direct plays
        Fate or free will? Star-crossed lovers meet their ends
on
          our stage
        I collect books and colored paper and old magazines
          filled with last season's styles
        The sign says, "Free! Take one!" and I take five
I am a gardener
        A slinger of worms, a creator of compost
        historian, social worker, environmentalist,
        janitor, secretary, athlete, activist
Sometimes I embrace democracy
Sometimes I embrace anarchy
Sometimes I reign in a monarchy where I rule as Queen

I seek answers in poetry, plays, short stories and novels
    from Conrad to Achebe
    from Mishima to Radnoti
    from Neruda to Allende to Szymborska
I have my own Top 100 list

I am a writer, a critic
My thumbs up or thumbs down determines futures
I must remember that

I love language
The new laughter it evokes when Pok
new to our country
greets the furnace man with a cry of
"Wazzup dude!"
The anger it releases when Vanessa
reads her poem on the anniversary of
her best friend's
suicide
I keep Band-Aids in my desk and
carry extra Kleenex to graduations and funerals—
I could go on but
because I suspect you want the short answer

I reply, "I am a public high-school teacher."

"Oh, that must be such a challenge."
And you walk off to get another beer.

SOURCE: *Bearing Witness: Poetry by Teachers about Teaching*. Edited by
Margaret Hatcher. Tucson: Zephyr Press. 2002. Reprinted here by
the kind permission of the author.

MARK SALZMAN

from *True Notebooks: A Writer's Year at Juvenile Hall:*
"Somebody"
(2003)

In spite of his initial reluctance and his lack of experience as a teacher, the novelist Mark Salzman (b. 1959) taught writing for a year to teenaged inmates in Los Angeles's Juvenile Hall. Fascinated by his students and they by him, Salzman described those tumultuous classes in one of the best, most consistently compelling books ever written on teaching.

Mr. Jenkins unlocked the bolt and pushed the steel-frame door to K/L unit open with his shoulder.

"Look who's back. Nice trip?"

"Very nice." I had just returned from my sister's wedding in Connecticut. "Did we lose anybody while I was gone?"

"Paulino's in the Box, but he'll be back."

"Hey Mark! Whassup?"

Three of the boys in my juvenile hall writing class were already in the library, their folders and notepads spread out on the table. Toa, a seventeen-year-old Samoan with a linebacker's build, stepped forward and gave me a hug. "So you bring us any maple syrup, or what?" he asked.

"Maple syrup?"

"I know 'bout that 'cause a watching *Mr. Rogers* when I was a kid."

Raashad's eyes opened wide. "You seen that show too?"

"Every kid seen that show, fool. Nothin' else to do in the mornin' 'cept break toys an' shit."

"Yeah, I was always like, where *that* neighborhood at? Nobody got drunk or beat his ass or nothin'."

"Yeah," Toa said, "but check it out: that show be *fake*. Know how I figured it out? People always be walkin' in and outta his door and he never locked it. He'd'a had all his shit jacked if it was real."

"Yeah! Homies be like, '*It's a beautiful day in the neighborhood*—now gimme that train set, fool.'"

"So how was your sister's wedding?" Antonio asked me as I handed out pencils.

"Beautiful. Perfect weather, too."

"Any fights break out?" Toa asked.

"At the wedding?"

"Nah, at the reception."

"No, no fights. Where are the rest of the guys?"

"The chapel. They got some kinda meditation retreat over there this morning. Could you gimme another pencil, Mark? This one ain't got no eraser."

Toa frowned. "'Cause you bit it off, fool. I just seen you."

"I didn't bite notin' off. It was already gone, I was just chewin' on the metal part."

"I went to that meditation thing once," Antonio said. "I went 'cause I heard the instructor was this hot female, but then I got there and it was some bald guy in a robe playin' a harmonica. Fuck that."

Raashad checked the eraser on his new pencil, then said, "Yeah, you suppos'ta close your eyes an' picture yourself goin' down some stairs into your workshop in the cellar where you got all yo' tools."

"Your tools?"

"Yeah, 'tools for life.'" Raashad rolled his eyes. "You suppos'ta choose what tools you need and put 'em on your belt, like you some kinda superhero. First of all, I say to myself: What nigga you know got a workshop? What nigga you know got a cellar? Right off I knew this shit ain't for me."

We joked around for a while, talked about a former class member who had just been sentenced to fifty years to life, then the boys settled down to write. After forty minutes, when they had all written something, I asked who would like to read aloud first.

"Let Carter start," Antonio said. Although I addressed them by their first names, the boys followed the example of the staff and referred to each other by last name only. "Carter got some good news last week."

Raashad nodded, propped his notepad on one knee, and read:

At about 2:33 a.m. the night staff came to my door and unlocked it. The sound of the key turning woke me up immediately, that sound always wakes me up alarmingly. The staff said, "Hey Carter, get up." I said, "Man what the hell." He said telephone. The first thing I thought was it was the police telling me someone in my family was dead. As I'm walking to the phone my heart was beating extremely hard like if you could see it beating through my shirt. When I picked up the phone I was relaxed by the sweet soothing sound of my companion and fiancée Amika telling me she just gave birth to a little girl. The feeling inside me was indescribable. It was amazing, she said she weighed in at 8 lbs 4 oz. I felt so happy my body felt so numb. I was astounded by the information I had just received. I feel so great. Ever since that day I've been happy and just waiting to see her. I heard her giggle on the phone, the feeling was great. I can't wait until the day when I can hold my daughter.

"Congratulations," I said.

He half-smiled. "I'm pretty excited about it. I just pray to God I win my case so I can get out soon."

Toa volunteered to read next, promising to take everyone's mind away from prison and back to the freedom of "the outs."

My family weddings are cool and all but my family can't get along. During the wedding it's cool and all but the party that's after it ain't nothin' nice. It's like warfare. As soon as they down a few cases everybody all of a sudden feels like Superman. For example my cuzzin's wedding was beautiful, everything's going smooth, even the party until my brothers showed up. Apparently my brother had shot one of the groom's cuzzins and he was paralyzed. And the best man was that fool's older brother. They weren't trippin' but my brother was. He banked the best man up on the dance floor in front of everybody. People was already drunk and shit so they start jumpin' in wanting to scrap too. My stupid ass cuzzin threw a chair in the crowd and it hit this old man. Everybody stopped right then and there because the old man was a priest. The priest's son started trippin' so we fucked that punk up in the parking lot. That's why I kinda hate family weddings.

As promised, the essay took Raashad's and Antonio's minds off their surroundings. They compared stories of family gatherings that had turned into brawls until we had only five minutes left for class, then Antonio read last.

I am lying in my room incarcerated at Central Juvenile Hall looking at the white painted walls in my room, and how my door is shut with a steel bolt lock to show that I am locked up. It's weird but this room relates to my life I once lived outside, over the walls laced with barbed wire. I was locked in a world where nothing would come in and noth-

ing would go out. I was trapped in my gang life, that's all I knew and all I wanted to know. I chose to stay in my room and not let anybody control me. I had too much pride to open my door and let somebody in. I neglected the people who really cared about me, my family and my loved ones. Sure, at the time it was all fun, but was the consequences really worth it? To me, no, but I was the steel bolt that kept myself from realizing that the world is a lot bigger than a room (my gang). There are a lot more things out there than your homies and homegirls. Don't get me wrong, I got love for them, but how are you going to be with people that are holding you back from blossoming and showing your full potential? I now realize how precious life really is. It's too bad that I am probably never going to be able to show the world what I have to offer. As I sit in my room thinking what would have happened if I would have opened my door and not just stayed in my room.

"This is why we get into so many fights around here," Raashad said. "You don't wanna be thinkin' shit like that, it's too depressing so you start somethin' with your roommate, and before you know it you both be poundin' on each other till you fall asleep. It's a distraction."

Mr. Jenkins tapped on the glass, letting us know it was time for the boys to return to the dayroom for lunch. Meanwhile, the inmates who had attended to the meditation retreat were just returning. They shuffled across the yard single file with their hands clasped behind their backs and most of their heads bowed forward. When everyone had come inside and the door to the unit was closed, one of the boys crossed the dayroom to say hello to me.

"How you doin', Mark? We missed you."

"I missed you, too, Santiago. It's good to be back."

"Sorry about not comin' to class today. I wanted to try meditation, see if it could make me relax."

"How was it?"

"It kinda sucked. The instructor was a guy."

"But you look happy," I said.

"I am happy! Something good happened to me today, Mark." Santiago grew serious for a moment. "I been feelin' really stressed 'cause I started trial last Friday. This morning the chaplain saw me and he asked me what was wrong. I said, 'I feel like a piece of shit stuck under somebody's shoe.' I told him how I had to hear the prosecutor say all this bad stuff about me in front of everybody. It was the worst day of my life. My whole family was there. I felt like I let everybody down. So the chaplain looks at me an' he puts his hand on my shoulder like this, an' he says, 'Diaz, you gotta remember something: *You are somebody.* Don't ever forget that.' So I thought about it, and I realized—damn, he's right! Nobody could take that away from me. I *am* somebody! I—"

"Diaz, get your ass over here so we can eat."

Santiago glared at the messenger and gave him the finger. The messenger pointed at Santiago and yanked his hand back and forth to simulate masturbation. The two boys exchanged threatening looks until honor had been restored, then Santiago turned his attention back to me.

"What were we . . . ?"

"The chaplain," I said.

"Oh yeah! I *am* somebody," he said once more, grinning this time. "Somebody awful!"

Mark Salzman. *True Notebooks: A Writer's Year at Juvenile Hall*. New York: Vintage. 2003.

This excerpt, Chapter 1, printed here by the generous permission of the author.

★ ★ ★

ELIZABETH STONE

"Acts of Revelation"
(2003)

Stone's beautiful memoir, A Boy I Once Knew: What a Teacher Learned from Her Student *(Algonquin Books, 2002), led her to reflect in an essay on the student she wrote about in that memoir, Vincent, and about writing students who share their secrets in personal essays: "Will you think me hopelessly naive if I tell you I had absolutely not expected to find this much pain in my students?" Stone, born in Brooklyn in 1946, is a professor of English, Communication and Media Studies at Fordham University in New York City.*

The first time I taught a course in personal journalism, I assigned op-ed pieces and, now and then, an autobiographical essay. Soon, I was reading piles of polemics in favor of lowering the drinking age, or improving cafeteria food, or ending all restrictions on opposite-sex over-night guests in the dorm.

The first personal essay to land in my pile was a laugh-out-loud piece by a young man who had recently survived Thanksgiving weekend with his girlfriend and her parents. They had taken his presence at their holiday table to mean that a potential son-in-law was in their midst. So while they talked turkey, my student gagged on his.

Then, I had an experience of my own that changed how I thought about my course. A long-ago student of mine named Vincent died of AIDS and, in his will, left me 10 years' worth of his diaries. I hadn't known that Vincent was ill, much less that I was one of his heirs. He'd been in a high-school English class I had taught 25 years earlier, while in graduate school. Vincent was bright, and we'd had a rapport, but, the next year, I became a TA, and, except for once, I never saw Vincent again.

During the decades that followed, we kept in touch with regular, if unrevealing, Christmas cards. All I knew was that this boy from

Brooklyn loved living in San Francisco, taking photographs, and traveling, but hated his job in insurance. Accompanying Vincent's diaries was a letter he had dictated from his death-bed but had not lived to sign. "Dear Elizabeth," it began, "You must be wondering why I left you my diaries in my will."

"I probably should just destroy them," he'd written, "but they contain my thoughts, feelings, and desires of my life for the last ten years." Vincent was dead, but he wanted the life he had lived remembered and affirmed.

Over the next year, I read Vincent's diaries, prompted by both curiosity and a sense of duty. As a diarist, Vincent was no Anne Frank, and he had lived neither wisely nor well, but, by the time I finished, I knew that he had made sense of his life and had arrived at some sort of peace with himself.

I spent the next several years writing about that posthumously developed student-teacher relationship because, to the end, especially in Vincent's dreams, I had remained his teacher. What I was learning from writing—about myself as well as about Vincent—informed how I taught a literature course in American memoir and autobiography. I came to believe the current literary theories about autobiography that I had been teaching my students—that telling our stories may change us, that utterance can mean mastery, and that experience is as much about personal coherence as about truth.

Meanwhile, I began to make assignments in my journalism class more personal. I set a few ground rules: Don't write about anything you don't want to write about, and don't write more personally than you're comfortable with. Only write about experiences you are willing to be asked about in detail and to explore thoroughly as writing. Maintain confidentiality, and so will I (which is why I've changed the names and identifying details in this essay).

"I'm not a therapist and this is not therapy," I cautioned, "and if I feel you're venturing into territory that seems emotionally risky for you, I'll encourage you to go to the counseling center."

Really, though, I wasn't expecting much in the way of risky disclosure. I knew most of the students in my class, either because they worked on the campus paper I advised or because they had taken other writing courses with me. They were fresh-faced, upbeat, and successful—campus journalists with good GPA's and prestigious media internships. So off we sailed into the semester. Right away, there were some wonderfully deft pieces—an antic essay by a young woman with a flock of brothers, all working in the family restaurant; a contemplative reflection by a young man, newly in love, driving home through the quiet night, thinking of his girlfriend and her emerald eyes. An otherwise talented writer named Pete turned in a perfectly awful piece, about how, if a guy wanted to score with a girl, he should put designer towels with satin edging in his bathroom.

During those first weeks, we experimented with various approaches to sharing and revising work, finding small groups were best. Soon, the groups took on distinct identities, as one member's piece inspired another. Charlie wrote about his little sister's long decline from cancer to death, when he was 11, and his own eventual depression, suicide attempt, and hospitalization. That prompted Julian to write about his own brother's death from an aneurysm. In another group, Jane wrote about her father's heroin addiction and how she, her sister, and her mother finally packed up and left. That impelled Iris to write about her parents' acrimonious divorce and how, for a while, she relieved her tension by nicking her arm with a razor blade and drawing blood. Other secrets emerged as well.

About two months into the course, Pete of the Fabulous Towels wrote about how his best friend, Jack, had killed himself during their junior year of high school. Jack was gay, and, the day before his death, he'd had a sexual encounter with a "straight" jock whom he idolized. Then the jock cruelly had turned on him and taunted him. In tears, Jack called Pete to tell him he'd swallowed pills. By the time Pete got to Jack's house, the boy was beyond saving, and his distraught parents didn't know what to think because there was no note. They hadn't known their son was gay, and Pete wasn't about to tell them. Now, in class, Pete acknowledged that he was gay, too, but his parents didn't know, so he hadn't been able to tell anyone about Jack's desperate phone call. Pete had kept his corrosive secret to himself.

Will you think me hopelessly naive if I tell you I had absolutely not expected to find this much pain in my students? Now and then, a student would come to my office, close the door, and fall apart. I knew the big picture, too—studies of rising rates of anxiety, depression, binge drinking, eating disorders, counseling needs, and psychiatric-medication use in college students. I knew those students existed, and I knew some of them attended my college. I just didn't think they were my students. There was no place for disclosures to come up naturally. And my students functioned at such high levels.

Despite the more than occasional somberness of the subject matter, the class tone was decidedly upbeat. The students became close,
their engagement with one another's writing was genuine, and their
writing grew in depth and texture. Meanwhile, I continued to impose structure—this week, how to use figurative language; next
week, flashback; the week after, dialogue.

Then, last spring, my department expanded the number of undergraduate creative-writing courses and started a creative-writing
track on the graduate level. Such alterations are part of a national
trend. According to the Web page of the Association of Writers and
Writing Programs, nearly 300 colleges offer undergraduate programs
in creative writing, up tenfold since 1975. Attending the recent annual meeting of the association, I overheard two women ahead of
me on the escalator talking.

"Remember when this was a small, intimate conference?" said
one.

"Yes," agreed her colleague wistfully. "I can't believe how many
people are here."

I began to put the pieces together. The rise in students' desire to
major or minor in creative writing seems in direct proportion to the
rise in reports about their emotional malaise. Not even for a moment do I think that means the most distressed students are drawn to
creative writing. But I do think that, for all our increasing protections
of student privacy, and the decline in colleges' responsibility to act
in loco parentis, our students want more than ever to be known by
us, their teachers.

Perhaps they want that even more because so much gnaws at
them—the pressure these days to complete a double major, the dim
and grim job market, the aftermath of the attack on the World Trade
Center. As adjuncts continue to replace full-time teachers and as
large cost-effective lecture classes increase, the chances of our students being known by us diminishes.

By now, some of you probably have grumpy phrases running
through your minds—maybe "navel gazing"? Or "self-indulgence"?
Or "therapy-nation"?

Those don't fit what happened with my own students (though
who among us hasn't had an irrepressible exhibitionist or two?), and
it isn't what my fellow writing teachers were suggesting in their off-
the-record grousing. Writing is not the act of a victim. Rather, the
writer works to make sense of experience (including victimization),

to master it if necessary, to triumph over it if possible, and to find a reader who will recognize it and understand it.

That's what I think Vincent was doing in the diaries he had flung into the waves like a message in a bottle from the desert island of his hospital bed. As for my class, Pete began what we came to call his "Chester series," an account of his first heady experience of falling in love. Each week my students would arrive at class like happy children at bedtime, waiting for the newest installment of his story.

SOURCE: *The Chronicle of Higher Education*. October 24, 2003. Reprinted here by the kind permission of the author.

DAN BROWN

"September: The Disharmony," from *The Great Expectations School: A Rookie Year in the New Blackboard Jungle*
(2007)

*After earning a B.A. in Film at New York University, Dan Brown (born in
1981 in Philadelphia) became a Teaching Fellow and taught fourth grade at
P.S. 85 in the Bronx from 2003 to 2004. He was twenty-two. He candidly
describes his first week's experiences in this episode from his memoir. He now
teaches at a public charter school in Washington, D.C.; he became a National
Board Certified teacher in 2011.*

On September 8, I woke up at 5:05, methodically showered and
dressed, purchased a bagel at the corner bodega, and boarded the F
train. I strode through the Great Expectations School entrance with
a quickened step, distributing good mornings to everyone I saw.

I had already prepared my chalkboard the previous Friday with
the heading:

September 8, 2003
Mr. Brown
4-217
<u>TEAM</u>

I knew that establishing the "team" classroom culture had to happen right off the bat. I needed to be firmest when I was the least
experienced, the paradoxical curse of new teachers. I hoped my
"make our own class rules" activity was the right kind of opener.

At 7:58, I descended the stairs to the basement level where the
students waited in the cafeteria. Each step down brought me closer
to the nether din of high-pitched children sounds. I cracked an excited smile, stunned that my weeks of training and years of youthful
experience had steered me to this unequivocally grown-up post. For
twenty-two years I had been on one path and twenty-five Bronx
children had been on another. Now we would meet. I needed no

284

more convoluted symbols like the blackout to interpret. The real moment was upon me.

"Don't smile!" Ms. Slocumb, a second-year Fellow, whispered forcefully. "Seriously, no smiling!"

Holding a pen and clipboard purely as props, I entered the lunch-room to meet the students. I took in the SpongeBob SquarePants bookbags, the girls' elaborate hair settings, jeans with winding embroidered flowers by the cuff, and the boys' Allen Iverson jerseys. Kids. They looked adorable, eager-eyed for the uncertainty-fueled first day of school. I circled the table, shaking each child's hand and introducing myself.

For the first of 183 times, we performed the morning lineup ritual: Mr. Randazzo raised his arm, the signal for silence. All responded by raising their arms in acknowledgment. Randazzo gave a perfunctory welcome speech, and the kids fell swiftly into two lines, separated by gender and ordered by height. He came around to give each class a rubric score of one to four depending on the degree of silence and neatness of the line. I marveled at the grand organization.

Line leaders Hamisi and Sonandia (two with encouraging blue cards), led the crew, halting every two doors in the corridor and every landing on the stairwell to look for the "go ahead" or "wait up" hand signal from me at the back. Meanwhile, I cased my problem-reputation kids. Imposing Lakiya Ray was the tallest in the class, a sour, tough-faced girl with tight braids. Eric Ruiz, whose previous teacher told me he was a "weird kid," was unreadable at first. Deloris Barlow, a skinny, pigtailed girl, was laughing a lot at the table before lineup but calmed down appropriately. Fausto Mason immediately tipped me off for trouble. Short and puffy-cheeked, he grinned and swaggered with a loose strut.

During summer training, I studied cases that made a convincing argument that students' achievement levels vary directly with their teacher's expectations of them, regardless of neighborhood or family background. I was determined from the first day to maintain high expectations for all my students, according everybody the blank slate I felt we all needed, even infamous Fausto Mason. After all, he had never had a male teacher and he had never had me.

I assigned the students to desks according to my carefully devised seating chart. Guided by the blue cards, I tried to arrange only one or two loose cannons per group. (City policy mandated that students sit in groups.) My class roster was also evenly divided between boys and girls and African Americans and Latin Americans, so I went for heterogeneous clusters.

After deflecting questions about my age, family size, and marital status, I launched into an even-tempered sermon about how 4-217 would succeed or fail as a group. "On the Yankees, either everyone wins or no one wins. If Derek Jeter has a great hitting game but doesn't back up his pitcher at shortstop, the team suffers. The Yankees are a strong team because they back each other up. They win because they work together. We need to help each other out for us all to do well. All I want to do is help you get smarter and have fun while it's happening. I'm very interested in trips, rewards, and games, but only if we work together. Does this sound fair?"

"Yes, Mr. Brown," the choral response resounded. The speech felt firm, and the kids sat silently with their eyes on me for every word.

"Excellent! Since we're a team, I thought it would be fair if we all made our class rules *together*. Who has an idea for a good rule for our team?"

Myriad hands shot up. I called on Cwasey, a shrimpy, bespectacled black boy with squinty eyes and a freshly shaved head.

"You should respect everyone. Like teachers and students and the principal."

"*Outstanding, Cwasey*! Brilliant! Respect for teachers and students and the principal. An outstanding first rule." I jotted it on the board. "What exactly is 'respect,' Cwasey?"

"Respect means you should treat everybody good, like you want to be treated."

I had a star. Cwasey Bartrum!

I called next on Sonandia, my line leader. "You should do all your work the best you can all the time."

Deloris said, "Nobody should steal nobody's stuff and treat everything like it's important."

Bernard piped up. "You should not fight in school cause there's better ways to . . . like . . . solve your problems."

"You should respect everyone," Dennis reiterated.

Lakiya prompted several giggles when she shouted in her bassy tone, "Do your homework!"

I ignored the chuckles because she had hit one of the key points. This wasn't going to be so lawless after all. These children were moral authorities! I consolidated their input into two broad rules regarding respect, effort, and honesty (rules I had of course planned from the beginning) and moved them to the "reading rug," a giant panther design I had bought on the Grand Concourse.

For the two weeks before the Success for All schedule began (when students would change rooms for their skill-level groups), teachers followed an introductory curriculum called *Getting Along Together.* For the first lesson, I had to read *Crow Boy,* an Eastern fairy tale about an outcast child who finds self-reliance. Introducing the story, I wrote the word "unique" on my chart paper, which Sonandia, my wordsmith, defined as "one of a kind." I told them we all have secret talents that we ourselves might not even know about yet. "Some of you on the carpet right now might be brilliant comic strip artists, creative writers, question-askers, room-organizers, or things we haven't even thought of. This year we will work together to discover those hidden gifts."

Two pages into my *Crow Boy* read-aloud, Fausto stood up and ambled leisurely toward the door, drawing the attention of the whole class. "Fausto. Fausto. *Fausto*!" I shouted. Fausto turned back toward the class.

"THAT STORY'S WACK, YO!"

I kept a straight face, but a majority of the class erupted in crazed laughter at Fausto's apparently genius comedic line. Fausto beamed while fifteen kids cracked up, Lakiya the loudest of all. She bellowed a forced, open-mouthed cackle, swaying violently in her seated position, knocking into classmates.

Ten seconds ago, we were all on the same page. Now it looked like a different class.

As the overwrought giggles receded, Fausto, now a superstar, still had not returned to his seat. I had to take this kid down. In deadpan, I said, "The story's not wack. Are you ready to stop acting like a kinder—"

"DAAAAAA! Mr. Brown talkin' gangsta, yo!"

"Mr. Brown said 'wack'!"

Destiny, Athena, Sonandia, and three others whose names I had not yet memorized sat patiently waiting for the story to continue. Everyone else was going bonkers.

"He say 'the story not wack'!"

Beads of sweat formed all over me. I looked at the clock: 8:43. Three hours and forty-seven minutes until lunch.

"Silence. Silence. Fausto! Sit!" I yelled at him as I would a wayward mutt.

Deloris piped up with a grin, "Mr. Brown, you turning red."

Bernard jumped in on my behalf. "Be quiet, yo! Let Mr. Brown read *Crow Boy*!"

Lakiya, still grinning, echoed Bernard's plea. "Shut up! Shut up y'all!" Suddenly, Fausto's face changed and he sat.

I had set myself against allowing "shut up" into the 4-217 vernacular, but my temperature was skyrocketing and at that moment I could handle the kids shutting each other up if it worked. And did Lakiya, a famous attitude-problem child, hold sway over other kids' behavior?

I battled through reading and discussing *Crow Boy*, often stopping mid-page because of rude laughter. One time, Fausto slapped Destiny on the shoulder, a minuscule harbinger of the intergender aggression to come.

When I sent them back to their groups to write a story retell, or regurgitation of the plot, I felt like I had scaled a mountain in simply getting through the short book. Sonandia and several of her pals seemed to enjoy the story. In fifteen minutes, though, I was back to the beginning of another new lesson and new fight. I calculated that I would teach at least seven hundred lessons this year; they could not all be like this stop-and-start scrape job.

Our opening math lesson regarding bar graphs yielded slightly better results. I made a model graph, polling the kids and charting their favorite TV shows in a data table and spelling out my procedure on the board. They copied everything in their math notebooks or blank loose-leaf sheets I provided.

P.S. 85 draws its students from one of the poorest neighborhoods in the Bronx, but almost all of the kids had cable television to watch their favorite shows: *That's So Raven, SpongeBob Squarepants, Kim Possible*. I soon learned that most of my students also owned state-of-the-art video-game systems. One teacher explained, "It's an investment in a twenty-four-hour babysitter."

Fausto got out of his seat eleven times during the twenty-minute math lesson. I tried to keep him at bay by calling on him when his hand was not raised. To my surprise, he had the correct answer every time.

After the kids answered the worksheet questions from the *Math Trailblazers* textbook and we had discussed them (although only ten of the twenty-one present completed the work), it was time for the Baseline Writing Sample. This would be a "before" example to compare with June work. The prompt was, "What would make a good teacher for me?"

Despite my coaxing, Lakiya, Deloris, and "weird" Eric again wrote nothing. Maimouna, my prolific student whose blue card warned about her tendency to "get lost by writing pages and pages," dutifully filled four pieces of loose-leaf with neon-purple ink.

One more lesson to go before the now direly needed lunch respite. Using a template devised during my summer training at Mercy College, I had created a "biography/autobiography" unit as an introductory meet-each-other literacy endeavor. For a model, I had a great kid-friendly biography of Martin Luther King, Jr. I decided on the spot that rather than read the whole book (an invitation for disruption), we would crawl one page at a time, charting the important elements of a biography.

PAGE 1: Birth date and place. Family background.
PAGE 2: Life before age 5.
PAGE 3: Life in elementary school. Friends, interests.
PAGE 4: An important experience or adventure as a young person. This may be a hint for something important the person does as an adult!

I stopped in the middle because after four and a half hours in the room together, we had made it to lunchtime. The kids jumped and pushed en route to the cafeteria. The mood was frantic and hungry and bore no resemblance to the beginning of the morning.

A phenomenon that lives only in our military, prisons, and elementary schools is the crucially serious transit *line*. I hated walking in line as a kid. I thought that if I could show I trusted my students to walk calmly and decently together, they would respect my trust and respect each other. Trust begets good teamwork.

When I reflected on the first hour of my first day, I realized everything I had done in that brief honeymoon period would come back to haunt me. My "team" spiel and my desire to offer everyone an evenhanded shake and social contract of respect were disasters of nuclear proportions. With my good-faith gesture, I had put myself in a position to be defied by one charismatic rebel, which of course happened immediately, opening the floodgates. Before I had won the respect and command of the class, I had allowed myself to be drawn into a graceless power struggle with the attention-seeking subverter. *From the Floor to the Moon* felt miles away.

Counter to my hopes, my lack of stern watchfulness during the first lineup enabled them to loudly screw off during future hall-walking time, since I had sent an initial impression that I was not fatally serious about our line. This resulted in a constant public fracas of shouting and shepherding the noncompliers during those formative first weeks. The disorder in the hall spilled wildly into the classroom, turning each morning, each return from lunch, gym, and computers, and each dismissal into an unwieldy and dangerous mess. I had been *too nice.*

The first day finished with forty minutes of doling out jobs—sweeper, dustpan holder, boys' line leader, girls' line leader, botanist, three librarians, two popularly demanded assistant librarians—and cleaning the floor, which had somehow become a cyclone scene of shredded papers, tissues, and pencil shavings. I handed out an exuberant welcome letter and supply list to parents that I had revised endlessly over the previous week.

I dismissed the kids out onto the subbasement-level blacktop as a gallery of legal guardians watched and waited behind the chain-link fence above. Seeing the adults waiting for us, my mood changed on a dime. I suddenly felt proud to be a leader in this procession of children, the first nip of excitement since my stairwell descent before the day even started.

The kids scattered immediately, and I headed back into school for the weekly eighty-minute Professional Development session. As soon as I hit the steps, I felt a shot of dull fatigue in my knees, as if they were about to give out. My heart throbbed and I felt a steely pounding in my wrists and forearms.

Barbara Chatton, my in-school mentor, advised me, "It's never as good as you think it is, and it's never as bad as you think it is. The day's over. Think of it as one door closing and another door opening."

That night I recounted the fiasco to everyone I knew. My roommate, Greg, and my neighbor Kadi wanted to rip Fausto apart. Their rage was contagious, and I started to feel worse. I called Jess.

I had only known Jess for nine days, but they were memorable ones. We had met while cavorting like fiends to Billy Idol's "Dancing with Myself "at a mutual friend's rooftop party in Brooklyn and had been more or less inseparable since. Meshing the stomach-tickling excitement of new romance with the annual end-of-summer dash for kicks, my feelings about Jess had quickly planted her very near to the center of my universe.

During the school day I thought I radiated failure, but Jess told me it's impossible to juggle so many flaming bowling pins of responsibility at once. I psyched myself up that this was a battle that I had asked for, and one that I was going to win. Now I knew their faces.

★ ★ ★

I decided two things. First, the kids would be disinclined to act out if there was a consistent reward system in place. This was something I had underestimated and thus had not implemented immediately on day one. Second, pleading with the collective for silence was exhausting and ineffective. I needed signals that could work efficiently and save my voice.

I made a "TEAM EFFORT" poster and divided it into halves for stars and strikes. If I counted to three, my newly hatched silent signal, and the room was still noisy, strike city! If they achieved quiet, star stickers all around. When the class accrued forty more stars than strikes (circa Halloween, I planned), we would have a 4-217 party.

I did not feel like smiling on my way downstairs for the second day.

Outside the 4-217 door, I sternly announced our new system to the line, translating their blank, tired looks as understanding. In the middle of my speech, a secretary tapped me on the shoulder and handed me three orange paper strips from the office, meaning I should expect three new students to arrive in my room in the next sixty seconds. Jennifer Taylor, Joseph Castanon, and Evley Castro dutifully appeared. Tall, mature-looking Jennifer shook my hand and said, "Nice to meet you, Mr. Brown." Evley had a sensitive face and shyly stared at his sneakers when I shook his limp hand. Joseph had a bowl haircut and an empty look in his eyes.

When chatter materialized during our bar graph lesson activity, I shook my head with slow intensity and boomed, "One . . . two . . . *I still hear talking* . . . THREE! That's a strike!" I felt like a jerk.

The kids reacted with spasms of disappointment, as if their final lotto number had failed to come up. They called out names of the offenders with twangy irritation. "Ber-NARD!" "Cwa-SEY!" "De-LOR-is!"

We had five strikes and one star when I realized I needed to doctor this whole operation. I started giving out spontaneous stars for strong individual efforts until we got the board even. Once the class received several stars, the kids started to like it.

Teachers are supposed to keep anecdotal records of misbehavior for documentation's sake. Mine quickly piled up.

SEPTEMBER 9

10:00 during *Simon Says,* Fausto punched Hamisi and Hamisi cried but did not fight back. Fausto did not apologize.

10:45 Lakiya will not stop talking no matter what! She makes mocking gibberish sounds when Deloris speaks.

11:30 Destiny says Joseph and Fausto told her they were going to beat her up at recess.

2:00 Unprovoked, Lakiya tells Tiffany, "I'm going to follow you home." Tiffany is terrified.

2:10 Randazzo tells the class "Mr. Brown is nice and you're taking advantage." I don't like that he says that.

SEPTEMBER 10

10:20 Destiny hyperventilating and can't stop. I send her to get water.

11:00 Had to scream at class. Lakiya completely rude and indignant. Laughing and yelling, "Preach!" Randazzo comes in, hearing the shouting, and lectures them. They're silent for him.

LUNCH (I'm not there) Fausto chokes Eric till Eric throws up. Gets in big trouble with Mr. Daly. Daly calls home and Fausto sobs. He says he will get beaten.

1:15 I have long conversation with crying Fausto about being a leader while I eat my lunch. Good man-to-man. He says he will step off confrontations. I believe him.

2:10 Fausto causes disruption in gym class immediately upon returning to group. Entire class game has to stop and wait.

2:35 Fausto pushes Destiny, she cries. *Lakiya* helps Destiny, very surprising.

2:45 Fausto picks up and drops Verdad in an awkward body slam. Verdad cries and becomes unresponsive.

I called all fifteen parent contact numbers I had. To the six I reached, I rambled praises and yammered about how I wanted us all to be working together. I encouraged the parents to read with their kids and to keep an eye on the nightly homework. I told Lakiya's mom about how Lakiya helped Destiny Rivera when Destiny was hurt and neglected to mention Lakiya's rampant disrespect during lessons. I wanted to win the parents onto my team now in the event that I would have to bring down the disciplinary hammer later.

Except for a few brief encounters in the parking lot at dismissal, this was my first contact with parents in the Bronx. As an outsider, my vague notion, fostered by Mercy College summer seminars, was that adults in the Bronx were either overworked, undereducated (hailing from P.S. 85 and the like), estranged from a spouse, tangled up with drugs, burnt out, or a combination of several. I did not know what to expect.

My initial impressions were that the parents wanted to hear what I had to say. Cwasey's mom volunteered to be a room parent on class trips. Lakiya's mother told me, "I appreciate your call." Tiffany's dad said, "I know Tiffany can get distracted, but she does good work when she's focused."

My two first-generation American kids from African families, Hamisi Umar and Maimouna Lugaru, had parents who spoke very little English. I knew Julissa and blue-cardless Gladys Ferraro's caretakers only spoke Spanish. I thought about ways to communicate with them. Then I passed out.

The following day was the anniversary of September 11, 2001. Some classes held discussion forums and responded to writing prompts about 9/11. Other teachers avoided the issue altogether because of the students' immaturity. Since many of my kids could not tell me their addresses, I opted against spending a chunk of class time on the tragedy. The self-censoring and expectation-lowering had begun.

At 8:30, Mrs. Boyd came on the loudspeaker and gave a speech about memorializing this day in history. Boyd got on the PA two or three times a day in September, taking her time on the microphone, incurring many frowns from momentum-losing teachers and spiteful comments from bored students. Instead of, "Mr. Randazzo, please call the office," we would hear, "I beg your pardon, teachers and students, and I apologize for this announcement in the midst of your literacy block, which I'm sure is making brilliant readers and writers out of you all [pause for guffaw], but Mr. Randazzo, would you please find a way to contact me, Mrs. Boyd, in the principal's office at your absolute soonest convenience. Once again, Mr. R., please contact the principal. Thank you and please return to your academic rigor and accountable talk."

Mrs. Boyd's 9/11 memorial message culminated with a prolonged moment of silence. I scanned the room, foreboding trouble in the pregnant quiet, but I was not ready for what happened next.

"SEPTEMBER 11TH IS WACK!"

Fausto leapt on top of the group three desks and jumped up and down, screaming incoherently. "FUCK SEPTEMBER 11TH!" he managed as I got my hands on him.

I grabbed him by the arms and yanked him down into a bear hug, blocking his path from any kind of crazed belly flop. Anything was possible. My face burned.

"I DON'T CARE, YO! GET THE FUCK OFF ME! SEPTEMBER 11TH IS BOOTLEG!"

I led him by the arm to Randazzo's office, telling Mr. R., "This one needs a time out." My physicality with Fausto surprised me, but the class cheered when I dragged him away.

With my biggest headache out of the room, I got reenergized to teach, as if I was on a hockey power play. My hopes got thrown in the gutter, though, when in the middle of our biography lesson, Eric suddenly lunged at Lakiya's face, awkwardly missing, and the two fell on the floor, wrestling viciously. I ripped them apart and angrily asked what it was about. Lakiya blurted, "He a faggot!"

At this exact moment I watched Lito Ruiz, the boy whose blue card identified him as "extremely susceptible to negative influences," heave a fistful of crayons at Verdad, my sullen, likable mathematician, who sat in the opposite corner of the classroom. "Liii–TO!" I shouted in what felt like comic slow motion. Verdad immediately retaliated by gunning his oversized eraser at Lito. He missed and hit Athena, who started crying. Several boys laughed maniacally, mocking Athena. Mr. Randazzo heard the noise and came in, shushing the class. The room went silent except for Bernard, who loudly sucked his teeth in an insolent snicker. Randazzo shook his head at me and blasted the class for being the most disrespectful group in the school. Sonandia covered her eyes.

Was this chaos my fault? I thought I had done everything I could to prepare to teach. My classroom was a print–rich environment. I modeled good character. I was organized and articulate in kid-friendly language.

I thought of a French movie that opens with a story about a man falling from the roof of a tall building. As he passes each floor he thinks to himself, "So far, so good, so far, so good." As his spirit looks down at his splattered corpse on the asphalt, he realizes it's not how you fall that matters. It's how you land. It's the mess that catches attention.

That night I decided two things: #1: Fausto was dead to me. His presence was cancerous. #2: I would aim high with content and ideas in class discussions (get back to those great expectations!), and if this amounted to blank stares all around, I would chalk it up. Jennifer and Sonandia would probably be able to follow me.

Decision #1 was rash and ridiculous. I could despise the kid, but I would still have to deal with his destructive actions. Also, he was a sad case. He said his mother beat the tar out of him. I felt sick for thinking so bitterly of an abused child. Decision #2 was built of virtuous intentions and horrendous logic. If I specifically geared activities toward the higher-achieving kids, I would alienate and lose the lower-achieving ones, who were already more likely to be discipline problems.

What was I supposed to teach to a room that held both Sonandia and Lakiya? Sonandia could read young adult books and analyze them critically with the right kind of guidance. She was capable of the higher-order skills in Bloom's taxonomy, a reference structure for teachers to analyze levels of abstraction in learning. Lakiya could not read a sentence fluently and refused even to write her name. The range of abilities in 4-217 was as wide as a Great Lake.

Upon arriving to P.S. 85 the next day, I got word that Fausto Mason had been permanently transferred out of my class. He was moving next door to Pat Cartwright, a tough black woman who had been in the army. This was Pat's second year as a teacher and first with a homeroom, and the administration felt she was better equipped to deal with Fausto than I was. I agreed. Pat explained, "He's just a rockhead. I'll whip him into shape."

With Fausto gone, I had my smoothest day yet. We began a *James and the Giant Peach* read-aloud. We reviewed the Martin Luther King, Jr. biography and wrote outlines on graphic organizers for our autobiographies. We made bar graphs from data in the *Math Trailblazers* textbook. We paraphrased stories that I had modeled aloud and some that I had typed on a homemade worksheet. We made a chart of components for "Good Listening" in our *Getting Along Together* lesson. We reviewed the parts of the scientific method introduced in a previous lesson by Mrs. Hafner. We read "A Spaghetti Tale" in *Highlights* magazine and talked about fiction and nonfiction. We looked at a map of New York City and reviewed the names of the five boroughs until each kid (except Eric) could recite them. We cleaned the classroom and copied our homework.

I felt familiar pangs of exhaustion in my knees and throat as I shepherded the kids down the steps for the fifth time, but something unexpected happened when I released them into the parking lot. Jennifer turned around and walked back. "Thank you, Mr. Brown," she said, putting her arms awkwardly around my neck.

I hugged her back, feeling my stomach drop in surprise and joy. "You're welcome, Jennifer. Have a great weekend."

"You too. See you Monday!" Jennifer ran off to meet her friends. The quick handful of words we exchanged were among the most cursory and common in our language, but unknown to Jennifer, those ten seconds at the very end changed the first week of my new profession and my new life. The knocks and bruises of the screaming and conflict in 4-217 vanished and I smiled on the subway home, a first.

LIST OF INTERESTING DISCOVERIES
AFTER WEEK ONE

1. Kids crave classroom responsibility. They compete for who gets to sweep and hold the dustpan. I need to use class jobs as rewards and withholding of jobs as punishment. However, sometimes the worst-behaved kids are the ones that benefit most from the tasks. I need to sort out a system with a publicly posted job board.

2. They love gym. Threatening "no gym" is a good threat to achieve temporary order. If I do cancel gym, though, I'm responsible for them, and I'll die if I don't get that afternoon prep after the 8:00–12:30 morning haul.

3. Many kids seem simply uninterested in academic achievement. For example, Eric, Deloris, and Lakiya do not do *any* work. They barely pick up their pencils. When I give an assignment, I need everyone working on it.

4. The kids are constantly touching each other and each other's belongings. At Mercy, this was mentioned as a byproduct of poverty culture; they have no personal space and very few personal possessions, so there is no sense of respect for those ideas. Should I lock up my stuff?

5. The administration is stretched very thin and has been undermined by the city with the region's "no detention, no suspension" policies. No one seems to know why we can't have detention or suspension; we just can't. I might be on my own to discipline them, but I don't know what I can hold over them. Bluffing a punishment would be a fatal mistake; I have to follow through on every threat I make. I hope Mr. Randazzo can help me.

6. Other teachers have the same problems I do. I need to look closely at what the successful teachers are doing and emulate that.

As I ushered the children into the classroom for the first day of week two, the assault commenced. "Good morning, ladies and gentlemen. Go immediately to your groups. Take everything you need for the whole day out of your bags. First group to show me they're ready gets four points. Take your homework out so I can see it. Yes, Gladys, you can sharpen your pencil. Destiny, wait till Gladys finishes and goes back to her seat. Verdad, you're after Destiny. And 'mines' is not a word. No, Lito, you can't sharpen your pencil. Yes, it is fair, the line is too long. Bernard, separate your desk from Hamisi. Because I've already given you too many chances. No, *separate the desks*! Here, I'll do it. Yes, Hamisi, because you're going to talk to each other at inappropriate times. Take out your homework, everyone! Which group is going to be first to show me they're ready and get stars and get to use the closet? Joseph, get back in your seat! I have called no groups over to the closet yet! Sonandia, you're setting a wonderful example. Why is group two the only group following directions? Tiffany, why are you staring at the ceiling? Group two is about to earn a star, and it looks like group one is going to get a strike. One star for group two! Let's make it two stars, I'm feeling generous. Yes, Lito, now you can sharpen your pencil. Well, it's overheated again because Verdad sharpened ten pencils. You'll have to wait. Lakiya, take your hat off, take your homework out, sit down, and close your mouth. That is not the way to enter our classroom. It's 'May I drink water?' not 'I can drink water?' Gladys, raise your hand if you have something to say to me, and please speak in a nice voice and not like you're trying to destroy someone."

Some people say, "Even when sex is bad, it's good." I found that even when my days at P.S. 85 were good, they were bad.

On Monday I got through all of my lessons successfully, but that didn't stop Lito Ruiz from punching chatty Julissa hard in the face during math. Barely suppressing my rage at the violence, I told the class, "It is never ever okay for a boy to hit a girl or a man to hit a woman. Never. A good man would absolutely never hit a girl. No boys in this room will *ever* hit a girl."

"Why?" Cwasey piped up. He wasn't being rude this time. He really didn't understand why this issue got me so fired up.

"Because it's cowardly, and no man I respect would ever raise his hand to a woman. It hurts everyone involved and it's not right and it's not okay and on top of that this is my room and that's my rule," I steamed.

I could tell by Cwasey's face that he didn't get it. Neither did Bernard, Hamisi, or Lito, who had their heads down. Lakiya cackled, "Preach!" She got a kick from mocking my impromptu speeches about decency and community.

I left for my prep disgusted. Barbara Chatton had arranged for me to observe Paul Bonn's fifth-grade class for the period, and Paul told me he could show a range of systems and routines he had in place to keep the order.

At twenty-seven, Paul Bonn stood five foot eight with a dirty blond goatee and untucked golf shirt. The first time I saw him I hadn't taken him for a genius.

Paul was a second-year teacher and not part of the Fellows program. His interview at P.S. 85 was fifteen seconds long. An administrator asked, "Are you scared?" He said he wasn't and was immediately informed of his hired status. Bonn was brought on as a cluster teacher, but in October, class 5-110 got out of hand, despite rookie teacher Ms. Elmer's large and intimidating physical stature. Kids were freely treating the furniture like an obstacle course, dancing, and fighting at will. The administration removed Ms. Elmer and gave her a cluster schedule.

It was a suicide mission. Unassuming, mellow-voiced Paul Bonn went in there, though, and straightened them out.

His first day, Bonn told Mr. Daly to clear the area in the parking lot outside room 110's windows. When the class got noisy in the first hour, Paul pretended to lose his mind and *threw a desk out the window.* The kids were silent for the rest of the day.

The second day, a notorious discipline problem didn't want to do his work. Bonn called the kid's mom, who showed up immediately to hold the boy's hand for the next three hours. The mortified student did not say boo the rest of the year.

The third day, a few kids started laughing in line. Bonn made the whole class copy the dictionary for two hours and write two pages about the importance of lines.

The fourth day was perfect.

Now he was one of the most respected teachers in the school, coordinating the faculty football pool and engaged to Melissa Mulvehill, a redheaded fourth-grade teacher whom he impressed more than anyone with the monumental turnaround of 5-110.

Paul Bonn rarely raised his voice because his class was a finely tuned machine. Two paper passers swiftly completed their appointed rounds with rehearsed precision. Class security guards, positions assigned to kids with discipline problems in their background, tabulated disruptions to be submitted for later punishments. They policed their own!

Bonn took his kids to the rug to read *The Blind Men and the Elephant,* a second-grade-level book about a gang of sightless geezers who decipher that there's an elephant standing in front of them by using teamwork. The reading was brief, and at the last word the kids immediately returned to their groups, hustling to get out their notebooks. Bonn gave group points on the chalkboard to the first group with all members who had written their name and the date. When Tiquan spoke out of turn, he had to copy a page of the dictionary. The class ran seamlessly. I was wowed.

What could I cull from this observation to bring to 4-217? Bonn had several advantages that I didn't have. Fifth grade was graduation year, so Paul had the NGL (No Graduation List), the most feared P.S. 85 punishment, at his disposal. Also, dictionary-copying fell into the broad reach of *corporal punishment,* a territory where I was reluctant to tread.

Corporal punishment, as I understood it, encompassed touching a child, forcing one to stand, making a student face the corner, and dishing out punitive assignments of no academic value. I slowly learned that P.S. 85 turned a blind eye to all of these practices in the name of avoiding "incidents." However, Barbara Chatton strongly discouraged me from engaging in them, especially in my first few weeks. I agreed. I did not want to become a teacher who dealt out these kinds of penalties, although my current methods were not exactly clicking.

I thought Paul Bonn's group points were perfect. Since I already had my stars and strikes that applied to all of 4-217, bringing in Bonn's group points would encourage teamwork and discourage academic laggards. ("Deloris is not writing her name and that's costing group three points right now!") I planned to keep track of the points in a box on the blackboard and give out candy bars or wildly popular Yu-Gi-Oh fantasy game cards to the winning group on Friday afternoons.

I also borrowed *The Blind Men and the Elephant.*

SOURCE: Dan Brown. *The Great Expectations School: A Rookie Year in the New Blackboard Jungle.* New York: Arcade. 2007.

PHILIP SCHULTZ

from *My Dyslexia*
(2011)

Philip Schultz (born in 1945 in Rochester, New York) is the founder and director of the Writers Studio in New York City; his book Failure *won the Pulitzer Prize for poetry in 2008. This excerpt comes from his memoir* My Dyslexia *(2011).*

When I taught poetry writing in grade schools I used the children's enthusiasm as a resource. Though many of their other teachers later came to enjoy the "magic" their students performed in class—perhaps, because of the "creative" focus of my job—they were often suspicious of me. What could this poet from New York City do that they couldn't? What was the purpose of teaching something as arcane and elitist as poetry in often overcrowded classes when so many of their students struggled with the basics? Although I didn't know about my dyslexia then, I did know that I would've loved being taught how to write creatively. I would've loved to put words together with feelings, through poetry.

Appealing to a child's imagination is perhaps the best way of fostering confidence in children. Kids who have already learned to mistrust their learning abilities can be reached through their love of surprise. I was often moved by the reaction of these children to my faith in their ability to climb the ladder of their own imaginative thinking. I didn't know that in teaching poetry I was reaching back toward the frightened lost child I'd been in order to rescue him.

Most teachers of writing teach what they learned through long trial and error, many prefer to work with those students who best reflect their own accomplishments. I work with gifted students, but I also work with those students who don't always readily shine. I work especially hard with those who—like me—have to fight tooth and nail to make any progress at all. In some ways, my method of teaching is designed with these students in mind. A number of years ago the

301

head of a prestigious writing program told me he believed the job of writing programs was to sort out the gifted from the merely serviceable. Surprised, I thought of *my place* in grade school. I asked him if he felt any responsibility to those others who don't demonstrate quickly an apparent gift, and if he ever feared he was failing them. His smile was answer enough. He didn't, not for a moment.

Albert Einstein, also dyslexic, said he wasn't the smartest person he knew—others had higher IQs—but he was the most creative. It's hard not to wonder what role his dyslexia played in his very original way of thinking. Dyslexics have to make up a great deal from scratch as they go along. Our minds turn most things into a game of one-upmanship in which blame is the main currency. Knowing something about the role fear played in my life, and the extent to which I was controlled by it, has given me insight into the length others go to avoid their own vulnerable feelings. I believe fear is the main reason why the majority of students stop writing, and why others are reluctant to write about those subjects they feel most passionately about. The Writers Studio is approaching its twenty-fourth year and not one of those years has gone by without some serious reassessment of its approach. I think of a line by Baudelaire: "The dispersion and reconstitution of the self. That's the whole story." We are constantly making and remaking and unmaking ourselves, an endless process of dispersion in which we find and lose ourselves in the current of an ever-changing story. A reconstitution of the self, and finding the right narrator to tell its story, is what I am attempting to do as a writer and a teacher. I no longer find it surprising that someone should feel little sympathy for a character with whom he most identifies. It's only surprising when he does.

My way of teaching is a long, intriguing, and complicated system of support. It sometimes seems as if I'm in the business of convincing people that they in fact possess the strength to reveal, in their work, the mystery of their nature. Great art does precisely that. Dyslexics perform some version of this in order to survive. Art's power of persuasion resides in the small personal details of one's own story, and if it weren't for my struggle with dyslexia, I doubt I'd ever have become a writer or known how to teach others to write.

SOURCE: Philip Schultz. *My Dyslexia*. New York: W. W. Norton and Company. 2011.